SPLENDID MOUNTAINS

SPLENDID MOUNTAINS

*Early Exploration in
the Sierra Nevada*

Compiled and edited by

PETER BROWNING

Great West Books   Lafayette, California

Cover design by Larry B. Van Dyke
Cover photographs by Peter Browning

Library of Congress Cataloging-in-Publication Data

Splendid mountains : early exploration in the Sierra Nevada / compiled and edited by
    Peter Browning.
        p. cm.
    ISBN 978-0-944220-22-1 (pbk. : alk. paper)
    1. Sierra Nevada (Calif. and Nev.)—Discovery and exploration—Anecdotes.
2. Sierra Nevada (Calif. and Nev.)—Description and travel—Anecdotes. 3. Wilderness
areas—Sierra Nevada (Calif. and Nev.)—History—19th century—Anecdotes. 4. Frontier
and pioneer life—Sierra Nevada (Calif. and Nev.)—Anecdotes. 5. Travelers—Sierra
Nevada (Calif. and Nev.)—Biography—Anecdotes. 6. Explorers—Sierra Nevada
(Calif. and Nev.)—Biography—Anecdotes. 7. Pioneers—Sierra Nevada (Calif. and
Nev.)—Biography—Anecdotes. 8. Travelers' writings, American—Sierra Nevada
(Calif. and Nev.) I. Browning, Peter, 1928-
    F868.S5S73 2007
    917.94'4044—dc22
                            2007030584

Great West Books
P.O. Box 1028
Lafayette, CA 94549-1028
Phone & Fax: (925) 283-3184
E-mail: peter@greatwestbooks.com
Website: www.greatwestbooks.com

Contents

Photographs

The photographs on pages 57, 59, 71, 92, 99, 101, and 103 are
Courtesy of The Bancroft Library
University of California, Berkeley,
from the Theodore S. Solomons collection.
Call Number: BANC PIC 1971.061:
Numbers 11, 15, 23, 39, 49, 50, and 60.

All other photographs, both color and black & white,
were taken by Peter Browning.

The front cover photograph is looking south from below
Bullfrog Lake toward the Kings-Kern Divide:
Junction Peak, and Forester Pass to the right of it.

The back cover photograph is of the Kings-Kern Divide
from the south, on the upper Kern River trail. From the left:
Mt. Ericsson, Harrison Pass, and Mt. Stanford and
Gregorys Monument close together to the right of the pass.

Introduction

The travels and explorations of William H. Brewer, Clarence King, John Muir, the California State Geological Survey, and the Wheeler Survey have been recounted many times and in great detail. For that reason they are not included in this volume. Most of the less well known early explorers of the Sierra Nevada were private individuals, rather than government expeditions or cartographers. The more literate ones had accounts of their achievements, adventures, and mishaps published in newspapers and journals, often accompanying them with photographs, drawings, and hand-drawn maps. Most of these wilderness travelers have been immortalized by having their names placed on mountains, lakes, and streams: Frank Dusy; Wales, Wallace, and Wright; Theodore S. Solomons; Bolton C. and Lucy Brown; Joseph N. and Marion LeConte; Lt. Nathaniel Fish McClure; Cornelius Beach Bradley; James E. Hutchinson. These are foremost among the few who pioneered the routes that are followed by so many at the present day.

Frank Dusy (1836–1898), born in Canada; educated in Maine; came to California in 1858. He was initially a miner, then turned to sheep-raising and ranching; took his stock to the mountains in the region of the North and Middle forks of the Kings River; discovered Tehipite Valley in 1869; explored the Middle Fork of the Kings River as far as the Palisades in 1878.

According to Lilbourne A. Winchell, himself an early explorer, Dusy was the only stockman of his time who seemed to take an interest in the mountain region for reasons other than stock feed. He was a man of intelligence and wide experience. He took the first photographs of Tehipite, 1879, carrying a bulky portrait camera, with studio tripod, wet plates, and chemicals. L. A. Winchell, in 1879, gave Dusy's name to the branch of the Middle Fork of the Kings River north of the Palisades: Dusy Branch, flowing out of Dusy Basin. Dusy Meadows and Dusy Creek, north of the Courtright Reservoir, are also named for him.

Frederick Henry Wales (1845–1925), born in Massachusetts; served in the Civil War; graduated from Dartmouth, 1872; Hartford Theological Seminary, 1875; came to California and resided in Tulare County for many years as minister, editor of *Alliance Messenger*, and a farmer. The

namesake of Wales Lake. **William B. Wallace** (1849–1926), born in
Missouri; his family came to California the year of his birth, and settled in
Placerville. He attended school in Sacramento County; graduated State
Normal School; taught school in Sacramento, El Dorado, and Amador
counties; came to Tulare County, 1876, and settled in Visalia in 1891.
He was an inveterate explorer and mountaineer in the southern Sierra
for twenty years. Namesake of Wallace Lake and Wallace Creek. **James
William Albert Wright** (1834–1894), born in Mississippi; served in the
Confederate Army in the Civil War; came to California in 1868. For
some twenty years he was a correspondent for various newspapers and
journals on agricultural and mining matters, and on travels in the Sierra.
The namesake of Wright Lakes and Wright Creek.

Joseph Nisbet LeConte (1870–1950) was the son of Professor Joseph
LeConte, the University of California geology professor who had con-
firmed John Muir's glacial theory of the origin of Yosemite Valley. Both
LeContes were charter members of the Sierra Club.

"Little Joe" LeConte served the Club for fifty years—as a director
from 1898 to 1940, and as the Club's second president, 1915–1917, after
John Muir and before William E. Colby.

He made many mountaineering trips in the Sierra from 1887 to 1928,
wrote extensively about them, and was an expert photographer and
map-maker. In his professional life he was a professor of engineering at
the University of California, Berkeley. Le Conte Point overlooking Hetch
Hetchy Reservoir is named for him. All other Le Conte features are
named for his father. Marion Lake and Marion Peak were named for his
wife, **Helen Marion Gompertz LeConte** (1865–1924).

Theodore Seixas Solomons (1870–1947) was the pioneer of the
northern half of the John Muir Trail. In three memorable trips in the
1890s, with three different companions, he explored, mapped, and established a route from Yosemite to Kings Canyon. On every trip he carried a
glass-plate camera, and created an invaluable photographic record of his
travels. The plates from the second of these journeys of discovery were
lost, but the others survived and are now in the Bancroft Library.

Theodore joined in the Klondike Gold Rush in 1898, then went to
Alaska for nearly a decade. He returned to the United States in 1908,
and in 1911 homesteaded west of Yosemite overlooking the canyon of
the Merced River. Many years later this homestead, called Flying Spur,
was owned and occupied by Shirley Sargent, the noted Yosemite writer.

Shirley's superb biography of Theodore, *Solomons of the Sierra* (1989), gave Theodore the recognition he deserved. In 1968, a peak just southwest of Muir Pass was named Mount Solomons.

Robert Martin Price (1867–1940), a charter member of the Sierra Club, and at various times its secretary, a director, president, and honorary vice-president. Obituary by William E. Colby in the *Sierra Club Bulletin*, v. 25, 1940.

Nathaniel Fish McClure (1865–1942) graduated from West Point in 1887. He was a first lieutenant in the Fifth Cavalry when he was stationed in Yosemite National Park in 1894 and 1895. He patrolled the remote areas of the park, preventing poaching and rousting sheepherders, and also scouted out new routes—particularly in the northern part of the park—and created maps in 1895 and 1896. McClure Lake, just south of Isberg Peak, is named for him. In fact, he probably named it for himself, since the name first appears on his 1896 map. The lake was within the park's boundaries from 1890 to 1905, but is now in the Sierra National Forest.

Bolton Coit Brown 1864–1936 founded the art program at Stanford University in 1891, and was its director from then until 1902. There he gained fame as a teacher and national recognition as a skilled mountaineer. He left California in 1902 and traveled to New York to explore the Catskill Mountains, and soon became affiliated with the Byrdcliffe Arts and Crafts Colony.

Brown went to England in 1915, where he learned lithography. He returned to America the following year and devoted the next ten years of his life exclusively to lithography. His expertise as a printmaker led to collaborations with some of the important artists of his time, among them George Bellows, Arthur B. Davies, John Taylor Arms, and Rockwell Kent.

Mount Bolton Brown on the Sierra crest northeast of Mather Pass was named for him in 1922 by the two men who made the first ascent. Lucys Foot Pass over the Kings-Kern Divide is named for his wife, **Lucy Fletcher Brown.**

Cornelius Beach Bradley (1843–1936) was born in Bangkok, Siam. His father, the Reverend Daniel Beach Bradley, was descended from a family which had been resident in Connecticut since 1644.

He attended Oberlin College, where he obtained the bachelor's degree in 1868. He remained at Oberlin as tutor for two years, pursuing at the same time the course in Theology. This he continued in the Divinity School at Yale University, 1870 to 1871. From 1871 until 1874 he was a missionary to the Siamese. He returned to America at the end of that period and in 1875 was appointed teacher of English and Vice-Principal of the High School in Oakland, California.

In 1882 he was appointed Instructor in English at the University of California, where he continued as Assistant Professor and Associate Professor of English Language and Literature, then as Professor of Rhetoric, until his retirement in 1911. He was honored by Oberlin College with the M.A. degree in 1886, and by the University of California with that of LL.D. in 1926.

Bradley was a charter member of the Sierra Club, and from 1895 to 1898 editor of the *Sierra Club Bulletin.* Mount Bradley, overlooking Center Basin, was named for him on July 5, 1898, the same day that he made the first ascent of Center Peak, on the opposite side of Center Basin.

James Sather Hutchinson (1867–1959) was a charter member of the Sierra Club, a director of the club from 1903 to 1907, and twice the editor of the *Sierra Club Bulletin.* He, Joe LeConte, and James K. Moffitt made the first ascent of the North Palisade, in 1903. James was an attorney in San Francisco for sixty years. He and a brother, Edward C. Hutchinson, made the first ascent of Mount Humphreys, in 1904. Hutchinson Meadow, at the juncture of French Canyon and Piute Canyon, was named for the Hutchinson brothers in 1922.

I know nothing about **George Gibbs.** His description of the descent of Tenaya Canyon is the finest article about a one-day, death-defying jaunt that I've ever seen. If you can survive that, perhaps you can live as long as the Splendid Mountains shall stand.

Kings River Canyon in 1868

E. C. Winchell

[Elisha Cotton Winchell was an early settler in Fresno County, arriving in Millerton in 1859. He practiced law, and became a judge. His son, Lilbourne A. Winchell, was one of the pioneer explorers of the Sierra Nevada. In the description of his trip to Kings River Canyon in 1868 the senior Winchell used a number of place names that no longer exist, and thus it is not possible to follow his exact route. Nevertheless, the route of access to that part of the Sierra, then as now, followed present-day state route 198 to the vicinity of the Grant Grove of Big Trees. From there one went eastward, north of the Kings-Kaweah divide and several miles south of the Kings River Canyon.]

Originally published in the *San Francisco Morning Call*,
September 11 and 12, 1872.

A Wonder of Creation—Sights in the Heart of the Sierras—"The Wonderful Valley Said to Have Been Discovered by Bierstadt"

My attention has been called to a letter signed "Dred," in *The Call* of September 5th, asking information regarding a "new valley" reported to have been found by the artist, Bierstadt, one hundred miles south of Yosemite, and excelling that cañon in grandeur; as well as to the editor's reply, that the report "lacks confirmation," and that "the existence of such a spot, though possible, is not probable." It was the fortune of the writer to have been one of a party of three who, in the Fall of 1868, visited and sojourned for two days in a stupendous chasm in the region which seems to have been indicated by the Eastern newspapers mentioned by "Dred;" and thinking it likely that not only he, but many others of your readers, may desire to know the truth concerning the "terra incognita" supposed to have been just discovered, I beg to submit to you, in as brief form as may be, a sketch of our explorations in that direction, in the hope that it may aid to turn attention towards a locality which, 1 think, is destined at no distant day to share with Yosemite the homage of the wonder-seeking world.

I am far from assuming that the cañon which we visited and which I shall attempt to describe, is the one said to have been visited by Mr. Bierstadt; for many a deep and dreadful abyss lies hidden in that Andean region, only thirty-three leagues southeast of Yosemite, where Mount Whitney, Mount Tyndall, Mount King, Mount Goddard and a score of other clustering peaks, each exceeding 14,000 feet in height, look down on the assembled sources of Kern River, King's River,[1] and the South Fork of the mighty San Joaquin; and the great artist, seeking new themes for his pencil, may have entered the portals of some granite gulf where, before, the foot of man never trod. But so far as my information extends, no gorge has yet been found in that part of the Sierra Nevada so extensive and so stupendous as the one to which I have referred.

I beg to correct "Dred's" idea that the "new valley" is at the head of the Fresno River, which is but a small stream rising near the Mariposa, Big Trees, only twelve or fourteen miles south of Yosemite. Its locality is the upper-part of the South Fork of "Rio del Rey,"[2] or King's River, in the extreme southeastern corner of Fresno County—about sixty miles, as the crow flies, E.S.E. from Millerton, the county seat—about fifty miles N.E. from Visalia, and about ninety-five miles S.S.E. from Yosemite. "Dred" can, if he desires, go by rail from San Francisco to Visalia in one day, thence in one day by carriage, over a good road to Thomas' Saw Mill, forty miles N.N.E. from that town, at an altitude of 5,000 feet, thence in one and-a-half days, by mules or sure-footed horses arid pack-train, thirty miles E.N.E. to the King's River cañon.

During a residence of several years in Fresno County, prior to 1868, the writer learned from a mountaineer, who had frequented the high Sierras, of the existence of an almost inaccessible valley near the head of King's River, said to contain forests of timber, which could be sent down

---

1. For many years "King's" was common usage, as though the river had been named for someone named King.
2. The Spanish gave the name *Rio de los Santos Reyes* (River of the Holy Kings) in 1805.

the stream to supply the increasing demand for lumber in the counties of Fresno and Tulare; and also said to contain valuable deposits of copper ore. Inspired by the triple desire of exploring so unfrequented and interesting a district, examining the forests and inspecting the mineral beds, the writer, accompanied by Capt. John N. Appleton, set out on horseback from the vicinity of Millerton, on the 22d day of September, 1868, and proceeded twenty-five miles southeasterly to Bensell's [Bensen's] store or trading-post, on Sycamore Creek, two miles north of King's River, where they were joined by their guide, William Haines, and completed their outfit for a twelve days' journey into the heart of the Sierras. Provisions, blankets, camp utensils and extra ammunition were packed on a sumpter mule, which, without leading, followed at their heels like a faithful dog. It appearing that no practicable route lay on the north side of King's River, because of the deep, impassable cañons of the North Fork and Middle Fork, which intervened, it was resolved to cross to the south side and proceed southeasterly for 25 miles to Thomas' Mill, the extreme outpost of civilization, and then turning north of east, traverse the northern flank of the huge mountain-spur which, lying east and west, divides the Kaweah River on the south from King's River on the north. Two days of delay occurred; and after fording the river, we reached Thomas' Mill by a pack trail, at noon, on Saturday, September 26th.[3] The pine forests here are strikingly beautiful, though fast disappearing before the insatiate steam saws that have been devastating them for fifteen years. The wagon-road from Visalia extends a mile or two beyond the Mill, to People's Creek, and to the first grove of big trees to be seen on this trip. Near the trail, on the left, is a hollow log, which the party explored on their return; and two miles on the right is said to he the largest tree yet found in California.

The "Pine Ridge" is a spur running down the north flank of the great "Kaweah Divide," just described, having Mill Creek on its west side, and People's Creek on its east, both flowing into King's River. A parallel but higher spur lies between People's Creek and Haines' Creek; a third, yet loftier, between the latter stream and Glacier Creek; a fourth, higher still, between this torrent and the Crescent Lawn and the final plunge in King's River Cañon.

---

3. The sawmill of Joseph H. Thomas was just west of the Grant Grove.

Across these high spurs, which corrugate the northern face of the Kaweah Divide, our course lay nearly eastward, midway between the crest of the divide high on our right, and the unseen bed of King's River, far down on our left. And from the first Big Trees on People's Creek we had three miles of up-hill travel to the top of the second spur, through trackless thickets and a labyrinth of fallen timber, where only the skill and patience of our guide could have found a way, then three miles of gentle descent through open woods to Haines' Creek, at the junction of Fern Creek, where, at sundown, we made camp by a strip of coarse grass, called the "Little Meadows," eight miles from Thomas' Mill. Bear hunters had been here some weeks before, and had left hideous trophies in the form of several skeletons of black and cinnamon bears. The hundreds of square miles of mountain jungle which clothe these spurs, are the haunts of numbers of these, as well as of the brown and grizzly bear; and the prudent hunter guards his stock of flour and bacon against their thefts at night, by bringing it near the fire, which they dare not approach. Our guide told us of a novice in woodcraft, who came up from Visalia to hunt bears, and who at night put a couple of Chicago sugar-cured hams under his pillow for safe keeping. He slept very soundly, and found, on waking at sunrise, that a brown hear had out witted him and carried off both the hams.

Our beds were of fragrant, feathery fern, our sleep unmolested. The mountain air grew keen before morning, and the dawn showed us our horses—accustomed to the warm climate of the valley— shivering over the frosty grass and icy pools in the little meadow. Leaving Haines' Creek before 7 o'clock, we at once began to climb a high hill—the third spur— whose top we reached in two hours. The dim trail often disappeared, and boundless thickets, filled with prostrate trunks of trees, made our progress slow and tedious. We were above the usual range of the Indians, and did not see one on the trip. The King's River tribes make occasional visits to the Monos and Owen's [Owens] River Indians, who now and then venture on this side in return; but this trail had not been used for years, apparently, and was often overgrown and obliterated. We at length found the dim tracks of two or three Indian ponies, made a month before, and these furnished a sort of clew to our way. Along Water-Spout Creek, a deluge from the sky had swept bare the solid granite in a strip fifty yards wide and a mile long, carrying away logs, trees, rocks and earth, like chaff, down a deep ravine into the river. Alpine Brook threads a dark forest in a wild glen, and falls into Glacier Creek, which also leaps into the river. Then comes the little stream Los Baños Frios, and Alsip's grove of Mammoth trees, which excel in grace and beauty, but do not equal in size, those of Calaveras and Mariposa. We ascended now another steep hill, passing the Druid's Altar, of granite blocks piled by Nature. Descending by gentle undulations we came into Evergreen Dell, where luxuriant foliage and cooling bowers tempered the blaze of the already fervent sun. At half-past 10, Avalanche Cañon presented a second track of desolation crossing our path. Shattered crags, mangled logs and trees, hideously mingled with dirt and debris, had plunged in chaotic column headlong down the rugged gorge, leaving a track of naked. slippery granite, one hundred yards wide, over which we got our animals with no little difficulty. In the midst of this frightful track, fast rooted to the firm rock, stood a stately "sequoia gigantia" [gigantea], or mammoth tree, uninjured by the torrent of debris that the storm and the mountain, in their most wrathful mood, had hurled against it. To this we gave the name of "Governor Haight." By the edge of this storm-path is Lamper's Grove, an assemblage of thrifty and graceful young "Big Trees." One of the larger measured sixty-six feet in girth. Continuing upward, we passed the summit of this Spur at 11 o'clock, and quickly descended to Glacier Creek,[4] a swift, bright stream, pouring, like all the former ones, down the north front of the Kaweah Divide into the hidden depths of King's River, five or six miles to our left. The steep banks, rough bed and rapid torrent endangered our horses in crossing, and we were obliged to wade and lead them. A mountain to be climbed presented itself at once—the *fourth* spur—and this was a steep, bad ascent, over, *under* and around fallen trunks of trees and through chaparral, requiring an hour's lively scrambling. Then followed a pleasant down-hill ride, through open vistas of superb pines and firs, for half an hour, to Crescent Lawn,[5] a spacious meadow encircled on the southeast by a grand arc of granite mountains thinly clad with pines. It was now half an hour past noon. We had been climbing, with no intermission, for six hours, had come nine miles under a warm sun, and were fatigued. We made a fire under the shade of the firs, had hot coffee with

---

4. This is probably Boulder Creek.
5. Horse Corral Meadow.

our lunch, and reposed for two hours. This spot is seventeen miles from Thomas' Mill.

Our course now abruptly veered to the north and northeast, leading us over the fifth and last spur, and rapidly nearing the profound chasm we were seeking.[6] Thus far, only once or twice had we seen the waters of King's River since fording it. Occasionally, through the leafy lanes of the forests, we could see the northern steep walls of its deep bed, and now and then the yawning gaps in those walls, through which, our guide said, came the North Fork and the Middle Fork. The rich sunlight that bathed the gray adamant seemed to transmute it into gold. We resumed our advance over a gently rising land through an extensive tract of forest, which allowed no view of the region ahead, though this was the highest point we attained, being perhaps 12,000 feet up.[7] In an hour the trail wound down the northern slope of a wooded declivity, and brought us, by four o'clock, to a grassy glade with natural wells of water,[8] in the heart of a noble forest where our guide halted us for the night, as it was yet, by the trail, five miles to the banks of the King's River, with no grass for our horses intervening. As we came down the slope just mentioned, our attention had been drawn to a remarkable peak of broken granite crags that rose, like a misshapen pyramid, or cone, high out of the forest before us;[9] and when it was found that our night halt was made within half a mile of its southwestern base, I set out, while my comrades were arranging camp affairs for the night, to climb to the summit before the sun should set. On reaching the apex—a smooth block of granite—I found that it commanded an outlook to the west over all the woods, streams and mountains we had passed, and that the San Joaquin plain would also have been visible but for the strange, misty veil, which, as thousands will remember, ominously hung over California for a month prior to the earthquake of October 20th, of that year. But the view to the north, to the east, to the southeast, and downward, was undimmed, for this peak rose abreast the lower end of the King's River Cañon, and looked down into its awful depths.

---

6.   The route of today's Don Cecil Trail.
7.   Barely 8,000 feet.
8.   Summit Meadow.
9.   Lookout Peak, elevation 8,531.

I regret that I cannot measure the grandeur of this scene by the features of Yosemite, which I have never visited; but no paintings of that gorge and its surroundings as seen from "Inspiration Point" or "Cloud's [Clouds] Rest," convey to my mind the idea of so sublime a landscape as that which, without warning, burst upon my vision as I looked over the granite block into a deep, dread, silent, stupendous amphitheatre, twenty miles across, crowded with adamant mountains, pinnacled crests, thunder-scarred cliffs, green lines of forests, snows in eternal sleep, horrid gorges and yawning gulfs. Eastward, the sharply serrated contour of the main ridge of the Sierras tore the twilight sky; northward rose the huge, massive barrier that fills the space between the middle fork and south fork; southward, the great, gashed Kaweah Divide bore to heaven its balmy forests; while *more than a vertical mile down,* in the midst of this vast arena, lay a granite trough ten miles long, half a mile wide, bordered by perpendicular cliffs rising thousands of feet. *A green mound of forests* hid the floor of the gorge, and a thread-like streak of water faintly gleamed out of it.

Awe-struck, I gazed till the misty veil of the plain drew nearer, and the weird gloom deepened. Silence the most profound brooded over the stony depths. Not a wave of air touched the sprays of the dark green forest which far below me enveloped our camp, nor swayed the straight column of light blue smoke that stole up higher than the trees from the deep-red star of the camp-fire. As the sun set I offered, with due reverence, from this exalted altar-stone the improvised incense of flame and smoke from both barrels of my gun, and before the myriad-echoed thunders had ceased their clamorings over the startled abyss I was descending the peak to rejoin my comrades.

Our hunter's repast of mountain quail, flapjacks and coffee, was soon over, and as the shadows fell, our horses, straying at will, were staked among the reeds and grass of the narrow glade. We made couches for the night by spreading our blankets on elastic twigs, trimmed from a fir laid low by Capt. A's axe, and carried near to a great log, which was set blazing from end to end. The night was a reign of beauty. No cloud marred the blue nor dimmed its gems. The full moon poured fluid silver through the sombre vistas, and tipped the giant pines with a splendid radiance—a frosted fire. Close about us lay compacted shadows, fitfully lighted by the wavering flames that anon leaped up and fell back again. Dark volumes of smoke rolled to the tree-tops, swarming with armies of golden sparks, which darted and glided hither and thither, crossing and recrossing, weaving and mingling their serpentine threads of fire, till they seemed to be myriads of twining snakes climbing up the smoky pillars to reach the stars. Standing around us like solemn genii the towering firs looked regally down. Their stately shafts were plumed with tapering cones of foliage, of so rare a grace, so exquisite a symmetry, as to command our unceasing admiration even in the prosaic glare of day; but the witchery of Night invested them with an unspeakable glory, and seemed to lift their lance-like points against the very dome of Heaven. As the firelight rose and gleamed, their forms were gilded and glowing; as it died flickering away, their sombrous shapes stood in sharp relief against the starry sky, while the frisky and irreverent sparks ever danced fantastically among their moveless branches.

At midnight there was a frosty keenness in the air, and the great log was burning low. We arose and heaped other logs and limbs upon the fire, which kept us warm till morning. Capt. A. desired to visit the top of the rocky pyramid before sunrise. Rousing early, we took a cup of hot coffee at dawn, and set off at five o'clock, through the frosty, spicy air to climb up 600 or 800 feet, and then down again, before breakfast. We reached the granite cap before the sun came over the Sierras. As the mists were dispelled, and the cold gray of the mighty chain melted into purple and gold, we beheld, in a direction south of east, and twenty-five miles distant, the forms of Mount Brewer, Mount Williamson and Mount Tyndall, with a more distant peak, supposed to be Mount Whitney.[10]

The eastern face of the peak where we stood was a sheer precipice for hundreds of feet, ending in a craggy pile of debris that sloped to a for-est-clad ravine, where wound the trail we afterwards descended. The northern front dropped yet lower, to a steep incline of smooth rocks slanting away for a thousand feet to a plunging gorge, which fell thou-sands of feet further to the floor of the cañon, where the tall pines seemed but shrubs. For three-fourths of a great circle about us, the view was unbounded, save by the mountain ramparts; and within those limits were embraced, in infinite variety, all shapes and forms of lofty height and unfathomed depth that cold and sullen stone can assume. Lordly and lonely obelisks rose along the Sierras' crest; majestic domes here and

10. Mt. Brewer is the only one of those peaks that can be seen from here.

there rested on wide exposures of granite; broad, mural tablets, gleaming like marble in the sunlight, lifted out of gloomy cañons; while there were hosts of beetling crags and buffeted cliffs that only scowled, even in the brightest hours. The largest areas exhibited only nude, primeval granite—cold, soulless and silent as death. Immortal snows lay cradled among the higher summits; and up the wide clefts, between the multitudinous spurs and ridges, were boldly thrust long, narrow columns of green forests, that dwindled to thin, spear-like points in the stern presence of undying frost. The central object of interest was the adamantine trough below us; so deep, its broad floor seemed but a few yards wide—its kingly forests a blended mass of shrubs—its river a contemptible rill. So high was this dominating peak, that, though half a mile back from the stream, it seemed possible to toss from here a pebble into the water.

The pyramid was now to he christened. A wicker-woven flask was produced, (its contents being tested to avoid possibility of mistake), and a generous libation poured therefrom upon the crowning block, while simultaneously was pronounced, in honor of Alexander Winchell, LL.D., State Geologist of Michigan, the name, "Winchell's Peak."[11]

Thus we followed the distinguished example set us by other explorers. Formal salutations were addressed to the witnessing mountains, and double charges of gun-powder fired over the cañon and forest, arousing crashing reverberations that leaped from cliff to distant cliff, swiftly redoubling on the morning air, till

> "Every mountain now had found a tongue;
> And Jura answered from her misty shroud,
> Back to the joyous Alps that called to her aloud."[12]

Rising, as it does, by the side of the only trail that can ever enter the King's River Cañon, this peak will doubtless he ascended by all tourists who desire to comprehend in a single glance a general view of the great

---

11. Alexander Winchell was a cousin of E. C. Winchell. Lil Winchell, unaware of this naming, in 1879 gave the name "Mount Winchell" to a peak south of the Palisades. That name was later moved to a peak northwest of the Palisades by the USGS

12. "But every mountain now hath found a tongue;/And Jura answers through a misty shroud,/Back to the joyous Alps who call to her aloud." (Lord Byron, *Childe Harold's Pilgrimage*, canto III, st. 92.)

gorge and its overlooking heights. Here is a subject for the skill of paint-
ers and photographers for all time; and it should be no marvel if, within a
few years, the pencils of Bierstadt and Hill, or the cameras of Watkins
and his brethren, shall have made this panoramic scene as familiar to the
habitués of Montgomery street, as are now the views from "Inspiration
Point."

A shout from our guide gave warning that breakfast awaited us in
the pillared saloon of the forest and we zigzagged down the steep without
delay. A genial sun was driving away the frost, and a bright day
impended. With keen zest breakfast was dispatched. Our horses were
quickly brought in and we eagerly prepared for a descent into the cañon,
a serpentine dive of four or five miles. By eight o'clock we were filing past
the southern base of the pyramid, and soon approached the head of a
broad but steep ravine, filled with pines, down which, in a northeast
course, we took our sinuous way. There was no little variety in our mode
of progress. We rode, we walked, we slid, we scrambled; we made sharp
angles to the right and left, ever plunging downward, downward—now, in
a faint trail, now, with no mark to guide us. Fortunately, the declivity was
clothed with a soil of crumbled granite and fine straw, which lessened the
toil and risk of descent. Crystal Creek rushed hither and thither athwart
our course, and leaped in white cascades down many a cliff.[13] The last
crossing, under the "Devil's Cataract," was attended with some hazard.
Thenceforward, no obstacle presented. At hall-past 10 o'clock we rode
out upon the sloping floor of the great gorge, having consumed
two-and-a-half hours in coming down from the base of "Winchell's
Peak," which now stood at a dizzy height above us. Half a mile over a
gentle glacis through a forest of pines in open order, led us to the long
sought river—the peerless South Fork—the very emblem of saintly
purity, on whose brink we halted.[14] Headquarters were established near
a fallen tree; saddles were stripped off, the patient mules unladen, the
animals loosed to roll and revel in the green, luxuriant grass; and when a
fire had been kindled and the camp set in order, we instinctively sought
the verge of the arrowy stream, and laved luxuriously in the wondrous
beauty of its transparent billows. So incomparably charming a stream

---

13. Sheep Creek.
14. At what is now Cedar Grove.

I never saw, though the Merced of Yosemite may rival it. Its thrice-polished sheen, its triple fineness, its infinitely lucent body, hindering no pencil of sunlight from irradiating its pebbly depths, its noiseless flight down smooth inclines, its purling voices where rocky ledges jarred its self-control, its utter peace and repose where shadows veiled its pools, and its delicate, ever-varying tints made it the object of our unceasing admiration.

In this primeval paradise, all day long we lingered mingling our sordid speculations in regard to the practicability of floating rafts of saw-logs down the river to the San Joaquin plain, with our feelings of wonder at the scenes around us. With our guns and fishing-tackle we rambled through the woods and by the stream in search of mountain grouse and mountain trout. Two miles below we found that the valley, which was three-quarters of a mile wide at the camp, contracted to a V-shaped cañon, only wide enough for the egress of the narrow river. No perpendicular cliffs border this western section, though the walls rise at a steep angle. Looking up the valley, we could see great cliffs that drew near each other, from opposite sides; but having no way of measuring altitudes, we could only guess at the elevations. Early the next morning, we pursued our way up the valley, on the south side of the river, which we crossed at a deep, swift ford, two miles above our camp. The cañon grew narrower—its sides more precipitous. A mile above the ford we passed the mouth of "Kettle Brook," which leaps into the gorge from the southeast, down a slope of 45 degrees, through an impassable ravine.[15] From here, onward, there was an unending succession of naked, perpendicular battlements, of various heights and forms, severed by breaks and gorges, out of which rushed foaming torrents. We were lost in amazement. There was a resistless fascination in those mural heights which impelled us to gaze fixedly at each new form, till it had passed and its successor rose to receive the like homage. We made many attempts to estimate the altitudes; but there were no data to guide us, and all our calculations failed. We believed the walls to reach thousands of feet above the valley, but whether 3,000 or 6,000, I have never dared to say. Opposite Kettle Brook are the "Pillars of Hercules," towering at the portals of the stony realm beyond; and next, on the same side, is "Appleton's Peak"—a sheer, blank wall, near whose

---

15. Roaring River.

top the great pines that plume it seem but a span long. "Leach's Peak," on the south side, fills the angle made by the Brook. The cañon here is but one-fourth of a mile wide, but rapidly widens again and contracts in ellip-tic form, making a rude oval, half a mile wide, and thrice as long, named "The Coliseum." Its lofty, fringing cliffs are yet nameless. At the eastern end a furious torrent darts out of a steep gully on the north side, with deafening roar, and gave us trouble in crossing, for which we repaid it with the title, "Thunder Creek." Further on is a second, irregular ellipse, a mile long, its northern wall a broad, angular peak, the "Pyramid of Cheops." On the south, "Three Sisters" correspond in form to the "Three Brothers" of Yosemite. Another stream emerges from a glen east of the Pyramid, to which, because of its proximity to the copper mine alluded to in the early part of this sketch, we applied the name "Malachite Creek." The deposit of ore crops out 400 feet above the valley on the east side of this rivulet, and appears to he of rich quality. A third swell in the cañon seemed so nearly circular, being only three-quarters of a mile long and of almost equal width, that we called it "The Rotunda."[16] Its enclosing heights are yet unchristened. Finally, beyond, is the noblest apartment of the series. The great cañon of King's River is here abruptly terminated by a magnificent granite tablet which stands across the valley and faces the west.[17] Two similar tablets uplift from the green floor, at right angles with the former, on opposite sides of the river, thus constituting the three inner walls of a vast Titanic temple, open to the setting sun. But through the enclosed, inner corners leap into this enchanted, and enchanting arena, two bold and glassy torrents from the north and the south—new-born of the snows—which, rushing together, instantaneously coalesce, forming the jubilant South Fork, and sweep in matchless beauty and wedded gladness down through the embowered and rock-walled valley.

---

16. To make sense of these fanciful names: "Pillars of Hercules" is North Mountain; "Appleton's Peak" is the unnamed cliffs west of Granite Creek; "Leach's Peak" is unnamed; "The Coliseum" is between Roaring River and Granite Creek; "Thunder Creek" is Granite Creek; "Pyramid of Cheops" is North Dome; "Three Sisters" is Grand Sentinel; "Malachite Creek" is Copper Creek; "The Rotunda" is the wide area at the base of Copper Creek.
17. Glacier Monument.

Here ended our advance; and here, at 11 o'clock A.M. of Tuesday, September 29th, we drew rein, and alighted in a delightful spot, where graceful pines and cottonwoods shadowed the green sward and the awful trio of cliffs seemed to bend over our heads. Words avail not to picture a scene like this. The Yosemite towers may, or may not, exceed these in height; it is immaterial. I cannot divest myself of the belief that no spot has yet been found on American soil where so much of grandeur concentrates in so small a space. The insatiate eye seeks again and again that trio of templed cliffs, and never tires of their supernal majesty. They seem to form Nature's own chosen cathedral, where deep organ-tones from sounding streams ever repeat the anthems taught by Deity.

Most reluctantly, as the sun stooped low, we turned our horses' heads homeward. At dark we slept by the "Pillars of Hercules," and the roar of "Kettle Brook" was our tremendous lullaby. Early the next day we crossed to the south side and hasted down the valley. Our leave of absence had expired, and ominous fleeces floated in the sky, which in a night might bury in snow our dim and difficult path. The ascent out of the cañon was made in less than three hours, and our camp that night was at Alpine Creek, fifteen miles from the "Pillars of Hercules." Our noon halt the next day was in the Big Tree Grove, two miles from Thomas' Mill. Our whole party took occasion to ride, in single file, fully armed and sitting erect on their horses, into the hollow log (before alluded to) for seventy-two feet, finding six feet of space overhead, and ample room at the terminus to wheel and ride out again. The faithful mule, as in duty bound, though heavily laden, voluntarily went through the same programme to the letter.

On the third day after, our journey was ended. We had been two weeks making the round trip, which, though a fatiguing one, has always been a source of delightful recollections. If "Dred" should resolve to undertake the journey, now is the golden hour of the year, when all the streams are at their lowest. If the trail from Thomas' Mill has been cleared since 1868, which is not unlikely, he could go thence to the valley in a single day, or in three days from San Francisco! He will miss the Yosemite Fall, the Vernal Fall, and the Bridal Veil, and may find no vertical cliffs so high as El Capitan; yet I feel it safe to predict that he will find, in other features of the King's River Cañon and of the encircling mountains, a most ample reward for all his toils and hardships.—E. C. W.

San Francisco, September 11, 1872.

A Trip to the Palisades, Through a Country Heretofore Unexplored

Frank Dusy

Originally published in the *Fresno Weekly Republican*, August 31, 1878

DINKEY, August 24, 1878

D r. Rowell[1]—*Dear Sir:* After parting with you in the South Fork Canyon, Peck and myself went to a point on the trail from the divide which overlooked the upper end of the valley, and took three negatives. Camped in the upper end of the valley. Next day we took the old trail and went to the summit between the two Kings. Here we took five negatives—one of White Mountain, one of Slate Mountain and Mt. Goddard, one of the Palisades, and an east and west view of the summit. Night overtook us on the second North Glazier Basin and we camped on short grass. Stopped at two different points next day on our way down the mountain and took views. Reached and camped early in the extreme upper end of the valley of the Middle Fork,[2] and prepared for our trip on foot to the Palisades. Here we left our horses.

Leaving the head of the main King's River Valley we found the northwest side of the river the best to travel on. For the first two miles the river ran through a narrow canyon with perpendicular walls from 20 to 100 feet in height. Here, on the east side of Slate Mountain[3] a small stream puts in from the north, which separates the slate formation of the west side from the granite on the east, as Goddard creek does the west side of Slate Mountain from White Granite Mountain. Here we were able

---

1. Dr. Chester Rowell founded the *Fresno Republican* in 1876.
2. Simpson Meadow.
3. Mt. Woodworth.

to travel along the river, the canyon beginning to assume the shape of a valley. **[See Color Plate No. 1.]** On the east, and a few hundred yards above Slate creek, another stream comes foaming down a steep slope over 1,200 feet high, which we called Cascade creek.[4]

The main river gradually turns till its course is north and south. About 8 miles from our old camp (mouth of Goddard creek) the river forks, about one-half coming from the east, in the direction of the Palisades.[5] We continued up the North Fork, and in about half a mile came to the lower end of a valley about half a mile wide and two miles long. The valley is level and is covered with the finest quality of grass, which now stands waist high. The meadow is bordered with tamarack, and the adjoining hill sides with a thick growth of brush. Here the mountains slope gradually nearly to the tops. The grouse which seemed to be the only occupants of this beautiful valley were as tame as domestic fowls, evidently never having seen men before.[6]

Four miles further up at the head of the valley the river again divided into four branches, one coming from the east being our course to the summit.[7] Climbing up a thousand feet we came to a small lake from which we could view the Palisades, and another thousand feet brought us to a lake 200 yards wide and two miles long. Here we camped and were entertained for some time by a small army of blood thirsty striped mosquitoes. From here to the summit,[8] which we reached the next morning, there is no timber. We reached the summit where the dividing range between the King's and San Joaquin rivers and the main summit unite, and found that King's river heads six miles east of the San Joaquin, instead of the reverse, as has been supposed. Bishop creek drains the north side of the Goddard ridge for at least six miles. We could see Mt. Goddard about fifteen miles in a due west course, and Long Valley extending north for a great distance. North from this point the Palisades ceased to be the divide, but south as far as we could see it is the summit.

---

4. A presently unnamed stream that comes into the Middle Fork about 0.5 mile north of Devils Washbowl.
5. Palisade Creek.
6. Grouse Meadows.
7. Dusy Branch.
8. Bishop Pass.

We estimated the peak at this point at 2,000 feet above the summit and over 15,000 feet above the sea, and attempted its ascent from the north. It is certainly the highest peak on the range.[9] We climbed up, first over immense rocks, and then over snow and ice until it was dangerous to go further. By clinging to the crags along the border of the ice drift we managed to reach a point about 400 feet from the top, where the ice blocked up every space through which the top could possibly be reached. From a shelf to the left, which we managed to reach, we could trace Owen's River for at least 50 miles. Big Pine could not have been over ten miles distant, for we could plainly see the houses and roads. Beyond the valley we could see three distinct ranges of mountains. Instead of being lava, as reported by Prof. Whitney, the Palisades are made up of a dark granite, checkered with veins of feldspar, and the ridges running down between the streams are of the same formation.

We descended with but little difficulty, and continued south along the foot of the main ridge and crossed a mass of ice a thousand feet wide with streams of water running down through canals worn in the solid ice. Crossing a ridge running west,[10] we came into a flat country of bare granite, and close to the foot of the Palisades found a beautiful lake, nearly round, very deep, and about a half mile in diameter.[11] Following a small stream which flowed from the lake, for a distance of four miles, we came to the east end of a long valley running east and west, the east end not over three miles from the Palisades. It was about six miles long, its lower end not more than one mile from the one first spoken of. This we named Palisade valley.[12] We found no fish above the canyon near the main valley. Our return to our horses, after three days of hard climbing, and subsequent return to our summer home at Dinkey was accomplished without unusual trouble. As compensation for the excursion I brought back 38 negatives of scenery entirely new, and have the satisfaction of having visited a region heretofore considered inaccessible. Sincerely, yours, FRANK DUSY

---

9.   Bishop Pass is 11,972. Mt. Agassiz, which they attempted to climb, is 13,891, and is far from the highest peak in the Palisades.
10. Probably through Knapsack Pass. **See Color Plate No. 2.**
11. The largest of the Barrett Lakes, in Palisade Basin.
12. Deer Meadow, along Palisade Creek.

A Trip to Tehipite Valley

"MONTERO"
Originally published in the *Fresno Weekly Expositor*, July 30, 1879

[Editor's note: Frank Dusy discovered Tehipite Valley in 1869. He was the leader of this foray, and also compiled a report of it, which was published in the *Fresno Weekly Republican* on August 2, 1879. It was somewhat shorter and less flamboyant than that of "Montero," who may have been Lilbourne A. Winchell. I have interspersed some elements of Dusy's report into the following, in italics.]

On the 11th of July, 1879, our party of five, *Thos. Hunt from the Toll House, Truman Hart from Millerton, and L. A. Winchell and T. Burks from Fresno,* equipped, armed and provisioned, left the hospitable mountain home of Mr. And Mrs. Frank Dusy, on Dinkey Creek, en route for the grand canyon of the middle fork of King's river. *In June, some miners from Mill Creek, Tulare county, found an old trail and took their horses and pack animals into the Valley. On learning this fact and getting the directions from those miners, I resolved to satisfy my long desire to photograph this dome and other views in the valley.* Our steeds were not of Arabic blood; two of them being the much abused and lowly donkey; consequently our speed did not compare favorably with that of Parole at the Ascot races. Nevertheless, with hopeful hearts, and amid the laughter of our friends who bade us adieu, we entered upon the arduous undertaking of climbing thirty-five or forty miles nearer the summit of the Sierra Nevadas; over a rocky and precipitous country, clad with chapparal and pine forests.

Those of our party who were mounted on horses experienced no difficulty in making headway; but not so with the unfortunates who bestrode the donkeys, for after going a mile in splendid style, the donkeys showed unmistakable signs of rebellion at the idea of ascending a slight acclivity. They ran first on one side of the trail, then on the other; now into a brush thicket; anon into a pile of rocks; and neither threats, blows, imprecations, entreaties nor kindnesses (of the latter they received scant measure) could induce them to move forward. Meantime our well-mounted companions were making themselves conspicuous by their absence, having ridden forward, leaving us and our donkeys, each to the tender mercies of the other. Finally, becoming exhausted and discouraged at our ill success, we dismounted, and, presto! the charm was found. Off went the donkeys at a rate of speed surprising for an animal so despicable, but, unfortunately for us, not in the right direction. They still persisted in going everywhere but in the proper course; however, by patience (?), we were finally victorious, and after getting within calling distance halloed for our companions to stop.

We soon overtook them, and adopted a new line of tactics, viz: one of the party went forward to entice the donkey, another behind to persuade. The persuasive argument was a small sapling, the size of a full-grown base-ball bat, daintily applied. In this way we forged ahead in fine style, as long as no hills presented; but as soon as one was to be climbed the donkeys would rebel, and the sapling argument would again be resorted to, with invariably good results. After six long hours of obstinacy on the part of the donkeys, and of toil and vexation on the part of the riders, we reached the North Fork meadows, sixteen miles from Dinkey, and our camping-place for the first night.[1] This is a delightful and romantic spot, in the valley of the north fork of King's river, one of the many oases of verdure in this wilderness of rude and ragged mountains. The valley, two miles in length, presents broad stretches of grassy lawns—is watered by bright and gleaming streams—framed in like a gigantic picture, with crags of massive granite. Here we gladly halted, and sought rest and refreshment after our weary initial day. Our animals were speedily unpacked and turned out to feed, and we commenced preparations for our evening repast. When supper was ready we were in no way afflicted with mock modesty nor vain ceremony, but did justice to the ample provision before us. Tired with our day's travel we rolled ourselves in our blankets at an early hour, and sweet and undisturbed was our slumber till morning, except on the part of one unhappy wight who ate too much supper, and suffered direful consequences in the shape of a vigorous nightmare.

---

1. Now named Long Meadow.

Rising early, we soon breakfasted, packed our animals and were once again ready to start. Suddenly one of our party rushed wildly into camp, with the thrilling intelligence that a bear—a genuine, living bear, in the flesh—not a black stump—was close at hand. Immediately all was excitement. Four of us armed and put out, following our informant to the spot where the bear had been seen. Looking for tracks, we discovered those of our comrade, pointed toward the camp, and nowhere more than ten feet apart. They turned not aside for rocks, logs, creeks or brush, so great had been his anxiety to inform us of the bear's presence, ere he escaped. Discovering Bruin's paw-prints, we followed them to a thicket, near the river. There the hunters separated. While three surrounded the brush, the fourth penetrated the thicket to flush the game. But, as thus "the boldest held his breath," bang! went the treacherous pistol of him in the thicket, and the hunt was up. The flankers rushed to the center to be in at the death, *we rushed to the spot and found him licking his hands—his revolver had gone off in his hands accidentally and burned his fingers,* and Bruin, sniffing the saltpetre and hearing the tumult, fled unharmed across the river. Be assured our chagrin and disappointment was great.

Leaving the North Fork we traveled seven miles in an easterly direction, across valleys and ridges, through meadows and forests, up hill and down, reaching Rancherie [Rancheria] Creek at noon. After dinner, and a two hours siesta, we resumed our two-fold labors of climbing mountains and delicately stimulating our long-eared Rosinantes. Traveling necessarily very slowly, we encamped for the night only six miles further on, at the Crown Mountain Meadows, so named from a mountain of white granite on the north, that rears its royal head more than 12,000 feet above the ocean level, and whose flat top is crested with a cap of rock resembling a huge crown.[2] *We camped at the Big Meadow near Crown Mountain, which is owned and occupied by the Collins brothers of Big Dry Creek.*[3]

The next morning, after a refreshing sleep and a hearty breakfast, we packed our provisions, blankets, etc. on the two donkeys and a mule, and leading them, made the rest of the trip on foot. As the rugged way now made it impossible to ride further, we here left our horses, staking one and hobbling a second, expecting they would await our return. But the

---

2. Crown Rock, overlooking Crown Valley.
3. The Collins brothers were sheepmen.

sequel showed that our confidence had been misplaced. Slowly toiling eastward about six miles, over a broken and rock-strewn country, we stopped for lunch and to take a rest before entering the stupendous canyon of the Middle Fork, which our guide, Mr. Dusy, informed us was only a mile distant. Reanimated by this assurance the space was quickly passed over, and at 4 o'clock P. M. of Sunday, July 13th, we stood on the brink of the cliff and gazed with wonder and awe upon one of the grandest views to be found in the Sierras. A grassy slope reaches to the very edge of the chasm, the bottom of which is more than a vertical mile below, and as one looks shudderingly down the giddy abyss he sees the majestic stream of the Middle Fork, appearing no larger than a brook, as it glistened in the sun. To the east we beheld mountains of solid rock, capped with snow, and increasing in grandeur and height as they near the summit, which was dimly outlined against the sky, in the far distance. Lingering with enraptured visions we were loth to withdraw our eyes from a scene at once sublime and awe-inspiring, at the warning by the lengthened shadows, that our time was limited, so with reluctance we left the spot and pursued our way down the steep and difficult route that led to the bottom of the valley.

No route has ever been found by which animals could be taken into the canyon of the Middle Fork till about a month ago, when some prospectors discovered a trail that evidently was made many years ago. It is said that about 1860 a party of Mexicans discovered gold in the canyon, and while engaged in mining there a party of white marauders encroached upon them, but were driven out. In return they caused the Mexicans to be murdered by the Indians, that they might become possessors of the gold. So much for rumor, now for fact. The path by which we descended winds around a ledge of rocks for a distance, and is very narrow. At one abrupt turn the ledge is broken off, requiring an artificial substitute. Here a tree has been felled across the break, then brush and rocks piled in to make a safe passage-way. Doubtless this work was done many years ago, as the stump and log are old and decayed, and the "blazes" on the trees marking the trail have grown over till they are scarcely visible. In the valley we found an ancient grave, an old campground, a venerable pair of boots, and remains of branches of trees used to make a corral, with other indications of an early habitation. As we plunged down the dangerous and flinty way, we came to a place where we were compelled to unpack our mule, in order to get around a narrow point on the ledge. But we determined to try the little donkeys without unpacking. So one of the party took a donkey by the head, while another seized his tail with a death-like grip, and in that manner, steadying the burro's nerves, made the passage in safety. The descent of two and a half miles is very tiresome, owing to loose soil and shifting rocks, down which the trail winds its tortuous way. But we arrived safely in the valley before sundown, tired enough to eat our suppers in haste and go to sleep.

As Mr. Dusy's chief object on this occasion was to take photographic views of the principle points of interest, we, early next morning, loaded ourselves with the camera, acids, glass, and other articles required to take pictures, and, guided by him, started off up the river about a mile, to where a vast amount of drift-wood has collected, forming a bridge across the stream, which here is divided into many branches. Crossing them without accident, and climbing up the chaos of rocks that for ages have been falling from the cliffs, on the south side of the canyon, we reached a suitable point, overlooking the valley, about five hundred feet above the river. Mr. Dusy was soon in readiness, and proceeded to take a copy of the Dome and the north side of the valley, but, owing to the hazy condition of the atmosphere, he did not succeed in getting a presentable picture. So we clambered down again to the river by a shorter route, wading nearly waist deep in the icy waters, across to our camp. The mountain air produced a singular drowsiness, and it was sometimes with difficulty that we could keep our eyes open, particularly after dinner. We arose next morning, with old Sol looking down upon us, reproachfully, as if chiding us for scorning the splendors of a mountain dawn. Hurrying through breakfast we again waded the river, and once more climber the rocky debris to our former point of observation. This time the artist obtained admirable representations of the Dome, the Valley, and the Falls under the Dome. Pleased with our success we returned to our camp, re-crossing the river at a place where it was necessary for us to partially disrobe, and to carry our boots and unmentionables, together with our photographic materials, in our hands. All but one crossed without disaster. The unfortunate stumbled in the swift current, and to save himself thrust downward the hand that held his wardrobe, thus dipping his boots full and sousing his clothes.

A general view of the valley, which is three miles long by one in width, is magnificent and sublime. Great white mountains of rock on either side, cleft by deep canyons, down which icy torrents tumble and roar; beautiful green meadows, dotted with copses of willow and oak; the bright colored flowers; the several branches of the river, with their transparent waters, bordered on one side with a bar of white sand, that glistened like snow in the sun, all combined to make one of the fairest pictures in Nature's gallery. The grandest feature of all is the superb and majestic Dome, which rises 5,330 feet above the level of the river, on the north side of the gorge.[4] The Indians call it "Tehipite," signifying high rock, and that name we decided by formal vote it should wear forever, and that the same name should also be applied to the valley. We recorded our resolve on a written notice, conspicuously posted, and also inscribed it on the blazed trunk of an oak tree. Be it known, therefore, to all the earth that the lordliest mass of granite in the Nevada range, is the Tehipite Dome, in the Tehipite valley, on the middle fork of King's river.

On the opposite side the rocks rise 6,000 feet high, though not vertically. The falls, under the dome, come from the waters of Crown Mountain Meadows, and pour over the cliff, in a series of cascades, and in three distinct falls. The lowest one is perhaps 300 feet high, and breaks into spray before reaching the bottom. Because of its great beauty we named it the "Silver Spray Cascade."

Our work being completed, we prepared to ascend again to the outer world, when at the last moment we found that our pack mule had eloped. After vainly trying to make our patient donkeys carry his load with theirs, two scouts volunteered to pursue the recreant. *Messrs. Winchell and Hunt volunteered to go and bring back the mule. Hart and myself joined a prospecting party that came in that morning hunting for a silver lead, while Burks remained in camp.* Wearily climbing out of the canyon, they followed his muleship six miles, and found him fraternizing with the horse we had staked four days before. Those that we had then turned loose, basely taking advantage of our absence, had fled homeward. The scouts brought the truant mule into the canyon the next morning. *Next day Winchell returned with the mule,* and we at once prepared to depart. At 1 o'clock P. M. of the 17th we began to struggle up the precipitous slope side of the gorge, and at 6 o'clock reached the summit without accident. We had to unpack the mule and steady the donkeys by ears and tail, as before, at a narrow pass. Here one of the donkeys lost his footing, and for a moment

---

4. About 3,300 feet.

was suspended by his extremities over a yawning gulf, 1,000 feet deep. Had either of those appendages failed him, or the grip of his drivers been less firm, sad would have been his fate, to say nothing of the precious treasure he bore in his panniers. He was fully conscious of his danger, and trembled all over when the crisis was past. At the summit we met and encamped for the night with Messrs. Doak, Tadlock, Sample,[5] and Collins brothers, who were on a prospecting tour towards Mt. Goddard and the higher Sierras.

Our next day's trip was on foot, sixteen miles to the North Fork, where we found our truant horses grazing on the meadows. Once more, on the morrow, we were all gaily mounted, and driving our faithful donkeys before us, we rode joyously out of the chaotic world of mountains, canyons, forests and chapparal which we had been exploring, into the more attractive region which borders Dinkey Creek, our point of departure.

---

5. D. C. Sample was another of the early sheepmen.

A Night on Mt. Whitney

W. B. Wallace

Originally published in the *Mt. Whitney Club Journal*,
Vol. 1, No. 1, May 1902.

"The hills were brown, the heavens were blue,
The woodpecker pounded a pine top shell,
The squirrel whistled the whole day through
For a rabbit to dance in the chaparral,
And the gray grouse drummed 'All's well, all's well.'"

The summer of 1881 was an exceptionally fine season for
mountain-climbing, and, having spent several weeks about Mineral King,
exploring its brown and gray heights, hunting deer in forest and silver in
vein, I longed for something new. "Things won are done. Joy's soul lies in
the doing."

It was therefore with a feeling of delight that I hailed the appearance
there of that genial, companionable soul, Captain J. W. A. Wright, of
Hanford, and, in accordance with a prearranged plan, we started, August
26th, on an excursion to Mt. Whitney. Rev. F. H. Wales, of Tulare, had
preceded us to Little Kern River, and there awaited our arrival.

On the south side of Farewell Gap we passed a patch of red snow,
something rarely seen. The largest area was three or four feet square, in
the middle of a great snowbank, and from this extended a line, like a
band of red ribbon, for a distance of fifteen or twenty feet. Its deepest
color was cochineal-red, shading off into a light pink. When crushed, in
Captain Wright's words, it looked "like red rock candy," and melted "like
water from a red watermelon." It leaves no stain, and is tasteless. This
rare appearance, naturalists tell us, is due to a microscopic vegetable or
animal form. The largest area of red snow I have ever seen was at the
head of the Big Arroyo, in 1882, where I walked across it for several hundred feet, leaving footprints that looked as if made in blood.

Our route for a considerable distance was along the Hockett trail.
The third day we camped on Whitney Creek, upon which we tried

unsuccessfully to impress the name "Volcano Creek," as that stream does not rise in the vicinity of Mt. Whitney. We lay over a day at this point to explore the craters of two extinct volcanoes and to feast on rainbow trout.

From there we traveled across the summit of the mountain range, in order to intersect the Signal Service trail, and passed a night in Diaz Meadows, Inyo County. It was the coldest and most cheerless camp of our journey. Its altitude is 10,000 feet, and bleak winds swept down upon us all night.

Captain Wright was the only fleshy member of our party. His ribs were encased in such thick layers of fatty tissue that, knowing his inability to freeze, we elected that he should sleep on the windward side of the camp.

Early the next morning we recrossed the summit and rode through Rampart Pass, where a grand view burst upon us. Spires and pinnacles and a great pyramidal mountain flanked with large bodies of snow arose above our horizon. The clear atmosphere brought us so near, apparently, that my companions thought it was Whitney. Closer scrutiny showed me that it was an old acquaintance, one on whose broad, massive sides I had had many a ramble. It was Mt. Kaweah. That night, September 3d, we reached Loomis Cañon and camped below and in full view of Whitney.

We were at an altitude of about 11,500 feet, in a little meadow, through which flows the clear, cold water of a creek heading at the foot of the mountain. This is the stream which we thought should have been named Whitney Creek. Toward the west we had an extensive outlook, but being in a close cañon the view elsewhere was cut short. The only timber there (for we were at the extreme upward limit of the timber belt) is the twisted pine, a regular corkscrew-tree, that will only split spirally. Old mountaineers delight in telling the story of a squirrel running down one of these trees and reaching the ground in advance of a streak of lightning, after an even start from the top.

This cañon is broad, wide-floored, rising gradually, and occasionally in terraces, and contains several lakelets and little meadows. At the head the walls are very precipitous. The southwestern wall, at the upper part, is perhaps two thousand feet high and deeply fluted, having the light reddish tint peculiar to that region. Much of the granite has a perceptible stratification, and most of it is porphyritic. The glacier-polished surfaces along tile creek are very beautiful, being dotted with flesh-colored,

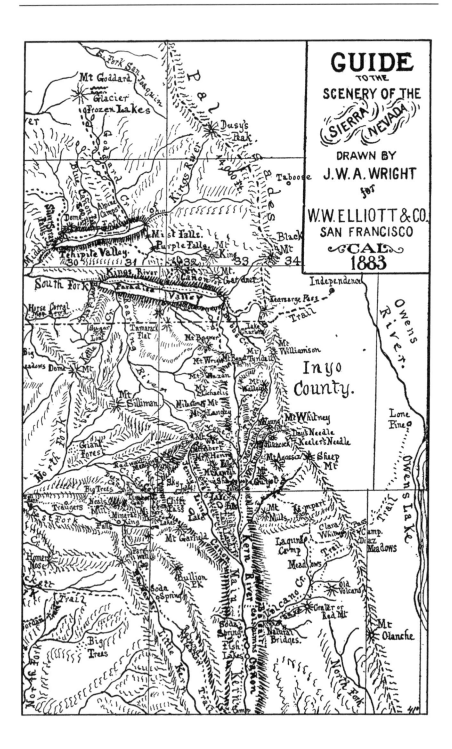

rectangular crystals from half an inch to two inches in length. The granite breaks into rhombohedral forms and occasionally large fragments may be seen nicely poised on sharp spires, holding their positions by a tenure so precarious that, apparently, a touch of the hand would dislodge them.

Mt. Whitney from our camp looked like a vast dome broken off almost vertically on all sides. Granite spires, or needles, range from it north and south and cling to its huge western flank. The most prominent of these is named Keeler's Needle. The summit of the mountain appeared to be accessible only by a trail which leads up a groove in its southwestern side, upon which some irreverent mountaineer has bestowed the name "Devil's Ladder."

On the afternoon of September 5th we set out to ascend it. Two miles higher up on the creek is a little lake, which, from the peculiarity of its shape, was named by Clarence King Guitar Lake, on the margin of which a temporary Signal Service station had been established, and a small detachment of U. S. troops was stationed there, under command of Captain Michaelis. There we met Professor S. P. Langley, now connected with the Smithsonian Institution, and the late Professor Keeler, since an astronomer at the Lick Observatory. They had come out from the East to make some astronomical observations and scientific experiments, principally to determine the color of the sun and sun-rays. They gave us a pleasant reception, and Captain Michaelis invited us to spend the night with him on the summit of the mountain, an invitation which Captain Wright and I gladly accepted. Leaving our horses at the foot of the Devil's Ladder, we started up that incline, each laden with an ample supply of provisions and bedding.

We were on top but a few minutes before the sun began to sink below the Kaweah Peaks, and had time only to take a few hurried glances about us before nightfall; but we speedily realized that we stood in the center of a grand circle of scenery. All about us were great granite amphitheaters and lordly mountains. Looking down into Owens Valley, but little more than ten miles away, and nearly 10,000 feet below us, we watched the lengthening shadow of Whitney as it moved eastward far in advance of the shadows of its neighbors. It crossed Owens River and dulled its glittering surface; it climbed the Inyo mountains and lay against the eastern sky high above the horizon, dark, solitary, and colossal.

We examined our picturesque surroundings until daylight faded into twilight and twilight merged into moonlight. The sun, like a glowing mass of fire, dropped out of sight, sending forth innumerable crimson lines to irradiate the west. Dining after dark, we sat around a camp-fire built of wood worth $140 a cord in that market; for it cost the troop $35 to get one-quarter of a cord to the summit.

Captain Wright narrated to an interested audience the story of the red-cement hunters, being the legend of a lost mine, and Captain Michaelis gave us a vivid description of the battle-ground of the Little Big Horn. He was the first white man to reach the body of General Custer on that ill-fated field.

The wind-storm which had raged about the mountain-top for several days had abated. The lowest temperature for the night was twenty-five degrees, and we experienced no difficulty in breathing the light air. The sky was cloudless, the moon was in the full, and we strolled for hours about the summit of this noble mountain, for which we were rewarded with many pictures that will long occupy a place in memory's gallery. There are about three acres at the summit comparatively level.

"The moon and her starry court" shone with increased brilliancy. Apparently more than double the number of stars were observable than can be seen from the valley, and while we know that every star is but a point of light without visible dimensions, yet in that clear, rarefied atmosphere the stars we see from below appeared not only brighter but larger. Here there was no obstruction to clear seeing. We were above the great body of reddish dust which forever hangs over the valley, and through which we see as "through a glass darkly." In the daytime we could see it below us. Then, in the words of Professor Langley, "we looked down on what seemed a kind of level dust-ocean, invisible from below, but whose depth was 6,000 or 7,000 feet. . . . It was evidently like the dust seen in mid-ocean from the Peak of Teneriffe, something present all the time and a permanent ingredient in the earth's atmosphere."

But resuming the moonlight scene: Outlines of all other great mountains in this region were visible, and the snowfields about Mt. Kaweah shone with subdued brilliancy. Owens Lake and Owens River presented dull, lead-like surfaces. The sides of Mt. Whitney are so precipitous to the north and east that in one place we looked almost directly down several hundred feet into the bosom of an oval lakelet—a feature of beauty in a form of grandeur. At half-past 12 o'clock, tired out, we lay down to sleep, and I think I never slumbered more soundly than during the following four hours. Awakening suddenly in the morning, I aroused Captain

Wright, and we hurried to the highest point, but fifty feet away. The sun was just appearing above the horizon, and soon lines of light were streaming through clefts and fissures in the mountain ridge, gilding granite domes and heightening the hues of crimson bands and red mountains far to the north and west. Another great shadow of Whitney appeared high above the Kaweah peaks, with the same pyramidal form and solitary as on the previous evening. Toward the east the scenery was equally impressive. Owens Lake was brilliantly illuminated, and river and lake, like a phosphorescent sea as the sunlight touched their surfaces, seemed starred and spangled with a thousand silvery gems. The valley is sprinkled with sand-flats and alkali patches. Beyond the lake we could see extensive lava areas, dark and forbidding, and to the north and east two or three ancient volcanic craters. We looked down upon Lone Pine, nineteen miles away, and we could trace the road to Darwin and the one leading up the valley. On the eastern rim of the valley are bright bands of metamorphic rock-white, gray, brown, and varicolored. The general desolate appearance of the valley is relieved only by a thread of green which marks the course of the river and by a few green fields in the vicinity of Lone Pine and Independence.

So high were we that it seemed like looking down into a lower world. For one brief period we were literally on top. The Inyo, Cerro Gordo, Coso, White Mountains, and Telescope Mountain, were in full view, and we could look down upon them all. Telescope Mountain is near Panamint, overlooking Death Valley. What a contrast between two points! Here we stood on the highest mountain in the United States, nearly 15,000 feet above the sea, and there, but seventy-five miles away, was that rainless, lifeless, bone-strewn valley, the lowest land in America—280 feet below sea-level! There

> "Not a flower lifts its head
> Where the emigrant lies dead;
> Not a living creature calls
> Where the Gila monster crawls,
> Hot and hideous as the sun
> To the dead man's skeleton.
> But the desert and the dead,
> And the hot hell overhead,
> And the blazing, seething air,
> And the dread mirage are there."

To Mr. William Crapo, who had remained with us over night, and to Mr. A. H. Johnson, who joined us that morning, both of Inyo County, we are indebted for much information regarding our environment. The latter pointed out a range of mountains on the Colorado River. Almost due south we could see the bold outlines of the San Gabriels near Los Angeles.

Mts. Williamson, Tyndall, Brewer, The Milestone, Kaweah, Miner's Peak, Olanche, Sheep Mountain, and Whitney form a great circle of towering heights, on the east rim of which we stood. Far to the north Mts. King, Goddard, Lyell, Unicorn, and Dana, and some in the near vicinity of Yosemite, were pointed out to us. One could not but gaze long on such a scene. [See Color Plate No. 3.]

We wandered about the summit studying our picturesque surroundings until hunger admonished us that we had not breakfasted. The mind had feasted, the soul had banqueted, but the stomach was neglected. I felt the sentiment of him who said, "Though the chameleon, love, can feed on air, I am one who is nourished by my victuals, and would fain have meat." After a good breakfast we resumed our observations, and witnessed some fine signaling with the camp at Lone Pine.

The year 1881, like the present year (1901), was one of national sorrow. President Garfield had been shot by an assassin. An inquiry as to his condition was signaled from the summit. The answer as flashed back was read, "The President is dead." Captain Michaelis ordered the flag lowered to half-mast. Later the question was repeated, and the answer, "No better," proved the former to have been misread. The sadness of our little group was modified, and we rejoiced at again seeing our national banner waving free from the greatest height at which it has ever been unfurled within our borders.

The height of Mt. Whitney, according to Clarence King's measurement, is 14,887 feet. The measurements made by Professor Langley were doubtless far more accurate, as he took readings from a fine mercurial barometer at short intervals every day for four or five days. He gives 14,522 feet as its height; but with this reduction it is the highest mountain wholly within the United States.[1]

---

1. The correct altitude is 14,494.

The Indians called Mt. Whitney "Too-man-i-goo-yah," which means "the very old man." They believe that the Great Spirit who presides over the destiny of their people once had his home in that mountain, and from that great height smiled upon the efforts of the good Indian, or, with a frown on his mighty brow, dealt swift vengeance upon the unfortunate *hombre* who transgressed the Pi Ute code of ethics.

On the eastern side of Owens Valley is Pi Ute Monument, a tall granite shaft. The Pi Utes have a legend that an old chief when dying declared that his spirit would reside in that monument, and as long as they were good Indians the monument would stand and they would prosper, but if they became bad Indians, it would crumble away and their tribe would cease to exist. We were told that the monument is crumbling away, and that that tribe of Pi Utes has well-nigh disappeared.

Kaweah was originally "Kah-wah," accented on the last syllable, and some Indians say it means "I squat here," or "Here I rest."

Before we seemed to realize it, the sun was declining in the west, and our time to descend had arrived. After one more long look, one sweep of the eye around our entire horizon, a last glance at the deep violet-hued sky above, a final salute to the flag on high, we dropped down the ladder to Guitar Lake.

The principal object of our journey was accomplished. About this time Whymper, of the Alpine Club, was boasting of having "polished off" Chimborazo and Cotopaxi and of tenting on the summit of mighty Sorata. We did not envy him, for we felt proud of a delightful experience in that line near at home.

The following day we bade our genial hosts farewell, retraced our steps down the creek for two or three miles, and then struck out northwest towards the head of Kern River. The second day we were on the brink of the cañon just east of the Milestone. I had assured my companions that we could descend into it near its head, but, as my confidence was not the fruit of my own experience, they were unyielding doubters from start to finish. Upon Mr. Wales asking a Frenchman whom he met on the plateau, the latter excitedly exclaimed, "Imposs'! imposs'!"

The next morning we broke camp and worked our way through brush and rock along a trailless route until we reached a bluff broken off vertically on the western side. Slipping out of my saddle, I dodged behind a bowlder heap, before my companions could compliment me on my success. Knowing that Captain Wright, whose motto was, "Blessed are they

Kaweah Peaks Ridge, from Mt. Langley.

that expect nothing, for they shall not be disappointed," would soon be lost in the study of the surrounding Sierra flora, I took time to examine the locality ahead very carefully. Finally discovering a way that was practicable, provided we could cross a mass of bowlders about three hundred feet wide, I set to work rolling the little ones between the big ones, and in two hours had a road constructed. Returning to my friends, the question, "What are the chances?" awaited an answer. "We must go down," I said. "Yes," replied Captain Wright; "but what are the chances?" "A Frenchman just told me it is impossible," remarked Mr. Wales. "The French," I replied, "have a saying that 'It is the impossible that always happens.' Let us verify it." We got our horses together, and we went down and rested that night at Junction Camp. In traveling less than eight miles we had descended about 4,000 feet.

Like a bird from the upper air, we dropped suddenly down from a cold, bleak, cheerless, wind-swept plateau into a new region of warmth and comfort. Junction Camp is a delightful place, 8,000 feet high, and there we found excellent fishing. From that point down for ten miles the cañon is closed in by walls that vary from 3,000 to 5,000 feet in height. There are five waterfalls on the sides from 1,500 to 3,000 feet high, the water of which drops three or four hundred feet at a plunge, to be dashed into spray on a succession of narrow shelves. We named the highest of these Shä-goo-päh Falls, after an old Pi Ute chief.

Along this cañon one in search of pleasure or relief from care may while away many an interesting day. The floor is dotted with flower-decked meadows, trout can be caught at nearly any point along the river, and a diligent hunter could find bear and deer. The only game we got here was a mess of fine quail. A great variety of flowers and many different kinds of birds are to be seen. Insect pests are not numerous, barring the omnipresent and belligerent yellow-jacket, that at all times seems like a boy with a chip on his shoulder, aching for a fight. Once I rode down Kern Cañon with a talkative friend mounted on a mettlesome mule. He was transported by his wonderful surroundings, and was rapidly exhausting a rare assortment of appropriate adjectives in expressing his views of the present beauties of the cañon and its probable condition before so much was removed by eroding agencies, when, in the midst of his rhapsody, a yellow-jacket touched him under the left ear and another paid its fervid addresses to his mule's flanks; and in an instant up went visions of primeval grandeur, forests, columns, colossal mountains, and heaven-born cataracts. It was a new feature introduced into a panorama of gorgeousness, and it evoked corresponding emotions. I have never seen a better illustration of the comic-magnificent.

From the sides of Kern Cañon come in many lesser cañons, reminding one of Major Powell's description of the Colorado—"Every river entering this has cut another cañon; every rill born of a shower, and born again of a shower, and living only in these showers, has cut for itself a cañon." The Kern River cañons are the result of erosion, and exhibit the great energy and working power of water. But water has only supplemented the efforts of a mightier agent, for ice with massive power has wrought extensively in that region. There the student of nature can find much that will sharpen his powers of perception and augment his store of knowledge; there he may see the first process in the formation of soils-nature's primitive efforts to utilize the mineral kingdom; and there, from ice-sculptured rocks, he may read the evidence of climatic changes, perhaps world-wide in extent. Our two days' stay in that place was restful and very interesting. We took many rare pictures for our mental galleries and we feasted to satiety on speckled trout.

Our course from Kern River lay south across a triangular plateau at the foot of Mt. Kaweah. The latter mountain we climbed, then went up the Big Arroyo near a point where the Kaweah, two branches of Kern River, and one of Kings River head within a pistol-shot of each other, and then, turning back, we ascended Cliff Pass, on the northeast side of Cliff Cañon. Thence, after one farewell glance at the Kern River basin, we commenced the descent into Cliff Cañon. Down, down we traveled over breakneck bluffs, through knee-tickling knee-brush, by the habitats of woodchucks, the surviving cave-dwellers, exciting the cheeping and electric-jointed chipmunks; driving, coaxing, and pushing our horses over slick rocks and along bowlder-strewn ravines until we reached Deer Cañon. The greater part of the 200 miles we had traveled was in the wake of the sheep-herder, and it was with a new feeling of delight that we rode towards Mineral King through ungrazed groves and meadows, where the tall grasses half hid our horses, where lovely tiger-lilies bowed approvingly as we passed along, and where every breeze was freighted with sweet odors. Our last camp was at our starting-point, where, after a good dinner, fatigued by a hard day's travel, we lay down to rest at an early hour and were soon lulled to sleep by falling waters and the sad, sweet music of swaying pines.

Notes on the King's River and Mt. Whitney Trails

(July and August, 1890)

Joseph. N. LeConte
Originally published in the *Sierra Club Bulletin*, vol. 1, no. 3, January 1894

[Before the age of automobiles, simply getting to the Sierra was a chore, requiring considerable time, effort, and logistical planning. And before there were maps, one needed articles such as this one—a forerunner of the present plethora of guidebooks. Note that the Kings River was often spelled with an apostrophe at that time, as though named after someone named King. The Kings River was named by the Spanish in 1805: *Rio de los Santos Reyes,* River of the Holy Kings.]

Fresno is an excellent place to start from, being on the main line of the railroad and due west of the King's River Cañon. We had considerable trouble obtaining donkeys here, and had to send as far as Raymond for them. Mules and horses, however, are easily obtainable. Excellent packsaddles and bags can be had (made to order) at any of the harness stores.

On leaving Fresno take the main Centerville road. This is one of the most frequently traveled roads in the county, and is surveyed due east on a section-line 17 miles to Centerville. Any one can direct you to the road. A streetcar runs out on it for a mile or so. There are many irrigating ditches along the way to furnish water. Cross the branches of the King's River a mile or two beyond Centerville. The main branches are bridged, but the smaller sloughs must be forded, which may prove a great inconvenience to pedestrians, if the river is as high as in June, 1890. A good camping-ground can be found anywhere along the river, with plenty of standing feed.

After crossing the last slough the *road forks*. Take the one to the *right* or *south*. A short distance beyond is the so-called '76 ditch or canal. Cross by a ford running as follows:

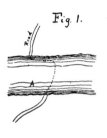

Fig. 1.

At A the water is deep. Still continuing east, enter between two barren hills, the first in the range. The one to the south is Mt. Campbell, while that to the north is Tcho-ne-tum-ne Mt. Beyond these hills is a large valley, cultivated over its entire extent. Soon after entering it the road forks again, and the right-hand fork is taken running along a fence for a short distance. At the base of the first real ascent is a small farm house where one may camp, but it is not the best of places.

Now comes a long ascent from the plains some 2000 feet into Squaw Valley. The road is steep, and there is very little water along the way. Squaw Valley is a very good place to camp. It contains plenty of standing feed, is covered with beautiful groves of oaks, and abounds in small game. A good camping-place is at Cherry's, 1½ miles beyond the school-house. From Centerville to Squaw Valley is 21 miles. The road now bears off to the right, crossing the ridge on the eastern side to the town of Dunlap. This is the last settlement before reaching Independence, in Inyo County. The road descends along a stream to the valley of Mill Creek. At the school-house the road forks, and you must take the one to the right running *up* the valley of Mill Creek. One can camp anywhere along this creek. (Altitude about 2100 feet). At the upper end of the valley the road begins to ascend by an extremely steep grade. It is a miserable road, badly washed out, and rarely used. The forest-belt is first encountered at an elevation of about 3500 feet, and at Happy Gap (5200 feet) we have sugar-pines and firs, and are in the heart of the forest. This is just above the Flooded Meadow, or the site of Thomas' old Saw Mill Ranch. You will strike here a good wagon-road coming in from Visalia, and running north to Moore and Smith's saw mill. *Do not follow it*, but take a dim road to the right, or, better yet, make your way down to the Flooded Meadow Lake, just below.[1] This, by the way, is a most excellent camping spot, with

---

1. LeConte's Flooded Meadow is Sequoia Lake, created in 1889 when the Kings River Lumber Company dammed Mill Flat Creek.

abundance of meadow land all around. From Squaw Valley to Flooded Meadow is 21 miles.

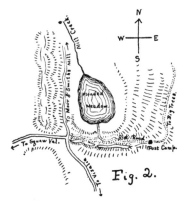

Fig. 2.

To reach the Big Trees, take the old road, which is at the southern end of the lake, and whose ruts can he traced to the spot where they disappear under the water. Strike back on this road up the hill, and branch off to the left at the summit of the ridge. This road will lead to a post camp in a grove of sequoias. The people here will direct you. Go on to the top of the ridge, and take the old skid road, which, in 50 yards, will turn into the Big Tree Road, which bears north. If desirous of reaching the Big Trees do not branch off on to any trail. In order to reach the Grand Cañon, turn off from the road on a trail to the right, about a mile before reaching the grove. This fork is at the crossing of a small stream, and the trail runs up along the stream on the northern bank for 50 yards or so, finally bearing off to north, and leaving the road to the west. One can camp anywhere along here, as meadows are abundant and the forests of the finest description. (From Flooded Meadow to Big Trees is 4 miles, to forks of trail is 3 miles.) The trail runs north for a mile or a mile and a half before turning up a steep, rocky hill to the east. Above this steep place is Round Meadow, which is an exquisite camping spot. Leaving Round Meadow, the trail, which is rather scattered here, turns north again, and runs up the slope in that direction for a few hundred yards. At the summit of the ridge the trail forks, and finger-boards on a tree direct the way. The *right*-hand trail goes to the King's River Cañon, the left to Long Meadows. The King's River trail turns eastward again, and preserves this general trend all the way to the cañon. Beyond the guide-post the trail descends a long hill to Little Boulder or Ten-mile Creek. While descending this hill, one obtains magnificent glimpses up the great cañon of the Middle Fork of the King's River or Tehipitee Valley. At Little Boulder Creek is the Bear Skin Meadow, and just where the trail crosses the creek is a grove of Sequoia gigantea. (From Flooded Meadow to Bear Skin Meadow is about 9 or 10 miles.)

Now comes an ascent of 5 miles to the summit of the ridge, between Little and Big Boulder Creeks, during which many groves of sequoias are encountered. The summit of this ridge is the highest point on the trail—over 7000 feet—and just below the top, on the other side, is a good camping spot at a fine large meadow. The trail now descends to the banks of Big Boulder Creek. This large stream comes down a steep slope in a succession of cascades, but there is usually a tree felled across, and it can probably he forded with very little trouble in most seasons, if the attempt is made early in the morning. After crossing this stream, take the trail up the tremendous ascent on the other side. Arrived at the top, the trail bears off over thinly forested, undulating country to the Horse Corral Meadows, 11 miles from Little Boulder Creek. The Horse Corral is a very large meadow, and is, of course, a most beautiful camping spot. After leaving this place the trail trends a little to the north, but there are no more steep hills till the verge of the King's Cañon is reached. Just beyond the Summit Meadows, at Grand Lookout, the descent into the cañon begins. The trail from here on is very rough and precipitous, descending 3000 feet in less than 3 miles. There are fine views along here of the Grand Cañon and the high Sierras to the east, and of the great "Divide" to the north. Arrived at the bottom, you are in the gorge about 3 miles below the Grand Cañon.[2] Follow up the trail a few hundred yards, to Fox's camp and meadow, just beyond which is a fine camping ground on the King's River. Fox leases the meadows from their owners, and makes a small charge for grazing stock. He also keeps on hand a small supply of provisions for the convenience of campers. (From Horse Corral Meadow to Fox's cabin is 6 miles.)

   The King's River is a very rapid stream, and fully 200 feet wide in the early summer. Fording or swimming animals is quite a difficult operation

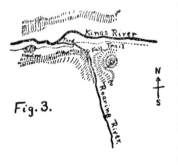

Fig. 3.

when the water is high. Fox endeavors to fell a tree across at some point each year, in which case there is no great trouble in pulling animals through. The trail contin-ues up the valley, on the south side of the river, for 3 miles to the meadow near the junction of the King's and Roaring Rivers. This latter, a stream about the size of the Merced, enters the valley through an

2. At what is now Cedar Grove.

extremely narrow cañon from the south. A short distance above its junction with the King's is the ford. Animals will have no trouble in crossing here, though pedestrians may have to fell a tree to get across. Where this river enters the valley there is a fine fall, about 50 or 75 feet high, but it can be viewed to advantage from the left or eastern bank of the river only. Both rivers abound in trout. After crossing Roaring River, the trail continues up the cañon, still on the south side of the main King's, to Big Meadows, 3 miles above. Here there was an immense sugar-pine felled across the main river, and it has remained in position for several years. At any rate, the river must be crossed here, and, as the water is comparatively quiet, there may be no great difficulty in pulling animals through. Just above the log the river makes a bend to the south, and on this bend

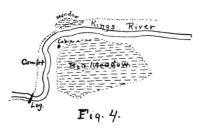

Fig. 4.

just across the log is an excellent place for a permanent camp. Big Meadows[3] is on the opposite side of the river, but there is also a small meadow on the same side as your camp just around the bend. The great cliff to the north of this camp is the face of North Dome, formerly called Mt. Ingersoll.[4] The high point on the south wall seen by looking from camp across the Big Meadow is the Grand Sentinel. The south wall can be best ascended by following up Avalanche Cañon, which breaks through the wall just where the log crosses the river. One may ascend the Grand Sentinel or Avalanche Peak by this cañon. Another way up the south wall is by the old trail in the gulch, just to the east of the Grand Sentinel, and this leads over toward Mt. Brewer. The north wall is best ascended by the Copper Creek trail, which follows up the left or western bank of the first large creek entering the river above camp. The distance from camp to the foot of the Copper Creek trail is about 1½ miles. This trail runs across the "Divide" into Tehipitee Valley. Paradise Valley can be reached by following up the left bank of the river. About 3 miles above camp the cañon comes to an abrupt end, the great mass of Glacier Monument blocking it entirely. The main King's River

3. Now Zumwalt Meadows.
4. Bob Ingersoll was a sheepherder.

comes down the rugged gorge from the north while Bubb's Creek enters from the southeast. At this point one must turn up the main stream, which can be followed without difficulty about 5 miles further, to Paradise Valley. There are many splendid cascades in the river on the way up.

The main trail to Independence crosses the King's River again, just above its junction with Bubb's Creek,[5] 3 miles above camp. There is a portion along the last bit of the King's River that is pretty rough and hard to follow, but it has probably been cleared out at present. In 1890 there was a log-jam across the river at the ford, so we had no trouble carrying our packs across. The river is broad and broken with islands. After cross-

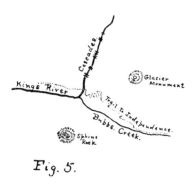

Fig. 5.

ing the river, the trail turns back along Bubb's Creek for a few hundred yards and then zig-zags up the hill to the left. *Do not attempt to follow along the stream-bank*, but find your trail and climb up the mountain-side. After attaining a height of about 500 feet the trail bears off on a level up the cañon of Bubb's Creek, gradually descending to the stream-bank again. There is no trouble in following it after this for the next 4 or 5 miles. Keep on the north bank. About 5 miles above the mouth of the cañon the *trail forks*—one branch keeping on up Bubb's Creek and the Independence trail turning to the left up a very steep hill. It follows up the left bank of the creek which drains Lake Charlotte (or Rhoda Lake), and which forms a waterfall of considerable size where it comes down over the side of the Bubb's Creek Cañon. The *other trail* crosses this creek on a sheep bridge which will help to distinguish the place. The trail from here on for about a mile is the worst on the journey—running in the dry bed of a creek filled with loose boulders. At the top of the steep ascent the trail follows along the stream again, through fine meadow land. The trail is very blind through here, but one need only follow along the left bank of the stream all the way to Lake Charlotte, which is some 9 miles above the upper end of the King's Cañon. This lake

---

5.   The apostrophe in the name is an error; the creek was named for John Bubbs, an early prospector.

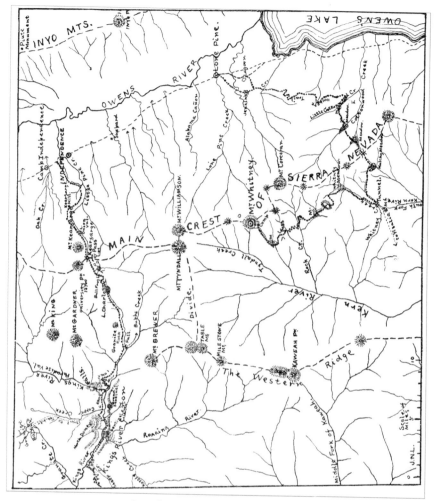

Joseph N. LeConte's map of 1890.

is a beautiful little sheet of water, a quarter of a mile long, set down amongst high, desolate mountains. It lacks trees and shade only to make it a fine camping spot. There are a few groves of Alpine pine (*Pinus flexilis*) on the margin, and also a narrow fringe of meadow about the lake. It abounds in fine large trout. Standing at the outlet, and looking toward the head of the lake, one notices a very fine peak standing up against the eastern sky. Our party called this University Peak, in honor of the

Kearsarge Lakes and Kearsarge Pinnacles. Beyond are South Guard, Mt. Brewer, and North Guard, on the Great Western Divide.

institution at Berkeley. It is over 14,000 feet high, and on the main crest. The altitude of Lake Charlotte is about 10,700 feet.[6]

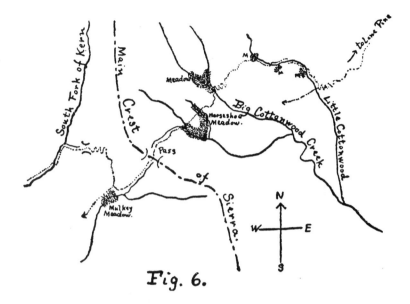

Fig. 6.

The trail passes around the left side of Lake Charlotte, and crosses the ridge at its head, keeping quite a distance to the left of the incoming stream at first, but approaching it again further on. There are several small lakes upon this stream. After crossing the ridge before mentioned the trail descends into the basin at the head-waters of Bubb's Creek, and passes around the left side of Bullfrog Lake. (Elevation 10,800 feet.) The rock scenery from this point to the foot of the Kearsarge Pass is rarely equaled in grandeur in any part of the Sierra. Only a few stunted pines grow amongst the rocks, but meadows are abundant. The trail is well beaten up to the base of the Kearsarge Pass. (Elevation of base 11,600 feet.) There is a ridge of loose rock at this point, and the trail runs diagonally up it for about 450 feet of ascent to the summit of the range. (

6. Before the first surveys by the U. S. Geological Survey, everyone over-estimated altitudes. Charlotte Lake is 10,370 feet; the peak is 13,005. In 1896 LeConte climbed a higher peak to the south, which he named University Peak. The peak cited here was renamed Mt. Gould for Wilson S. Gould, a member of the party.

Horseshoe Meadow.

Elevation of the Kearsarge Pass 12,056 feet.) The view from the top, which extends over the roughest portion of the Sierras at the head-waters of the forks of the King's and Kern Rivers, is the most sublime which it is possible to obtain in any part of the range. The summit ridge is not over 10 or 12 feet wide, and is very much shattered.

The trail starts rapidly down on the other side, amongst the loose debris to the left, passing around the northern edge of a frozen lake known as the Devil's Pot-hole. Just beyond this lake is a great drop in the cañon bed, but the trail is tolerably good, and beyond this place there is no trouble whatever. There are six lakes upon the stream (Little Pine Creek), and the last, which is by far the largest, is called Onion Lake. All these lakes abound in trout.[7] Just beyond the old Kearsarge Mill, the trail turns out of the cañon over the low ridge to the north, and descends into Owen's Valley by another cañon. The last portion is a wagon road, running directly east over the sage plain to independence. The distance from Lake Charlotte to the Kearsarge Pass is about 3 miles, and from this point to Independence 15 miles.

The road to Lone Pine is a continuation of the main street. It runs due south and to the east of a low mass of hills (the Alabama Hills), which are about 13 miles distant, passing between these hills and the Owen's River. There are several farm houses on the road after leaving

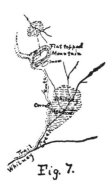

Fig. 7.

Independence, but none after coming within 6 miles of Lone Pine. After rounding the point of the Alabama Hills, the town of Lone Pine is still 4 miles distant. (From Independence to Lone Pine is 16 miles.) Continuing on through Lone Pine our road passes to the left of a little lake, or lagoon, of the river, and then forks. Take the branch to the right at this point, as well as at the next fork a short distance beyond. This road passes up through the Alabama Hills, and across the plain beyond to Jenkins' Ranch, running nearly west. The Hockett trail starts from

---

7. Little Pine Creek was the original name for what is now Independence Creek. LeConte's "Onion Lake" probably is Gilbert Lake.

this ranch, bearing southwest.[8] The first water is $2\frac{1}{2}$ miles from Jenkins', where a fine stream crosses the trail, and after this there is no more for 8 miles. After crossing this creek the trail runs diagonally up the hillside to the south, and then turns back into the mountains. The Hockett trail is well built, but the climb is a tiresome one, owing to the absence of water. The first water is at Little Cottonwood Creek; but there is no feed at this point. Follow the right hand branch of the trail which forks here, keeping up the stream on the right hand bank. Half a mile above are fine meadows and good camping grounds. It is 12 miles from Lone Pine to Little Cottonwood Creek. The trail runs up the creek, sometimes on one bank and sometimes on the other, and then turns to the left over a ridge to Big Cottonwood Creek. There are fine meadows and plenty of golden trout at Big Cottonwood, which is 17 miles from Lone Pine. The Hockett trail crosses Big Cottonwood and runs up the opposite hill, bearing a little to the left. *Do not* follow *up* the creek. The trail crosses a low ridge into another meadow—a very large and fine one—called Horseshoe Meadow. After crossing this portion of the meadow the trail passes over a low, wooded ridge, and down into another arm of the same meadow. It skirts around the right hand, or upper, edge of this, and then follows up a small stream coming in from the west. After reaching the top of the ridge at the source of this, we cross the main crest of the Sierra at an elevation of about 11,000 feet.[9] The trail is well blazed all along here. It then descends along a small creek to a large flat below, which is green in the middle and sandy about the edges. This is the Mulkey, or Mulchy Meadow. Cross a large sand hank, and then turn to the right, taking that fork of the trail which bears north, up the sandy plain. Continuing north the trail enters a dry valley, covered with sagebrush and scattered timber. Two miles above the Mulkey Meadow the trail turns to the left and crosses the ridge on that side, descending on the other side in a dry cañon to a large creek, the South Fork of the Kern River. Our route is first down the left bank for a short distance; and then crossing the stream, continues on the right side, the creek running in a deep gorge. Finally, the trail emerges on a

---

8. The Hockett Trail, built by John B. Hockett from Visalia to Lone Pine in the early 1860s. Portions of the trail can still be seen on the hillside that is traversed by the road to Horseshoe Meadow.
9. Trail Pass trail, which crosses the Pacific Crest Trail at about 10,500 feet.

sagebrush flat, still keeping near the South Fork till the "Tunnel Fork" is reached. At this point Whitney Creek and the South Fork approach within a few hundred feet of one another, and a tunnel has been cut, draining most of the water of the former into the latter. As the trail passes along the top of the low ridge over the tunnel, one may easily miss this place, which is a most important landmark. Here the Whitney trail branches from the Hockett trail and turns back up Whitney Creek.[10] At the "forks" our party put a blaze on a tree on the north side of the trail.

From Big Cottonwood to Horseshoe Meadow is 1 mile, and from here on to the Mulkey Meadow is 3. From Mulkey Meadow to the South Fork of the Kern is 3½ miles, and the trail follows this latter stream 4 miles to the "Tunnel Forks." Whitney Creek and the South Fork abound in golden trout.

Turn back toward the mountains again, taking the trail up Whitney Creek. At first the trail keeps well up on the ridge, and then descends to the south bank of the creek. A mile and a half above it crosses the creek and keeps on the other bank all the way to Whitney Meadows.[11] These meadows are at the base of Old Mt. Whitney, or Sheep Mountain.[12] You follow along the left, or northern edge of the meadow, and watch carefully for a sheep corral. It is built substantially of logs, and is set a little back in the forest, so that it can easily escape detection. Just here is a small stream, upon the bank of which is a U. C. cut upon a tree. From here on for a distance of 2 or 3 miles there is a gap in the trail, so one must cut across country, following prominent landmarks. Cross the little creek and ascend along the ridge upon the other side, bearing north. Then incline slightly to the right, getting finally into the cañon of another small creek flowing parallel to the first. At the head of this creek may be noticed a flat-topped mountain, which, in ordinary seasons, has a large patch of snow near the top.[13] *Ascend to the top of this mountain* with your animals, by keeping to the left of the patch of snow. On the summit will be found quite an extensive area covered with loose boulders. At the foot of the mountain on the other (northern) side will be seen an

---

10. Present-day Golden Trout Creek.
11. Big Whitney Meadow.
12. Mount Langley.
13. Siberian Pass.

The old trail across Guyot Flat.

extensive meadow with sandy margins, and our route is down the rocky slope into this.[14] Once at the bottom, make toward the point where the stream[15] leaves the meadow, at the northwestern corner. After following this stream down for a few rods on the left bank you will strike the trail which leads all the way to the base of Mt. Whitney. Two hundred yards from the edge of the meadow the trail crosses the creek, and on the other side it is well-beaten into the sand. For 1½ or 2 miles the trail follows near this creek on the east bank, and then it bears off more to the right, crosses a large lateral moraine, arid descends into a deep cañon to the banks of Rock Creek. Follow down this large stream for 1½ miles, till you come to a sheep corral. A hundred yards or so below this the trail crosses the creek on a sheep bridge, and on the other side it runs directly up the mountain northward. The starting point near the creek is marked by a blaze on a tree, thus: Δ P I E B. The trail zigzags up the mountain toward a saddle just to the right of a large peak,[16] crossing on the way up another fine creek.[17] Cross the pass at the saddle,[18] and then descend to a sand flat on the other side.[19] Cross this and follow the trail through forests of *Pinus flexilis* along the hillside for 3 or 4 miles, and then down a very steep, rocky slope, into the cañon of the creek which flows from the base of Mt. Whitney.[20] At the foot of the trail is a fine, large meadow.[21] Two creeks flow into it, one coming in from straight in front,[22] and the other (by far the larger) entering from the left. Where this latter meets the meadow is a series of narrow, vertical blazes on a tamarack.

From here to the base of Mt. Whitney there is only the remnant of a trail, but no difficulty will be encountered in following up the left (northern) bank of the large creek. A quarter of a mile above is another very fine meadow. About a half mile from the base of Mt. Whitney a beautiful lake will be passed, which is just at the timber line. (11,000 feet.) At the

14. Siberian Outpost.
15. Siberian Pass Creek.
16. Mount Guyot.
17. Guyot Creek.
18. Guyot Pass.
19. Guyot Flat.
20. Whitney Creek.
21. Crabtree Meadow.
22. Crabtree Creek.

Crabtree Meadow (lower center) and the basin of Whitney Creek.

The west and southwest sides of Mount Whitney, from the lake below Guitar Lake.

very base of the mountain is another lake and small meadow, where one may camp, but there is very little wood about. At this lake the creek forks. *If you keep up the southern branch*[23] for a quarter of a mile you will come to the site of the old Langley camp. From here to the summit may be found evidences of an old trail. Keep well to the right, ascending the slope to the south of the main peak.

Distances are as follows: Tunnel Forks to Whitney Meadows, 5 miles; Whitney Meadows to Rock Creek, 8 miles; Rock Creek to large creek flowing from base of Mt. Whitney, 9 miles. Follow this latter up for 3 miles to the foot of the mountain. From here to the summit is 3 miles.

During the whole trip from Lone Pine the true summit of Mt. Whitney cannot be seen anywhere along the trail till the descent into the cañon of the last creek is begun. On the way up this creek, however, the mountain is constantly in view. From Independence to Mt. Whitney is about 70 miles by trail.

23. The creek flowing from the Hitchcock Lakes.

Among the Sources of the San Joaquin

Theodore S. Solomons
Originally published in the *Sierra Club Bulletin*, vol. 1, no. 3, January 1894.

On the 17th of May [1892] the writer, accompanied by Mr. Sidney S. Peixotto, started from San Francisco for a five months' sojourn in the High Sierra. Previous to reaching the Yosemite Valley we traveled in a wagon drawn by mules, which were also accustomed to the riding and pack-saddle. After six weeks' travel among the summit regions of the northern and middle Sierra counties, we reached the Yosemite Valley toward the end of June. Here we were joined some weeks later by Mr. J. N. LeConte, and our party of three made a ten days' trip to Mt. Ritter, which we ascended, and then pioneered our way down Rush Creek to Mono Lake, returning to the valley by way of Bloody Cañon and the Yosemite Trail. Mr. LeConte then left the valley, and on August 9th Mr. Peixotto and myself packed a carefully selected outfit and three weeks' provisions on our two mules (named respectively Shasta and Whitney, in honor of the two dominant peaks of the range), and started upon a trip to the region south of Mt. Ritter, which appeared, from the splendid view of it we had obtained from the summit of that peak, to be an exceptionally wild and rugged country, with many indications of remarkable scenic features.

As far south as Ritter the crest of the range was explored some ten years ago by the United States Geological Survey during its reconnaissance of the Mono Lake Basin. South of Ritter no systematic survey has ever been made, and, although the region includes the southeastern portion of the Yosemite National Park, and gives birth to one of the two principal rivers of California, the greater portion of its surface is *terra incognita*.

Unfortunately, when we reached the Tuolumne Meadows, it became necessary for Mr. Peixotto to return, and, rather than abandon the proposed expedition, I decided to continue on alone—a most foolhardy undertaking, I afterwards realized; but one which happily resulted in no accident. I selected the more experienced of the two mules, and packed upon his back as much of the provisions as he could carry, in addition to the large camera brought along, and the remainder of the outfit. For the benefit of any club members who may possibly profit by my experiences I might state that I did not use the ordinary pack-saddle and bags. My saddle was an old army saddle, small, but very strong, and with a sort of horn, or peak, at each end. Two boxes, 2½ x 1½ x 1; one containing provisions, the other camera and outfit, were hung on each side of the mule by straps of suitable length, fastened to handles on the ends of the boxes, and hung upon the saddle peaks. Of course, the breast strap and breechings were also used to keep the boxes in place while ascending and descending. The box method obviates the perpetual nuisance of packing and unpacking. The boxes opened on the side by hinged lids, which swung down, disclosing compartments. While on the march it was simply necessary to halt, unlatch the lid and take out the camera or other article, replace it, close the lid and proceed. The boxes also served as a perfect protection to the camera plates and other comparatively breakable articles against bumping into trees and rocks.

The trip to the summit of Lyell and the photographing of its glaciers need not be described, as the route to the summit and the topography of the adjacent region is well known.

As a warning to those who may attempt the ascent of the mountain late in the season, it might, however, be pertinent to refer to the changes which take place on the surface of the glacier toward the end of August and the beginning of September (according to the amount of snow which has fallen during the previous winter). On the 16th of August, when the writer crossed the glacier, the portion adjacent to the terminal moraine was extensively hollowed out, which was evidenced by the sound of rushing water under the surface, by its varying degrees of opacity, the profusion of little green pools, and also by holes in the crust, which I did not yearn to explore. Farther up, about midway between the moraine and the cliffs, I encountered several little crevasses, stretching directly across the path to the summit. Not anticipating anything of the kind, I had been plodding up the sloping glacier, my eyes fixed upon the distant cliffs, when, happening providentially to glance downward I saw, with horror, that I was upon the very brink of a crevasse. A few feet further and my brief career in the high Sierra would have abruptly terminated. The crack extended some 200 yards on either side, with an average width of 3 or 4 feet. I leaned over the edge, but could not see the bottom, nor upon dropping in a stone could I catch the sound of its striking; but it is not unlikely that it fell upon snow. The opposite side of the crevasse, the lip of which was somewhat overhanging, was serrated with icicles of most fantastic form, some resembling blades, others appearing as spears of all sizes, up to great pointed poles of ice, hanging 30 and 40 feet into the depths. Tints of green and blue shaded the interior of the crevasse, and portions of the walls were stained crimson, due to the presence of protoccus,[1] as we are told by Whitney and Russell. Beautiful beyond description are these crevasses, but the cold shiver which invariably gambols down the spinal column of the beholder is not always to be regarded as a purely æsthetic sensation. The highest point of the glacier is a little névé tongue, which the traveler usually crosses before taking to the cliff. This tongue, though rather steep, is usually firm and safe. When I reached it, however, the snow was rotten, and seemed undermined by the drainage. Before I had mounted far the surrounding snow vibrated like jelly After floundering about a few moments I discreetly descended and took to the cliffs, a few hundred feet eastward. It will be seen from the foregoing that the ascent of the mountain, at this season of the year, is fraught with no little peril, especially to the unwary.

The following day, August 17th, was devoted to photographing the glaciers and terminal lake, and early on August 18th I crossed the Tuolumne from the main camp at the upper end of the Meadow, and made my way over substantially the same route as that pursued by our party three weeks before.

Upon the eastern side of the stream which dashes down the mile-long gorge, from the melting point of the lower glacier, and flows out upon the Tuolumne Meadow, a rude trail which is, in fact, scarcely more than an interrupted series of blazings, may be followed up the first and more difficult two-thirds of the length of the cañon. The ascent of the eastern wall presents no difficulty to men, but is a rather ticklish matter for animals. On our first expedition we followed up the cañon to quite an extensive flat, situated nearly at its head. On the present one, however, I turned at the first piece of meadow, which is about half way up the cañon. A terminal moraine of the old, retreating glacier, distinguished as usual by a kind of embankment of boulders and debris, had dammed up a lake, which, gradually filling, has at length become a little meadow, level as a floor,

---

1. A genus of microscopic unicellular algæ.

and furnishing a delightful camping ground. Among other smaller trees and bushes, four large trees are conspicuously seen to lie in a straight line up the western side of the cañon. This line of trees I had noticed from the slopes of Lyell the previous day, as marking the location of what seemed the most advantageous place of ascent of the entire mile of cañon side. I found it indeed quite easy on Whitney, although, as a result of my own carelessness, he fell twice.

Once out of the cañon, a treeless, sloping plateau, walled in on the east by some very old and very interesting cirques, must be traversed before the divide is gained. The lowest point of the ridge is easily reached, and here a very pretty little lake lies almost on the divide.[2] A splendid view is obtained of Lyell and McClure, and, in fact, of the entire basin of the Tuolumne. To the south a lofty and snow-covered line of peaks extends from Mt. Lyell to Mt. Ritter and its twin, Banner Peak, where the ridge abruptly ends. Between the observer and Mt. Ritter lies the upper basin of Rush Creek, which has been most fantastically eroded from a continuous mass of greatly metamorphosed sedimentary rock. The basin derives its waters from the snow and ice of this lofty ridge.

Here, on the very crest of the mountain, on the true divide between the eastern and the western slope, there are evidences of the former presence of moving ice. For a distance of some hundreds of feet the glaciation is continuous, the divide having been planed down until level as a floor. Slabs of rock displaced by subsequent disturbances, together with glacial boulders and other residual debris, are profusely scattered over the surface. This little pass, then, is one of quite a number of low places on the main crest which appear to have been completely covered by ice during the glacial period.

The journey to the base of Mt. Ritter from the divide is comparatively easy, with the exception of the first descent to the upper plateau of the basin. A steep and ugly bluff fractured and roughened by storm and torrent, must be descended, and very cautiously, too. It would be next to impossible to take an ordinary horse down this hill, and it is very trying on a jack or mule. It is well to keep on the western side of the stream, and sufficiently near it to take advantage of the little patches of soil which the water has washed into the numerous holes.

The tree line is reached at the lower margin of the upper terrace of

2. At Donohue Pass, not named until three years later.

Ritter group from Island Pass. (Photograph by Theodore S. Solomons, August 1892.)

the basin; and here the whole region is one great camping ground. The structure of the basin is, I believe quite unique. The terrace-like formation is noticeable, not only in the way that the basin is divided into several well marked plateaus, or benches, but each of these, and even the main lower basin itself—their confluent, so to speak—is divided into little grassy terraces, separated by low, rounded masses, and running into each other in a most bewildering fashion. The easiest route from the base of the steep bluff described, is to keep curving in toward the slopes, maintaining the level as much as possible, and avoiding the steeper descents.

On the summit of the hill the main crest is again reached.[3] Here the traveler is on the divide between Rush Creek and the head waters of the main San Joaquin River, which heads in a shallow, island-dotted lake, lying at the northeastern base of the Ritter group.[4] The view of these majestic peaks, mirrored in the little lake on the very summit of the divide, is something so awe-inspiring, so indescribably impressive, that, however extensive may have been his travels in the Sierra, the spell- bound beholder will murmur "At last!" when the full scene bursts upon him.

The desolation of the landscape is but little softened by the effect of the few trees in the foreground. That desolation of rock, shattered and torn, carved and sculptured, with its cold, white mantle of glacier and snow field, is relieved only by the very majesty of the mountain peaks themselves, with their forcible suggestion of life and personality. The sweeping, upward curve of their slopes, the sharp outline of the summits endow them with a dual sovereignty. Mt Ritter and Banner Peak stand the king and queen of the Sierra, dominating a crest that stretches from Shasta on the north to Mt. Goddard in Fresno County, on the south.

The divide here is so low and flat that a wagon road might easily be built over it. The Ritter group is not situated upon the main crest, but is the termination of the lofty ridge which extends southward from Mt. Lyell At a point on this ridge, about half a mile north of Ritter, the divide shoots off in a nearly easterly direction for about 3 miles, then turns abruptly southeast, thus enclosing the isle dotted lake and its outlet stream.

Following up the rivulet which flows down the northern slope of the mountain and empties into the lake, I camped at the highest patch of grass, where a clump of stunted tamarack bushes provided shelter and fuel. Next morning I slung the camera and four plates on my back and started up the mountain. The route to the summit is a go-as-you-please one, but very trying, at best. On our first expedition we kept well up on the slopes of Banner Peak, crossed the main glacier slantingly and tackled the precipitous side of Ritter, instead of going to the very head of the glacier, from which point the final ascent is most easily made, as we

---

3. Island Pass.
4. Thousand Island Lake.

Banner Peak from camp.
From an elevation of 11,500 feet.
(Photograph by Theodore S. Solomons, August 1892.)

afterward discovered. We soon found ourselves in the same predicament as that alluded to by John Muir in a description of his ascent of the mountain twenty years ago. We reached a point on the almost vertical cliff from which it seemed equally impossible either to continue the ascent or to descend. We did not experience that sudden inspirational agility which came to Mr. Muir just in the nick of time; but by great care and good management—as we prided ourselves—succeeded in accomplishing the ascent. Once on the narrow backbone of the peak the summit was only a matter of climbing, which, at times, seemed like navigating a picket fence.

The view from Ritter is not greatly superior to that obtained from the summit of Mt. Lyell, but it is different. The southern Sierra is nearer. The Fresno mountains are spread out as a vast panorama. Ten or fifteen miles to the south is the great trough of the San Joaquin, its irregularities of topography nearly indiscernible on account of the distance; and the country for miles seems a great, rolling valley. The junction of the main and south forks with the "balloon dome" of Professor Brewer, seem quite near. Farther to the southwest, through the great depression, the course of the river may be traced until lost in the purple obscurity of the foothills; and on a clear day the haze of the San Joaquin plain is a long, yellow spot on the western horizon. Down the crest of the range, stretching southeast in zigzag lines, many peaks may be identified with a little patience and careful sighting. We believed we had located the Palisades and several even more southerly points.

On the present expedition I climbed along the bed of the stream which feeds the lake, jumping upon large, angular slate boulders, surmounted the final barrier of rocks which dams up the lakelet into which the glacier flows, and on the shore of the lake took my first photograph.[5] On our former visit this lakelet was partially frozen. Small icebergs floated on its bosom, and the ice and snow which nearly covered it were a beautiful cold green. The lake is drained on the west by the streams which form the north fork of the San Joaquin. In climbing around the northern and western base of the peak quite a chain of similar lakelets are encountered, located on a kind of circular shelf or terrace. Above towers Ritter's dark and frowning cliff, while below the waters of the lakelets plunged down the steep mountain-side, uniting their several streams in the gorge below. In several cases these streams, before leaping over, had burrowed through the snow which still filled their channels, forming tunnels through which a man might easily pass.

---

5. Lake Catherine.

The last of these lakes is a beautiful sheet of clear water, filling a basin of smooth, solid rock, having the western face of the peak for its eastern shore and the southern glacier as its source of supply.[6]

The latter glacier exhibits several small but interesting crevasses, a well-defined ice cascade and other curious features, but it is not so extensive a body as the northern glacier.

Being unable to walk around the lake, I was obliged to ascend the cliff, my intention being to cross the backbone of the mountain, a little to the north of the summit, descend to the head of the main glacier, and then make straight for camp, which I hoped to reach before dark. In gaining the summit of the cliff, nearly twice as much time was consumed as I had calculated upon. It was ten minutes of six, and, instead of an easy descent to the northern glacier, I found myself on the edge of a perpendicular cliff which walled in the third or southeastern glacier. This is undoubtedly the body of ice referred to by Clarence King as located in a "deep *cul de sac* opening southward on the east slope of Ritter, and covering an area of 200 yards wide by about half a mile long." The view was wild almost to a suggestion of cruelty.

There remained one unexposed plate in the camera box, and, realizing that I was in for it anyhow, and that a few more minutes could make little difference, I set the tripod on the edge of the cliff—the only possible place—then leaned over and drew the cap off the lens with one foot swinging in air. If my shoe had fallen off, which I am thankful to say did not happen, it would have dropped something like a thousand feet before touching the rock.

My only hope of descent lay in first climbing the remainder of the way to the summit, which I reached in ten minutes. By taking to the glacier at the nearest possible point, and running down its ridgy surface at full speed, I managed to make the upper edge of the rocks just as the sun had set and the long shadows had deepened, and merged into twilight. Climbing the highest boulder, I fortunately caught a glimpse of Whitney,—a black speck in the distance,—and, setting my face squarely in his direction, commenced a race with the darkness. I kept right on, over slippery surfaces and boulders, across patches of snow, jumping from flinty edges, over icy cataracts, turning neither to the right nor left for fear of losing that precious direction; and, just as it became too dark to see to

---

6. Southernmost of the Ritter Lakes.

jump—I fairly ran into the mule.

Next morning we passed down the slope of the mountain to the lake, with its hundred islets, and wound among little hillocks of brown and red volcanic rock along the northern side of the lake. The basin is so broad and flat, considering its location in the very heart of the summit region, and the mountain rises so majestically above it, as to form an almost ideal Alpine landscape. One unconsciously looks along the shore of the lake for the ubiquitous Swiss Hotel.

At a distance of about 3 miles from the base of the mountain the lake pours its waters into a wonderful cañon, which, in its lower parts, is sunk several thousand feet below the general surface of the surrounding mountain mass. Its eastern wall forms a portion of the main crest, as does that of the cañon of the Lyell fork of the Tuolumne. You leave an inhospitable region of rock, snow and ice, and, upon descending rapidly into this beautiful gorge, enter groves of tall trees, skirt the banks of lakes, fringed with water lilies and embosomed in emerald meadows which are beautified by the most luxuriant flowers, ferns and grasses. Truly a little paradise hidden deep in the earth. The remains of an old sheep trail relieves the traveler of much of the labor of picking his way, and leaves him free to observe and enjoy the scenery.

The cañon trends almost due southeast, and is about 12 miles long. A quarter of a mile from its head another stream, draining a lake situated similarly to that along the shore of which I had recently passed, comes tumbling down the western side of the cañon, and, being deflected neither to the right nor left, may be followed by the eye for a great distance. On the same side of the cañon, a few hundred yards further down, is a perpendicular wall of most marvelous and varied hue, extending continuously nearly half a mile-nowhere less than 300 feet high, and often twice and thrice as lofty. Its entire surface is formed of beautifully striated metamorphic slate of every conceivable tint, which has been polished by the ancient ice so that it shines like glass. The beauty of this unique cliff is quite beyond description.

Through the entire length of the cañon the stream runs in a deep and narrow channel, which, in its general form, and in the proportion of its dimensions, is almost an exact reproduction of the cañon itself,—a sort of gorge within a gorge, similar in many respects to the main cañon of the upper Kern and the gorge through which the river flows. The cause of this singular similarity may be traced to the fact that the entire formation of mother rock is to a great depth quite homogenous, at least as to the dip of the strata, so that the erosion of the present water-course has resulted in exactly the same sort of excavation as the mighty torrents of a more remote period. The angle of cleavage of the rock in the little gorge is seen in some places to be identical with that of the main cañon side, and the basaltic character of the formation is also quite obvious. Along the course of the stream are many falls and cascades, none of which, however, are of great height.

Half way down the cañon I came upon its most extensive lakelet, which I found to be most singularly formed. In the middle of the floor of the cañon extends a kind of wall or dyke of rock, perhaps 30 to 40 feet in height; and where it suddenly ended, the stream, which had been flowing between the wall and the western side of the cañon, had backed its waters round the wall, and formed the lake, which thus occupied the level space between the wall and the eastern side of the cañon. The inlet and outlet of the lake are nearly at the same point.[7]

At the margin of the lake, in the center of a lovely grove of tamarack, juniper and red fir, I found an old hermitage. There was a rude forge and bellows, some peculiarly shaped frames and tools, the remains of a canvas-covered hut and empty cans innumerable—the latter rather spoiling an ideally romantic scene. Evidently some misanthrope, who imagined himself on the verge of a mechanical discovery, or perhaps an old prospector, had retired to this lofty wilderness, away from the prying eyes of the vulgar and curious. If his object were to isolate himself from mankind there is little doubt that he succeeded beyond his most sanguine expectation.

Treading the devious and occasionally obscure trail, now passing through narrow groves and meadows, again clinging to the side of bluffs which projected boldly across the cañon, after traveling perhaps 5 miles farther we emerge into the valley of the main San Joaquin, where the stream, leaving the main crest, turns abruptly south and maintains this course for many miles, gradually, however, deflecting to the southwest. At the point we entered the valley the stream receives some small tributaries, and we were now in more frequently traveled country, being indeed on the old mammoth trail to Owen Valley. The once celebrated Pass—one of the best in the range—may easily be distinguished as the

---

7. Olaine Lake.

lowest point of the divide.

The floor of the cañon is here composed wholly of nearly pulverized pumice, so light as to float upon water.[8] For miles there is no soil other than this ghastly grey pumice, and though not barren of vegetation, the region is not exactly a fertile one. On the higher slopes, the trees are fairly thick and tall considering the altitude.

Following down the river from the mouth of the cañon, the banks become exceedingly precipitous in places, the bluffs showing granite outcroppings from the surface of pumice-the first pure granite I had seen since leaving the Tuolumne River. I crossed the turbulent stream with much trepidation, leading the mule slowly from pool to pool between the boulders. Upon the opposite bank it was smooth sailing for a while, until it also became precipitous; when, tantalizingly enough, as I glanced across the river, I saw that the bluffs on that side had ended, and the bank was traversable. Looking about for the least dangerous place to cross, to my intense joy I saw blazings on some trees near the water's edge, and taking the hint, crossed the river at the indicated point. Still following the blazes, twice more we crossed from bank to bank to the infinite disgust of poor Whitney, to whom this sort of thing was exceedingly monotonous.

At length, after traveling about 3 miles from the main crest, we came upon a perfect wilderness of pumice in the shape of an open rolling valley, its floor sparsely covered with trees, its distant slopes more thickly timbered. Here were many cattle trails, and among them a well-defined horse and mule trail, which latter it is of the greatest importance to identify and follow if one would avoid losing the route pursued by the cattle men.

Some miles farther down the river, near the place of crossing of the Mammoth trail, there is a splendid specimen of columnar basalt, which was photographed many years ago by Mr. J. M. Hutchings while crossing the mountains. In every scenic freak the sheepherder recognizes the handiwork of his Satanic majesty. This formation is therefore known to local fame as the Devil's Woodpile. Before reaching this point, however, the route I had been pursuing led me away from the river, so that I did not encounter this remarkable fuel.

Continuing down the pumice-covered valley, its western side grows steeper and gradually approaches the river. Finally it becomes almost a naked granite wall; and as the floor of the valley changes to low rolling

8. Pumice Flat.

hillocks, looking upon this western wall, we observe, flashing among the trees that grow upon the cañon side, a series of cascades plunging down from a notch in the wall. Back of the notch we suddenly catch sight of some sharp black teeth, standing out, in wonderful contrast, against the grey of the granite and the ashen hue of the pumice. One word escapes the lips—"Minarets!" And yet, according to the map of the State Geological Survey, on which alone the position of these peaks are indicated, the Minarets are only 3 miles south of Mt. Ritter; and here we are nearly 3 days' journey from that mountain.

From Ritter, however, our route has been northeast, southeast and south, and now the Minarets are as nearly, as one might judge, from 3 to 5 miles due west. A little figuring shows the position of these remarkable pinnacles to be about 8 miles southeast of the Ritter group. But are they the Minarets of the old survey? Probably not. The lofty crest which extends from Lyell to Ritter practically terminates with the latter peak, although its extension southward may be traced as a series of crags and pinnacles of gradually diminishing altitude. From Ritter only an endwise view is obtained of this line of pinnacles, and it is therefore quite impossible to judge of the comparative sharpness and isolation of the different groups, or pick out the Minarets with any degree of certainty. From the west, however, a group of needle-like pinnacles are observed close to Mt. Ritter, and these are undoubtedly the objects represented on the old map and called the Minarets. They are situated about 5 miles northwest of the group at the head of King Creek, and are probably not so striking in appearance as the latter, especially when viewed from the east. The King Creek group are the Minarets of the sheep men, of the traveler crossing the Mammoth Pass, and of the prospectors who named the mines found in their vicinity after the peaks. Which are the "Minaritos," a picture of the "pass" through which, appears in an old magazine article by John Muir? The probable fact of the matter is that, upon a near approach, the whole crest from Ritter southward will be found to be thickly studded with pinnacles similar to the two groups which now bear the name The Minarets.

It was 3 in the afternoon when I reached the river, opposite the falls. Removing the gun and boxes, I packed a day's provisions in a canvas saddle-bag, fastened it on one side of the saddle, and the camera-box on the other, forded the river—here a stream of about the size of the south fork of the Merced—and led Whitney up the cañon wall to the north of the cascades. The pumice was, as usual, an exasperating annoyance, but once upon the summit we had nearly level ground. The stream I subsequently found to be King Creek, or Minarets' Creek, sometimes so called. It rises in the snow fields at the base of the Minarets, and flows straight west for about 3 miles, when it tumbles over the cañon wall of the San Joaquin and joins that river. For the first mile or more the ravine of King Creek exhibits all the external characteristics of the ordinary granite country of the Sierra-boulders of all sizes, flat, ice polished surfaces, a naked, rocky stream bed. Suddenly the superposed volcanic rock is encountered, and the line of demarcation is strikingly definite. I noticed several outcroppings and even free boulders, whose upper portions were of a dark volcanic material, the lower portions being of ordinary granite.

The Minarets themselves are of a hard black flinty lava, rising from a general surface of dark red and brown volcanic rock, which in its turn sets upon the granite, as just described. In the ravines and gullies the metamorphic rock extends farther down than it does on the hillsides, showing that the volcanic material was poured out upon the granite to an uncertain depth, and flowed down in all directions, naturally traveling farthest along the course of the streams.

I soon came upon a trail which had been recently traveled, I afterward discovered, by a party of mining men who were then negotiating for the sale of the valuable iron mines discovered near the Minarets. After passing a very pretty lake and meadow, the trail avoided the creek and zig-zagged along the hillside. 1 made camp near the main stream, and the next morning strapped the camera on my back and after a couple of hours' hard walking reached a suitable point of view, from which I photographed the pinnacles; and then, returning to the San Joaquin, repacked Whitney with the boxes, and continued on down the river.

The afternoon shadows found us toiling through a magnificent fir forest on the southern slopes, far up over the river, which, from the point where the trail leaves it until it reaches the foothills, nearly 60 miles away, is quite impassable for animals, and, in places, nearly so for men. About a mile or two from the river, as the trail began to ascend, I encountered a recently deserted military camp, the first graphic suggestion of human occupancy that had greeted my eyes since leaving old Lambert's cabin in the Tuolumne Meadows. Some stakes driven into the ground, and a placard posted on a tree, gave notice that here was the boundary (and I think the corner) of the Yosemite National Park. Standing thus on the line separating the prohibited from the unprohibited,

I waited in vain for a deer or other eatable animal (provisions were distinctly low), to appear south of the line, for, of course, I would not have discharged my rifle within the limits of the Park!

Through the shady forest of spruce and fir, [of the latter the brilliantly beautiful red variety (*Abies magnifica*) predominating,] we pursued our way until camping time. I made a glorious fire, which illuminated the forest for many miles around; and, after supper, Whitney approached it and winked contemplatively at the cheerful blaze for several sober hours. We were in a Sierra forest again, in all its virgin beauty, not a vandal buzz-saw within 50 miles. So fine and tall were the trees as to make one forget that, after all, it was only an Alpine forest, and no part of that magnificent lower sugar-pine belt which is at once the pride and the wealth of the whole southern Sierra.

Through the trees, far down the forest slopes, next morning, we caught an occasional glimpse of the great cañon, and toward noon, after passing some pretty little sylvan lakes, the trail wound down, and we again approached the river, now a majestic stream, flowing between frowning walls of granite. A ticklish bit of trail was the final descent to the willow flat near the river, where the sheep men had completed a natural three-sided corral and made a sheep camp.

I calculated that I must be still about 15 miles above the point of confluence with the south fork, and should travel southeast again in order to explore the intervening country. Fortunately, the trail led in precisely the desired direction. Leaving the river, it led among rocky bluffs, skirting an occasional terrace of basalt, and, upon turning southward and rounding a hill, I beheld a miniature Yosemite Valley, whose stream joined the main river some 2 miles west. I gazed in spell-bound admiration. The same winding silver ribbon, the same bright bits of meadow, the talus slopes, and lofty grey granite walls surmounted by rolling forests. Directly opposite was a wall not so high as El Capitan but almost identical with it as to color, carving and perpendicularity.

Also on the opposite side, and at the lower end of the cañon, a stream came tumbling down the bare granite wall, alternatingly in foamy dashes and green, ribbon-like glidings. Far up over the brow of the steeper portion oi the wall it could still be seen, the whole cascade seeming fully half a mile long; but the season was so far advanced that the volume of water was small. I should like to see that cascade in June.

There was a kind of crazy trail leading down the shattered, under-growth-covered cañon side nearly as long and quite as steep as the old Indian Cañon trail of the Yosemite. Forgetting it was long past lunch-time, down we went, Whitney allowing me to place his feet for him when the trail grew all too much for even his sagacious ingenuity. The brightest meadow spot, as seen from above, upon reaching and fording the stream, turned out to be a swamp of the most villainous description.[9] At the base of the cañon wall a stream divided, both branches ultimately flowing into the river and enclosing the swamp, which had become such through the continual inundation of the subsoil by the circumfluent rivulet.

As I crossed the river something jumped at a fly; and, still oblivious to the now imperative demands of the inner man, I must needs ransack the pack for hook and line, bent on ascertaining the nature of that some-thing. It turned out to have been a trout. One hook proving inadequate to the demand 1 tied on another, and began hauling them out, as fast as I could whip the stream, two at a time, and not one under eight inches in length.

The presence of trout said very plainly, "No more falls down stream on the San Joaquin." For the sheepman does not, as a rule, waste his precious time stocking streams. Apropos of the sheepmen, I afterward learned that such of the fraternity as had visited the cañon were less strongly impressed by its scenic features than by the abundance of trout; hence they gave the stream the name Fish Creek, ignoring the cañon completely, except (possibly) to recognize it as forming the banks of the creek.

The valley, though of not more virgin freshness than other places which have once been afflicted with the disease called sheepherder, was enticing enough to hold me for two days, during which I fished, sketched and photographed, living the while principally upon trout and wild goose-berries, and so avoiding injudicious inroads upon my remaining slender stock of provisions.

On August 28th I climbed out of the valley on the opposite or south-ern side. I had spent several hours the previous day in searching for miss-ing portions of the nearly obliterated trail, which as a whole corresponded exactly to descriptions of the famous Chinese puzzle. And, to add to the difficulty, it maintained the steepest angle at which it was possible for a

---

9. Fox Meadow in Fish Valley.

laden beast to ascend—at every jump Whitney literally drew himself up by his fore feet. At a point about half-way to the summit a kind of promontory jutted far out into the valley, and here I took my last photograph of one of the finest bits of cañon scenery to be found in the Sierra Nevada.

Above the cañon the trail was lost in a million sheep tracks, but 1 traveled south, following the stream which I have already alluded to as descending to the valley in a remarkable cascade. At a distance of some 3 or 4 miles I crossed, and, upon climbing the hill, found myself on the divide overlooking the great south fork of the San Joaquin. I camped on the shore of a little bench lake, whose western shore, save for a fringe of trees, formed the horizon line in that direction, and into whose waters dipped, seemingly, the setting sun.[10]

From the divide the topography of the country was spread out to the view as upon a map. For miles in either direction the country shelves down very evenly to the south fork, whose numerous tributary streams, flowing westward down the long, regular slope, furrow it with deep, trough-like corrugations. For two days I tried in vain to cross the river which, as far as the eye could see, flowed in a perpendicular gorge, which through the ages the stream has carved out for itself in the solid granite. I saw no traces of glacial action.

In the morning of the last day I had left Whitney tied to a sapling, while I descended to the river in quest of a place of possible descent and re-ascent on the opposite side. I made my way down the mile or two of rolling forest slope, taking my bearings very hurriedly. Arriving at the edge of the gorge I skirted along for an hour or more, several times half descending [to] the river. Some distance up stream I found a likely place, and soon worked out a possible route of descent, carefully marking the way as I advanced by piling monuments at every turning point. It was late in the afternoon before I had finally connected the forest above with the stream bed below and, my task done, turned my weary steps in the direction whence I supposed I had come. No mule—no familiar granite outcropping—and I soon found myself completely at sea.

Night was almost at hand. I had eaten nothing since morning but a few berries; my clothing was light and the nights were cool. I had only my

---

10. This apparently is at the John Muir Wilderness boundary, half a mile southwest of String Meadows.

compass, pocket knife and perhaps a dozen matches to assist me in reaching civilization in the event Whitney should break away before I could find him. The latter contingency troubled me greatly—indeed, 1 thought it more than probable that he had already twisted himself loose from the sapling and wandered off. At last I struck the trail near which I had tied him, but before I was able to determine which direction to pursue, the darkness obscured the trail—one difficult to follow in daylight—and I was confronted with the responsibility of deciding whether it would be wisest to use my few matches in the doubtful effort of following the trail, or save them for the nights during the enforced journey west, should I fail to find the mule in the morning. The matter did not seem as trivial then as it sounds now; and, not being able to choose between the two, I effected a compromise, so to speak, by using half the matches on the trail. They helped me on about a hundred feet. Then I groped my way to the first gulley, supped on water and raw gooseberries, taking the two courses in about the proportion of a gallon of the former to a gill of the latter, built a three-cornered fire, and, in spite of my anxiety, slept till morning, for I had been sorely fatigued.

In the twilight of the dawn I sat on a log waiting until it should grow light enough to follow the trail. My eyes were sore from the smoke and glare of the fire, my face, hands and clothing were dirty, and all inside was a gnawing indescribable. The excitement of the night was gone. I was wrapped in the cold, grey dawn of another day, and the ashes at my feet were dispiritingly suggestive.

It was soon quite light, and, pulling myself together, I turned in the direction of the trail. Over a mound of granite, around a big yellow pine, and then I stood rooted to the spot, for there was Whitney, the pack on his back, dragging his lead strap, and quietly browsing near a pool. What a rise in the thermometer of my spirits! Let us draw the curtain over the scene of the greeting, which was quite too affecting for words.

Across the gully, and a little way up the opposite bank, I found the sapling, peeled and twisted from its all-night struggle with the famished mule. I had fasted and shivered within 200 yards of food and blankets! To add to my joy, a sheepherder—the first human being I had seen for nearly a month, and the handsomest mortal that was ever created—rode over the hill, and, in broken English, conveyed the joyful intelligence that the sheep bridge was on the main river, a few miles above its confluence with the south fork. To surfeit me with bliss, he actually told me of a trail

Sheepherders camp in "Basaw" Meadows.
(Photograph by Theodore S. Solomons, September 1892.)

leading thither.[11] That day the forest rang with songs certainly strange to its ear and long unfamiliar to mine; and, at precisely 6 o'clock in the afternoon, I had the squarest meal that I had allowed myself for two weeks.

The entire country included between the main and South Forks is

---

11. Now named Cassidy Bridge and Lower Miller Crossing.

rolling, and in no respect unlike the granite country elsewhere in the Sierra. The gorge of the main river is however deep and strikingly savage in appearance. While descending to the excellent log bridge, which solved the problem of the last 40 miles, I caught several glimpses, and likewise did the camera, of Prof. Brewer's balloon-shaped dome, situated at the apex of the angle formed by the two forks. The most perfect dome in the Sierra he called it; but as the writer has not seen all the domes in this mountain range of rounded granite formations, it is difficult either to corroborate or deny the assertion of the enthusiastic geologist of the old survey. From the north and northwest it is much more perfect than any of the great domes of the Yosemite and surrounding region, and in dimensions and general setting I considered it by far the most impressive and imposing object of the kind I had ever seen.

Alter two day's journey across the meadows of Jackass Creek and the Chiquita Joaquin, where I again fell into the Mammoth trail, I ran across a most hospitable sheep camp just as the food question was beginning to assume colossal proportions, and I had begun to harbor wicked thoughts respecting the capacity of my rifle to transform into beef some innocent cattle I passed on the trail. Out of gratitude to three of the kindest and most genial herders who ever superintended the transforming of Sierra grass into mutton, I took a picture of their camp in the Basaw[12] Meadows, besides filling an aching void in one of the molars of the packer, which I did by way of heaping coals of fire on the latter's head for having chris- tened me "The Photographer with the Appetite."

The Basaw Meadows lie just over the divide from the Madera Flume and Trading Company's Mill, situated on the headwaters of the Fresno River. From the old mill a wagon road runs north to the Soquel Mill, of later construction, and at that time busily engaged in the laudable under- taking of removing all traces of the old Fresno grove of Big Trees from the face of the earth. Here a well-chosen trail skirts the Merced divide into Sheep Camp on the main road from Fresno Flats to Wawona.

Early on the evening of September 10th I shook hands with Mr. Galen Clark, in the Yosemite Valley, who kindly informed me that my friends there were about organizing a relief expedition to rescue me or kill the bear.

---

12. Beasore Meadows, named for Tom Beasore, the original settler, who lived until 1953.

A Search for a High Mountain Route from the Yosemite to the King's River Cañon

Theodore S. Solomons
Originally published in the *Sierra Club Bulletin,* vol. 1, no. 6, May 1895

The writer and his companion, Mr. Leigh Bierce, had tramped it in the Sierra last summer [1894], from the 20th of July. By way of hardening ourselves for the serious expedition we proposed later to take, we had made, among other trips, a descent of the Tuolumne Cañon, in the middle of August, photographing the principal scenery of that remarkable locality, and meeting with many experiences,—including a three days' fast,—which will serve to keep that little expedition almost as green in our memories as the one which forms the more especial subject of this article. Thoroughly equipped, we left the Yosemite on the 1st of September, bound for the King's River Cañon, via the High Sierra.

Two years previously, the writer had accomplished a portion of this journey. A description of the route followed was given in an article in the *Sierra Club Bulletin* of January, 1894. The writer led a mule from Mt. Lyell, past Mt. Ritter, and down the head-waters of the main San Joaquin to its junction with the South Fork, thence returning to Yosemite. It was our present intention to resume and complete this journey from the southernmost point attained on that trip, by continuing along the crest of the mountains—or, at least, sufficiently near the crest, to be still in the High Sierra—to the Great Cañon. We proposed to keep between the South Fork of the San Joaquin and the main crest, which run nearly parallel; then, if possible, to pass between the crest and Mt. Goddard; and finally to descend the highest practicable fork of the King's to Tehipitee Valley, from which our destination, the larger cañon, is easily accessible.

Such a high mountain route, practicable for animals, between the two greatest gorges of the Sierra, has never been found—nor, indeed, sought, —so far as my researches have revealed. The journey is usually made by crossing the mountains, either by the Mono or the Kearsarge Pass, and traveling across the hot and monotonous desert to the other pass. The trip has occasionally been made through the mountains—notably by a party among whom were John Muir and Galen Clark. Their route, however, avoided the High Sierra almost entirely.

After seeing the Yosemite, to enter the Californian Alps and to travel in them uninterruptedly to the grand gorge of the King's River would be a journey fit for the gods. As a scenic mountain tour, I doubt if the world affords its like. The Sierra Club member is sufficiently acquainted with our marvelous mountains to be able to picture to himself the glories of such a journey, and I need not therefore enlarge upon the subject.

The last fifty miles of this route, whatever may be the exact course of the zigzag to be worked out, must necessarily he extremely rough. One must travel right into the High Sierra before he can gain an adequate conception of its peculiarly rugged character. That portion in which head the several branches of the King's River and the South Fork of the San Joaquin, is the very climax of the Sierra in loftiness, in wildness, in desolation, in grandeur of view. Yet each rocky barrier has its vulnerable point, each pinnacled divide its cranny or gap through which the mule or jack may be led; and as travel in the Sierra becomes more general and popular, the route will be worked out, blazed, and mapped, and yearly traveled by the fortunate few, until its fame becomes world-wide.

To make the journey, a pack-animal is a necessity; for though there are probably few localities which offer any serious impediment to the passage of men, and a not too heavily laden pedestrian could make the trip very comfortably, the distance to be traversed is such that he could not possibly carry sufficient food to keep him strong enough to complete the journey. To go west to the forest settlements at intervals on the journey would hardly meet the difficulty; for the Pine Ridge stores, the only settlements which would be accessible to him, are fully seventy miles from the crest in any traversable line. It is an "animal route," therefore, which must be found before the average Sierra tramper will be likely to care to attempt the trip.

Our equipment was, I think, very complete, save that, at the last moment, we were obliged to substitute a small horse for the mule we had intended to take. The horse carried the boxes (improvements on those described in the previous article referred to), while the jacks, "Lyell" and "Kid," bore the reserve stock of supplies. The bulk of our provisions was purchased at Fish Camp and at the store of the Madera Flume and Trading Company, thus saving our animals thirty-five or forty miles of transportation from the valley. We amply provided against a possible six weeks' trip by taking over 200 pounds of food. Included in our outfit were a hand-shovel, small ax, fishing-rod, Winchester, 6½ x 8½ camera (with six plate-holders, case, tripod, and seven dozen glass plates), a few emergency remedies and surgical applications, tools, rivets, straps, and few clothes. Our saddles and packing paraphernalia were the best and strongest that are made, and our beds were eider-down, canvas-covered sleeping-bags that weighed next to nothing.

The route we followed to the southernmost point reached on my previous expedition is the same as that by which I then returned to the Yosemite, and it need not, therefore, be now described. We took the road to Wawona and to Fish Camp, the trail to the Madera Flume and Trading Company's mills, and the Mammoth Trail to the Basaw Meadows, to the Chiquita Meadows, and to Jackass Creek, where, leaving that old and well-worn bridle-path, we struck south to the trail which Miller & Lux have built to their sheep-range, and followed it across Granite Creek to the main San Joaquin, about three miles beyond which is the Castle Meadow.[1] Though it was quite dark when we approached them, I recognized the Meadows by a certain peculiar natural corridor cut through the basalt. At their upper end the ruddy blaze of a sheep-camp fire was a welcome sight to our tired animals and their hungry masters. Fresh mutton and mythical topography were our evening's entertainment.

The sheepman is at home in every part of the High Sierra in winch he happens to have herded, but you cannot read his mental map. He is a good guide, but is nearly worthless in directing others. He will draw diagrams on the sooty bottom of the "fry-pan," which you must vow are lucid, though you know in your heart they are ridiculous. Moreover, the country immediately beyond the precise limits of his range is stranger to him than Afghanistan to a Bowery bootblack. Yet his contempt for your maps—though not altogether unjustified for other reasons than his—is as

---

1. Cassidy Meadows. Solomons may have misunderstood the name.

ill-concealed as it is profound. The nomenclature, too, of the mountains and rivers, changing with each new generation of herders, adds another clement of confusion.

The High Sierra, south of the section delineated by Mr. W. D. Johnson during the reconnoissance of the Mono Lake Basin some twelve years ago, is practically unmapped. Originally, the State Geological Survey, in 1865, made a hasty examination of a portion of it, and named a few peaks. Their map gives only a very general sketch of the topography, and is totally unreliable, where it is not, indeed, entirely wanting in detail. Subsequently the U. S. Land Office surveyors encroached upon the summit region here and there, but many of the township plats have been rejected for suspected fraudulent surveys, and the others are to be taken with many grains of allowance. Other than from these two sources, little data is to be had, the county maps adding nothing, and the Geological and Geodetic Surveys, whose atlas sheets are everywhere regarded as the most complete and reliable mountain guides, not yet having entered the region. This section of the Sierra is therefore a real *terra incognita*, save to the nomadic and ubiquitous sheep-herder. If it were magically scooped from its foundations and set down anywhere in Europe, it is safe to say that not two years would elapse before its every acre would be explored and mapped.

The vicinity of the junction of the south and main forks of the San Joaquin is, in some respects, a unique locality, and an interesting one from a scenic point of view especially. For several miles above their confluence both forks flow in narrow, notch-like gorges of bare and generally smooth granite, which at the junction of the streams unite to form a single similar gorge of considerable length. A mile or less in equidistance from the forks, and standing upon a pedestal of sloping glaciated granite, is the matchless Balloon Dome, reference to which was made in my previous article. From the sheep-camp a day's trip was taken to and around the dome, and to the "Notches," or river gorges, during which a number of negatives were secured, that, later, suffered the fate of all the other views taken during the trip.

The chief representative on the sheep-range of Miller & Lux looked aghast when we told him our destination; and he warned us against the early snows, which were imminent. As a matter of fact, we had started rather late in the year, owing to delay in the Yosemite; but we determined to hazard the trip anyhow.

The route we selected led along what is called the "Upper Trail," which runs south-east and well away from the South Fork, to the end of the Miller & Lux range, which is some sixteen miles in length. Here intelligible trails ended, and we made our way around to Mono Creek, a large stream which rises on the main crest, flows southwest for about twenty miles, and empties into the South Fork. It was this creek that the old Geological Survey party descended, on re-entering the mountains from the Owen's Valley; and the Indian trail they followed is still used every summer by the few remaining Indians of Madera County.

It was while camped on the forest slope above Mono Creek, one beautiful evening, about two weeks after we started, that a singular adventure befell us. We had spread our canvas—our sleeping-bags thereon— about thirty feet from a dead, though standing, yellow pine of immense size, and had built our camp-fire of its fallen branches. We had spent the evening laughing inordinately at the caricatures in some humorous papers. In due course we went to sleep, those dreadfully funny periodicals still by our side.

In the dead of night I awoke with a strange sense of deadly fright. A crackling sound had aroused me, and my unconscious faculties interpreted it. The base of the dead tree had caught fire, and it was falling upon us. I yelled to Bierce as I stood up in the prison of my sleeping-bag, and had time to hop twice when the air quivered above me and a deafening crash chilled the blood in my veins. Something lightly touched my hair, and then there was again the perfect stillness of the Sierra night, and a pitchy blackness reigned.

"Bierce," I shouted in dread.

"All right," was the cheery response, in a ringing voice; "and you?"

"You bet," I replied, getting bravely mundane in a moment.

Moving my head, I found the thing that had touched it was rigid. I put my hand up. It was a foot-thick branch of the fallen tree. A few inches from my side there was another branch, and between Bierce and myself, who were not more than six feet apart, there was another great limb; and Bierce was hemmed in by them, as was I. He had been similarly awakened by the warning crackle, but not taking time to rise, shrewd youth, had rolled in his bag about as far as I had hopped, or about six feet from where we had lain. Two feet back of us was the giant trunk lying across the canvas on which we had been sleeping. Stumps of its branches had pierced the canvas, and were deep in the earth. Seeking new lodgings, we finished our night's rest. In the morning the tree was merrily burning, telling us plainly that had we not perished at once on being struck by the trunk or impaled by its sharp limbs, a slow roasting to death would have been our fate. The branches of the fallen tree were so numerous that in no other positions so near the trunk, excepting the particular ones we had chanced to occupy when the monster fell, could two persons have been standing and not been struck. Of our many remarkable escapes during that summer, this must surely be reckoned as one peculiarly miraculous.

The middle portion of the creek flows through an extensive flat covered by a growth of tamarack and other trees, which give it a park-like appearance. This flat is at least five miles long by a mile in average width. From the color of its soil, we christened it Vermilion Valley.[2]

From the high ground above Mono Creek we had carefully examined the country to the south-east, and had decided upon attempting the passage of what appeared to be a cut in a range of peaks which, though rugged and crest-like in character, we concluded was only the divide between tributaries of the South Fork, and must jut out from the main crest. This proved to be the case; for, upon crossing Mono Creek and ascending the divide—of which more anon,—we found ourselves overlooking Bear Creek, the southern ridge of which was our summit-like divide. At the head of the principal arm of Bear Creek was our gap, thenceforward to be our objective point.

The southern side of Vermilion Valley rises quite steeply for a few hundred yards, and is then rolling to the divide between Mono and Bear Creeks.[3] It took us all of an afternoon to surmount this first acclivity. We led the animals a little at a time, each in turn. When nearly up, the "Kid" lost his footing in the loose, treacherous soil, and went literally heels over head, pack and all, down the hill, bouncing like a rubber ball from rock to tree, boxes of photographic plates the while whirling through the air; while the other jack brayed in sympathy and terror. The "Kid" finally brought up against a bank of chaparral, and in a moment we were at his side, certain lie had been killed a dozen times,—jacks have more lives

---

2. Vermilion Valley is now under the waters of Lake Thomas A. Edison.
3. This essentially is the route of the John Muir Trail south from Quail Meadows.

than cats,—and so he must be quite dead. Instead, we found him in a sitting posture, winking contemplatively in the direction of the plains. Kneeling down, I reached my hand under his shaggy breast to the region of his heart. Heavens! it was thumping like a steam hammer. Though unhurt, the poor little fellow was evidently frightened almost to death. Singularly enough, none of the plates were broken,—a worse fate being in store for them.

Bear Creek rises on the main crest, not more than eight or ten miles north of the Palisades. Running at first north-west, it curves gradually to the west and south-west, maintaining the latter course until it joins the South Fork five or six miles above the confluence of Mono Creek. About the head of these streams—especially of Bear Creek, since the latter is nearer to the divide between the two great rivers,—the crest region is truly sublime. Between their upper cañons there stands a castellated and pinnacled mass of pure white granite, like a colossal barbaric dagger, set deep in the rugged mountain, and piercing forever the indigo vault of the sky—a finer peak of its kind than any I had ever beheld, though much resembling the Castle Peak of the Tuolumne Sierra.[4] Yet this magnificent pile is not within five miles of the true crest, whose peaks and those of the intervening territory are everywhere, if possible, richer and grander in sculpture.

Fine though it may be, the summit region of the Merced and Tuolumne Rivers is as much inferior to that of the King's and San Joaquin, as the former is superior to the low and rounded crests of the Sierra north of the Central Pacific Railroad. The crest region about the head of Bear Creek —or it would be more correct to say, the crest-like region—is a belt ten or fifteen miles wide, the outer half resembling the highest and finest peaks and divides of the Sierra east of the Yosemite, the inner, or true, crest resembling nothing that the writer's imagination had conceived.

The descent to Bear Creek was down a hill quite as trying as the ascent from Mono, and in accomplishing it, our little horse, a willing, plucky animal, broke his leg, and we had to shoot him and divide his load between the jacks, which then carried not more than 130 pounds apiece. We next ascended the upper course of the creek, the lower appearing to

---

4. This probably is Bear Creek Spire.

lie in an impassable gorge. As the creek turned south and approached our pass, its valley forcibly reminded us of that of the Lyell Fork of the Tuolumne, which is ascended by climbers of that peak. The upper valley of Bear Creek is, however, much rougher, and having generally no grassy floor, is, rather, an open, rocky trough than a valley. Its glaciation is more striking than in any other similar locality I have ever examined. The ice seems to have melted only yesterday.

At a distance of perhaps ten miles from where we first struck the creek the valley ended and the stream forked, its larger branch coming through our pass—a term which we hasten to corrupt to "impass,"—the smaller draining a remarkable group of chains of lakelets which lay upon a number of terraces, or plateaus, to the south and west. The south wall of the gap we found to be the side of a peak, the eccentric shape of which is suggested in the name Seven Gables, which we hastened to fasten upon it—the second and last of our gratuitous christenings. We climbed the Seven Gables on the afternoon of our arrival at the head of the valley—September 20th. There was a dash of snow on its chimney-like pinnacle, which must be upwards of 13,600 [13,075] feet above the sea.

When we gained the edge of the slanting, roof-like crest of the peak and looked out east, we both experienced a sensation that is hardly to be described, though it will be understood by those who have traveled in the Sierra or the Alps.

I was too awed to shout. The ideas represented by such words as lovely, beautiful, wild or terrible, cold or desolate, fail to compass it. Words arc puny things, and the language of description quite as impotent as the painter's brush. Roughly speaking, one might say that the sight was sublime and awful. I can scarcely conceive of another scene combining the peculiar qualities of that view in a higher degree, and I believe I was then looking upon the finest portion of the crest of the Sierra Nevada Mountains—their scenic culmination, their final triumph. I am led to this belief by the fact that in extent of view, in general topographical character, and in the shape and proportion of the dimensions of the objects constituting the view, no essential difference seemed to exist between the landscape before me and those pictured in photographs I had studied, taken from Mt. Whitney, Mt. Tyndall, and the vicinity of the Kearsarge Pass, which constitute the culmination of the range in altitude; while there was added an clement of variety and contrast of form and color, due to the volcanic and other metamorphic masses which here are blended with the granite. and which quite disappear farther south.

We were standing on the very edge of a thousand-foot precipice that ran on south for some distance. Below were some frozen lakes in a bare, glacier-swept basin between our peak and those immediately beyond. Stretching north-east, perhaps five miles, and north-west and south-east as far as the eye could reach, there lay a territory of solid granite and darker-hued metamorphic rock, the surface of which was rent, upheaved, and disheveled into a bewildering confusion of peaks, walls, detritus-piles, pinnacles, and cliffs, massed and fairly crowding upon the view; and among them, like jewels, were patches of snow and cold lakes, like black-blue eyes, and here and there a little, gnarled tree, which was almost painful in the landscape, because of its suggestion of a nether world of things that live. Yet, in spite of that reminder, you may imagine your world dead, cold, turned to a moon, and nothing from pole to pole but those hard, frigid monuments watching the eternal sky, oblivious of all other existence. It seemed the very end of terrestrial sublimity.

Mt. Goddard was hidden by an intervening divide, but Mt. Gabb, Mt. Abbott, Mt. Humphreys, and Red Slate Peak were probably all in view, though we could not pick them out. I doubt if they will ever be identified among hundreds of equally prominent and striking crest-masses; and, for lack of adequate published description, the old State Geological Survey will likely have named those four peaks in vain.

But the animal route! Well, our animals not being mythological beasts with wings, a glance sufficed to convince us that the Bear Creek divide was quite impassable. Yet, being within thirty miles, as the crow flies, of our destination, we determined to stick to our undertaking, and to dodge this ugly place by going a little farther from the crest and passing, if necessary, a little to the west of Mt. Goddard, which is the sentinel that guards the watershed between the two rivers.

I shall not have space to describe our movements during the next few days.[5] Suffice it to say, that on the 28th day of September, after weathering several little flurries of snow, which were to be expected at that season of the year, and which therefore we did not seriously regard, we again

---

5. Solomons and Bierce may have attempted the South Fork of Bear Creek, but found themselves at a dead end at Three Island Lake.

found ourselves camped very near the Seven Gables. Not having been able to pass down the gorge of the lower Bear Creek, lack of provisions had forbidden any greater retrogression to a new starting-point, and we therefore determined to give our animals to a belated herder who was "feeding" up the creek, and to conclude the journey on foot, carrying our luggage on our backs. Experience in the Tuolumne Cañon had demonstrated that, hardened as we now were, we could carry fifty pounds and make good time; and allowing liberally for delays, we thought we could make the journey on the food we could carry, after subtracting from our combined capacity of 100 pounds the weight of camera outfit, blankets, and other absolutely necessary articles.

It snowed next day quite heavily as we neared the head of the valley, which was the place where we were to leave the jacks and strike out alone. Our fire-logs had to be pulled out of the snow, and, though we had no difficulty in maintaining a fire, the heat melted the steadily failing flakes and soaked our sleeping-bags, so that we got almost no rest, and had to wait patiently for morning. The cheerless dawn came at last, and its gray light revealed to us a most alarming situation. From the edge of the melting circle of our fire out over the cañon, the surrounding crests, and as far as the vision extended—from horizon to horizon—Mother Earth was buried under nearly four feet of snow. Fully nine-tenths of it had fallen in the single night, and it was still falling. It enclosed us and our fire and the remnants of our outfit. We were on top of the Sierra, some seventy-five miles of nearly waist-deep snow between us and the nearest settlements. It was late in the year; the ground was cold; and, even assuming that no more snow would fall, fully two weeks must elapse before the mass already on the ground could melt. And then there would still be ahead of us the toilsome march across cañons and rivers to the lower mountains. On the whole, it was patent that our provisions were insufficient to warrant an attempt to weather the storm. How we hated to give in! But the silent, insidious enemy sifted deeper and deeper as we deliberated, and we surrendered to a cold and ominous necessity, and prepared to retreat. The "Kid" had strayed; "Lyell" we shot, to keep him from freezing or starving to death. Then we made up our packs, discarding everything we thought dispensable. When we struck out into the snow my camera-case and my companion's knapsack each weighed about eighteen pounds; and our sleeping-bags, wrung out as dry as we could get them, about twenty pounds each, or quadruple their weight when dry.

After struggling through the drift about fifteen feet from camp, we stopped, obeying a common impulse, and looked at each other; and then, without a word, floundered back again to the smoldering logs. We were now fully alive to the gravity of the situation. It was a matter of life or death. Away went bedding; away went camera and the precious negatives secured at the pains of so many hours of patient climbing; away-flung out upon the snow-went everything except half of a threadbare saddle-blanket apiece, absolutely necessary cooking utensils, and some twenty-five pounds of food. Thus lightened, we took our last leave of the remains of a once proud camping outfit,—I remember how yellow the flour looked against the absolute white of the snow—and struck out through the soft drifts.

Simply to walk was a complicated operation; for at every step the foot had to be raised clear of the snow before being reinserted, the body meanwhile precariously balanced on the other leg. We constantly ran foul of hidden snags, slipped from treacherous rock-surfaces concealed by the snow, and were tripped by logs too small to be indicated by long snow-mounds, as the larger ones were. Crystals showered down our necks as we jarred the laden trees; and often we could not see a hundred feet in front of us, and had to navigate by compass a creek-bottom, savagely rough and difficult to traverse when free of snow. The brawling stream had frozen over in the night; for the cold had been intense. It was yet snowing; our hands, though swathed in socks for mittens, were blue and stiff, and we had often to rest from the unwonted exertion of lifting at every step the weight of our legs, extra-weighted by the tenacious snow. We were sleepy; the hours went swiftly by, and our progress was alarmingly slow. Though we never lost hope,—if we had, we should have been incapable of the exertions we were making—yet when discussing our chances, we were forced to admit that they were no better than about even.

At noon we succeeded in clearing a space, lighting a fire, cooking some oatmeal and chocolate, and drying ourselves. This consumed two hours and a half. In the afternoon it ceased snowing. We climbed the north wall of Bear Creek; and, as the dismal night closed threateningly around us, exhausted, cold, and dispirited, we stood in the snow prison that had clogged our limbs since early morning, and looked for the shelter and bed, by comparison with which all the things the great round world could then have offered us would have been contemptible. A big tree had fallen over two small bowlders, between which was a space only partly filled with snow. Bierce descried it; and we worked there till long past dark, scraping bare the ground of the cubby-hole, and roofing it with branches. Shelter we must have. As an effective preparation for slumber, we had previously found burrowing in the snow to be a delusion and a snare. The darkness deepened. Our shelter, when finished, was not snow-tight. Of the big pile of branches we had collected, little remained for firewood. My companion was taken with a severe chill, and I stood up, hour after hour, alternately warming the two rags of blankets, and making hot coffee. The night was freezing cold; the sky still ominous. Would it snow, or would it not? It was the critical hour of the whole adventure. At twelve o'clock, when nearly asleep, though still holding the blanket before the feeble blaze, I looked at the sky for the thousandth time, and thought I saw a star! I rubbed my grime-filled eyes. Yes, it was a star— three stars! As long as I live I shall never forget the shape of the triangle they formed. I shouted. Bierce and I watched that hole in the shroud of the sky. The three stars returned our steady gaze for a moment, then twinkled—twinkled alarmingly—and, finally, the shifting blackness blotted them cruelly out. But just then Bierce shouted, and pointed to the opposite portion of the sky. It was jeweled with stars! In ten minutes the whole firmament was lit with them. The storm was over.

Bierce's chill left him; we tore down the roof of branches, and con- verted it into fuel; we slept a little, and rested until late in the morning; ate breakfast, and struck out for the South Fork in a glare of sunlight that was dazzlingly reflected from the snow. The great Sierra world was robed in virgin white. Never have I seen a sight so purely and transcendently beautiful. To feel one's self a mere animal, seeking warmth, food, and self-preservation; and suddenly, as upon that morning, to be confronted with a sight that touches to the quick the æsthetic nature, and thrills the immaterial soul within as it had never thrilled before-what a lesson in the duality of man!

The first day we had made perhaps five miles; the second, eight or ten; the third, we waded the icy current of the South Fork, and, climbing wearily up the other side, accomplished much less. By way of exercise, after our work of the day, each night we were compelled to devote two or three hours to collecting and arranging wood enough to keep us suffi- ciently warm to sleep. We had not a sufficiency of nitrogenous food to enable us to withstand these unusual inroads upon our strength, and on the fourth day we experienced the unique sensation of weakness without either sickness or particular fatigue. On the fifth we ran across a storm-bound sheep-herder; and mutton, in more than allopathic doses, restored us to full vigor. I venture to say that that sheep-herder had never got hold of more ostentatiously credulous listeners to his outrageous yarns. Generous with his edibles, superabundantly supplied with blankets, our pastoral Munchausen found us willingly—nay, anxiously—gullible; and in return for the contempt with which he doubtless contemplates our memory we continue to retain only the most innocent admiration, alike for his imagination and his mutton.

The next thirty miles was simply a run down the forests to the Pine Ridge settlements, on reaching which we learned that we had been overtaken by the most severe early storm that had ever occurred within the memory of the oldest inhabitant. Our satisfaction over the incontestable fact that we were still living, was such as to prevent any vain regrets over failure and loss of outfit; and we jolted indolently down the Pine Ridge road on a lumber team, reaching Fresno on the 8th of October.

As soon as circumstances will permit, the writer intends to resume the search for a high mountain route from the Yosemite to the King's River Cañon.

Mt. Goddard and its Vicinity—in the High Sierra of California

Theodore S. Solomons
Originally published in *Appalachia*, vol. 8, no. 1, 1896.

It is not without some sense of humiliation that a native and resident of California is obliged, even by implication, to refer to the unpardonable indifference with which that State has neglected the survey of the Sierra Nevada Mountains. Yet it is impossible to avoid that implication in an article narrative of the journey in those mountains of private persons fitted out with barometer and compass. It may be said that in time the United States Geological Survey will map and describe this portion of the country; but that a Commonwealth at once so populous and prosperous as that of California should for nearly half a century trust to the delay and uncertainty of the National Survey to publish to itself and to the world the story of another Alps, is to convict it of something very like a public crime.

In the just arraignment of California for this offence one mitigating circumstance is, however, to be noted. In the childhood of the State, the Legislature of 1862 directed the organization of the Geological Survey of California, and appointed as its chief Josiah Dwight Whitney, who, in full cognizance of the popular clamor to be told by science where mammon lurked, went systematically to work to describe the whole territory comprised within the boundaries of the State, and without entire disregard of such unmerchantable resources as beauty, grandeur, and sublimity. The result was that before the niggardliness of a succeeding Legislature had routed the Survey, and drove Professor Whitney eastward in profound disgust, a considerable portion of the more accessible regions of the High Sierra had hastily been examined; and to-day all that is extant in map or book descriptive of the locality which it is my purpose here briefly to describe is to be found in the unfinished annals of the State Geological Survey published a quarter of a century ago. Those few volumes are now out of print. The younger generation has not read them, the older has mostly forgotten what it read; and less is known at the present time of the California Alps by the people who live within sight of them than was known twenty-five years ago. The *raison d'etre* of the Sierra Club, then, is obvious; nor in future will it lie in the mouth of a sluggard people, who may possibly awaken some day to map-making and trail-building, to tell that Club that its members have erred in their altitudes or blundered in their meanderings. Our work is necessarily erratic; and its results, so far as our maps are concerned, temporary and makeshift.

The twelfth day of last July [1895] found the writer and his companion, Mr. Ernest C. Bonner, engaged in emptying cereals into canvas bags, trimming chunks of ham, compressing dried fruit into small compass, and other like labors. The rather unusual scene of these prosaic occupations was the polished floor over which, in bygone ages, the great glacier of the South Fork of the San Joaquin—in size and importance the second river in California—slid silently, resistlessly, titanically. Its puny successor, the present South Fork, now swirled madly by, in its narrow, throat-like channel, cut in the solid granite. The picturesque sheep-bridge, constructed of slender tamarack trunks, which spans the river here, is called Jackass Bridge, and the succession of flats just below are correspondingly the Jackass Meadows. They are nearly eight thousand feet above the sea.

A two-weeks course of training, during which Bonner and I and our sober old pack-mule had explored many an alpine recess and climbed many a peak at the head of South Fork streams, had so strengthened our muscles and lungs that when we had completed our preparations and arose with our knapsacks on our backs, the one hundred and twenty pounds they weighed together seemed not half so much of a burden as our sceptical friends had predicted on our departure from San Francisco. In truth, however, we were not lightly loaded; but there was no alternative.

During two previous summers I had forced my way south from the Yosemite Valley, bound to worry out somehow, somewhere, a high mountain route connecting that valley with its twin in grandeur, the King's River Cañon, nearly a hundred miles away. Between lies the larger part of the Southern High Sierra, an uplift of alpine crest, the loftiest, wildest, and most rugged within the boundaries of the United States, and that takes rank scenically among the few most magnificent mountain masses on the globe. When within twenty miles of the head of the South Fork and forty of my final goal, snow and ice, gorges and frowning pinnacle-crowned cliffs, had defied me, until, lingering obstinately among them, a late autumn storm of unprecedented violence had driven me and my then companion to the lower mountains, glad for mere life on any terms of failure. Pondering the matter during the winter, it occurred to me that I could do more toward finding passes over those walls if I were to go on foot instead of trying to lead animals; and accordingly the following summer we prepared for a knapsack trip.

After our course of hardening (which was not without the additional fruit represented by the exploration and mapping of an important portion of the crest), we resigned our mule, surplus outfit, and a number of exposed but undeveloped photographic plates to a sheep-herder, who subsequently conveyed them for us to the settlements, and incidentally subjected the plates to such further and less judicious exposure as to fog them completely. I shall always maintain that in disregarding my humble entreaties not to open that box, the stony-hearted fellow merited more condign punishment than that of his disappointment at finding the pictures quite invisible.

While a smaller quantity of provisions than we took would have been sufficient for a direct journey from our starting-point to the King's River Cañon, it would have been impossible to make side trips, and otherwise to provide against delays in discovering the route sought. Our knapsacks, which were of stout canvas arid home-made, contained sleeping-bags formed by doubling eider-down quilts, and weighing four pounds apiece; light cooking-utensils; emergency remedies, including kola-nuts and a few strong antiseptics; 4 x 5 Poco camera, tripod, and five dozen glass plates; a small aneroid, compasses and level; lines and hooks; two Sierra Club register-cans; straps, buckskin, et cetera; socks and one "sweater;" and a little over sixty pounds of food, consisting of ham, canned salmon and corned-beef, flour, white corn-meal, oatmeal and hominy, dried apricots, prunes and apples, raisins, coffee, sugar, chocolate, condensed milk, butter, salt, and baking-powder. Each of us wore a felt hat, overalls, woollen under and over shirt, and the very stoutest shoes with slightly projecting hob-nailed soles.

The region we were about to explore, like many other portions of the High Sierra, was represented on the map of the county in which it lies, partly by blank spaces and partly by townships drawn in such a way as to indicate to one made wise by bitter experience that the topography thus indicated was mythical, and the purported survey of the Land Office fictitious and fraudulent. This proved to be the case. The only other source of information was the atlas-sheet of the old Geological Survey of California, on which, however, only a rough sketch of the topography was to be found. This represented Mt. Goddard as situated on the northern wall of the cañon of the South Fork of the San Joaquin, which, sweeping by it, headed on the main crest of the range some six miles east of the peak. This, with the addition of tributary streams whose graceful curves and perfect regularity suggested "conventional" detail, constituted the only data by which we were to be guided on our travels.

I have found that such foods as condensed milk and butter, by imparting a greater palatibility (sic) and zest to the plainer foods, insures better digestion and assimilation of the latter, and so more than compensates for their extra weight.

The sheep-herding fraternity, to whose unloving care the groves and meadows of the High Sierra have for many years been given over, have made rude trails to their principal pasture-grounds; and it was into one of these uncertain paths that we soon fell as we threaded the uneven bottom of the South Fork Cañon.[1] The first day out we made some seven miles in the morning, and devoted the afternoon to lazing in a hospitable sheep-camp and trying to translate into terms of topography the descriptions of our densely ignorant host, "a Portoogee," who, as we expected, could speak only the language of grass. He did know Mt. Goddard, though, and assured me it lay on the northern side of the cañon and at its very head, whereat I was rude enough to smile.

During the second day we crossed a large northern tributary of the South Fork which entered the cañon by means of a deep gorge through which it rushed in foaming rapids (elevation 8,400 feet).[2] Nowhere Yosemite-like in character, the walls of the South Fork Cañon, nevertheless, are lofty and rugged, and the rock of peculiarly striking colors. This

---

1. Solomons did not return to the point reached the year before, but rather followed up the South Fork of the San Joaquin, thus bypassing the eventual route of the John Muir Trail over Selden Pass.
2. Piute Creek, about 8,000 feet at this stream juncture.

is due to the fact that the rocks composing this portion of the slope of the
Sierra are metamorphic slates, and also of volcanic materials. Nor was the
granite again encountered until we ascended out of the cañon to the valley of the Middle Fork. This stream, which also enters the cañon from the
north, we reached toward evening, after having travelled that day something like fourteen miles (elevation 8,700 feet).[3]

Judging the entering stream to carry a larger volume of water than
the stream in the cañon itself, we resolved to explore it. Accordingly next
morning we cached all but three days' provisions, and, our knapsacks
thus lightened, climbed the gorge of the big tributary. Gaining a point
from which the stream suddenly became visible throughout its entire
descent, we paused as though petrified. Swelled by the fast melting snows
of its high sources, its volume that of a small river, the stream hurled
itself with torrential force over a series of falls and cascades the most
striking and magnificent I have yet encountered in the Sierra, excepting
only those of the Tuolumne Cañon. If the whole course of descent of the
Middle Fork, from the valley above to the cañon beneath, which must be
nearly a third of a mile, could be divided into so many separate falls and
cataracts, these would number at least a score and represent all the various shapes and forms assumed by falling water. The grandeur of the picture of which the uppermost of these falls form the central feature is
greatly enhanced by the blending with the dark slate of the now reappeared granite, and also by the presence in the right background of a
massive rock which rears its head at the angle formed by the cañon and
gorge. This rock, which we have called Emerald Point, is of a bright green
color, and, I take it, is similar in composition to other masses of like colored rock which are composed of a highly metamorphosed sandstone.

Surmounting the falls, a spacious valley delighted our eyes.[4] In a
plushy meadow the river swam lazily as though unsuspectingly to the
brink of its plunge. On either side an alpine forest formed groves, which
clothed the lower and gentler slopes of the valley, and climbed the
steeper sides with picturesque irregularity. This valley I account one of
the fairest paradises of the nowhere unlovely western slope of the Sierra;
and the State is to be congratulated that the difficulty of its approach has

3. Evolution Creek, joining the South Fork just above 8,400 feet.
4. Evolution Meadow in Evolution Valley.

saved it from any serious hurt by sheep and sheep-herders. In altitude its lower end is about 9,200 feet, its upper a little over ten thousand. Threading the meadows and woods with a buoyant step, we reached the head of the valley in a few hours, and, ascending its rather steep northern side, attained a commanding position. From its highest fountains to the cañon brink whence its collected waters are precipitated into the main river, the whole Middle Fork was spread out before us in the greatest detail. The valley of this stream ran east and west. On its southern rim, and near its head, a colossal, sugarloaf-shaped buttress of fractured granite stood sharply up, the advance guard of the host of peaks presently to be described, yet so conspicuously separated from them as to suggest the name The Hermit. The head of the valley was formed of an abrupt, semi-circular wall over which two streams poured in thunderous cascade. The smaller of these emerged from a snow-choked, rounded, trough-like basin, which reached back due south a distance of five miles, where it widened at the base of a line of jet black peaks, whose northern faces formed a continuous wall, against which was piled a great mass of snow and probably ice, for the central portion of this belt is undoubtedly glacial in character. Above this central and most extensive ice body, the wall rose as a fine pyramidal peak, which, though we could only suspect it at that time, was afterwards determined to be Mt. Goddard. The larger stream, or main Middle Fork, came over the end wall of the valley in broad, ribbon-like cascades; and a mile below another stream, draining a very elevated snow basin on the north, coursed down the valley's side —here not so steep—in seven or eight distinct branches unconfined by any definite channel.

Above the ribbon-like cascades, which have a fall of about six hundred feet, the Middle Fork drains an alpine area of surpassing grandeur. A few stunted tamaracks (*Pinus contorta*), scarcely to be discerned in a general view, are the sole remnants of vegetable life, save only the alpine grasses; and the stern landscape is one of snow, ice, and granite. Southward the view was limited by the black wall, which, as it trended eastward, merged into granite, and joined the main crest, which forms the eastern and northern boundary of the alpine area, about six miles from where we stood, and some seven or eight miles from Mt. Goddard. This six miles of crest was uplifted as a peaked and pinnacled wall, varying in height from eight to fifteen hundred feet above the cirques that scalloped their bases, and fully twice that height above the general surface of the

"Head of the Middle Fork of San Joaquin River." (Photograph by Theodore S. Solomons, 1895.) Evolution Lake and Mounts Darwin and Spencer.

lake basin into which was collected the drainage of the entire area. Immediately upon our right towered a long, thin ridge of reddish buff granite, fully two miles in length, whose crest rose into several peaks, the whole upper surface of the wall being crowned with fantastically shaped pinnacles. This fine mural mass, which we called Mt. Darwin, is quite precipitous on both sides and both ends, and its pinnacled spine is in places so sharp as to inhibit the climber who might scale its western end from passing forward to the eastern and highest point of the peak. The wall of Mt. Darwin continues in a direction east by southeast as a much lower but even sharper ridge for about three miles. At a distance of two miles it rises perpendicularly five or six hundred feet, forming Mt. Haeckel, and a mile beyond again rises several hundred feet higher, though not quite so sharply, forming the peak called Mt. Wallace. Here the lofty crest, now fairly bristling with minaret-like pinnacles dips, and trends abruptly south for a half mile, where again it turns cast by south, zigzagging in that direction, while still flinging aloft its sharp teeth in splendid confusion, to the Palisades, some fifteen miles distant from Mt. Darwin. A mile south of Mt. Wallace, Mt. Fiske (named after the distinguished American historian and writer on the Evolution Philosophy) rears a dark granite pyramid into the clear sky. These peaks and crests are during the summer quite laden with snow and ice, which clings to their sides and bases wherever the acclivity is sufficiently gentle to permit its lodgement. Endowed, in seeming, with the personality with which their whole aspect invests them, it is not difficult for the fancy to see in them a band of gaunt Titans rising from beds of snow and shaking the clinging white from their bare backs and ribs. [See Color Plate No. 4.]

From the six-mile stretch of reddish buff crest, several parallel spurs run down to the bosom of the basin. These, singularly enough, are of much purer granite; and two of them, which start respectively from Mt. Haeckel and Mt. Wallace, are rendered conspicuous by the splendid peak which rises from the middle part of each. These are Mt. Spencer and Mt. Huxley, between which there exists a wonderful similarity, not only in the analogy in their positions, but in the peculiar resemblance they bear to each other in size and shape, in the sharpness of their summits, in the snow-gorges that flute their sides, and in the smoothness and purity of the cream-colored granite out of which the peaks are sculptured. Indeed they are beautiful monuments rather than mountain peaks. The gorges between these spurs carry torrents that drain the extensive névé-fields filling all the amphitheatres and glacial basins between the summits of the peaks. At the bases of the spurs these streams empty into a beautiful lake which, though narrow, is fully two miles long, and which curves from the spur of Mt. Huxley northward and westward to the head of the valley of the Middle Fork. This fine sheet of water is thus the reservoir which pours its icy flood over the dam-like wall at the head of the valley forming the ribbon-like cascades which have already been noticed. The altitude of

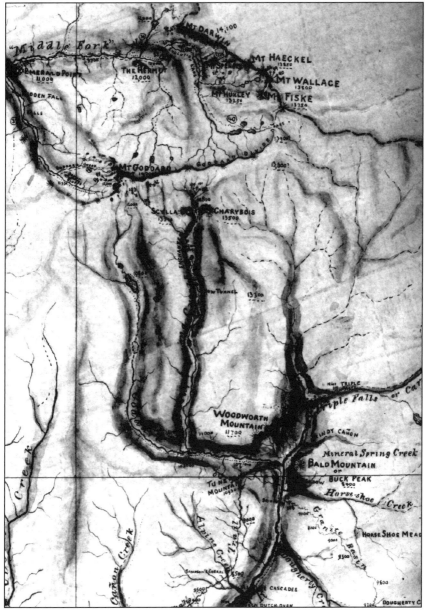

A portion of Theodore Solomons' 1896 map. Solomons and Bonner came up the
"Middle Fork"—now Evolution Creek—and after climbing Mt. Goddard they
eventually went down Disappearing Creek to Goddard Creek and Simpson Meadow
("Big Meadow"), and from there on south over the known route via Granite Pass to
Kings Canyon. The present route of the John Muir Trail is up Evolution Creek, past
Evolution Lake and the cluster of the then unnamed lakes at the head of the creek,
and over Muir Pass, which is marked by two small lines and the word "pass," just
south of Mt. Fiske. A peak directly south of the pass is now named Mt. Solomons.

the lake is about 11,000 feet.[5]

By far the largest stream which supplies the lake is one which enters it at the upper end after rather a steep descent over a granite bluff. This stream drains the spacious lake-basin lying at the northern base of the wall previously referred to as bounding the alpine area on the south. The bottom of this basin is one great snow-field, through which crop up bosses of granite, straggling lines of morainal boulders, and heaps of other detritus,— the accumulations of countless ages of erosion. Many large lakes lie in the basin's trough, some few bright with limpid water, others glittering with snow and little icebergs; others still dull with a thick coating of ice that the long siege of the midsummer day's sun is incapable of dissipating.

Such is the birthplace of the San Joaquin; such the origin of that river which turns a hundred mills, irrigates a million acres of grain, fruit, and vine, and which imparts fertility and beauty to the largest and richest of California's valleys. The Sierra crest is nowhere grander, and nowhere more generous is the recompense that awaits the wearied traveller, than here among the sources of the Middle Fork of the San Joaquin.

Sleeping that night at the base of Mt. Huxley, warmed by our fire of gnarled juniper, I dreamed of my task fully done. A well-marked trail led from the distant Yosemite past the long lake, up the snow-basin, and over the divide to the King's River. I hope my dream was prophetic. The way, at all events, is clear. Only the trail waits to be built.

Next morning we climbed Mt. Wallace. Sliding down a long snow-slope to the frozen lake at the bottom of the amphitheatre at the base of the peak, we avoided a bath by the merest luck, and toiled up a rock-filled chute that led to a splintered wall whose highest point was the summit. By nine o'clock I had the camera set up, while Bonner levelled the compass. The aneroid read 13,900 feet [13,377]. Noon found us back at our camp, eating lunch and photographing Mt. Huxley; and the late afternoon sun flung the shadow of Mt. Spencer over us and over the large frozen lake which is set deep in the granite at the base of the highest crest of Mt. Darwin. But we did not set foot on that crest. The sun had nearly set when after two hours' hard climbing we finally came upon a little platform of rock from which farther ascent is barred to all human beings; and

---

5. Sapphire Lake, elevation 10,966.

though descent seemed fraught with imminent peril, descend we must and descend we did. Before doing so, however, I took the altitude. The barometer read 13,950 feet, and, as nearly as I could judge, we were between two and three hundred feet of the summit.[6] Reaching the névé just before dark, we slid a full half mile in less than a minute, seized our knapsacks, and after a quarter of an hour's struggling in the darkness, kicked a thicket of tamarack, and camped.

The following day, July 17th, was devoted to photographing arid general exploring; and late in the afternoon we returned to the South Fork cañon, where, in a little cavern at the base of a fifteen hundred foot cataract that comes tumbling over the south wall, we had hidden our provisions, safe from molestation by wild beasts. Continuing up the cañon, its slaty structure changed to one of basalt. For a number of miles the descent of the river is much more rapid, and the strong current had ripped out of the basalt a deep channel, the bottom of which was formed of a series of steps, over which the stream poured in a succession of falls. One of these was fully a hundred feet high, and in its descent the water scarcely touched the rock. In this locality the walls of the cañon exhibit a beautiful glacial polish; and the striæ, which also tell of the passage of ancient ice, were visible to a great height.

After having travelled about seven miles from the confluence of the Middle Fork, most unexpectedly we reached the head of the cañon, at an altitude of 11,700 feet. It opened upon a glacial valley, the bottom of which was fairly submerged by melted snow. Thus we were surprised at finding that the main cañon of the South Fork headed, not upon the crest, but at least eight miles west of it, and that the assertion of our sheep-herder that Mt. Goddard stood at the head of the cañon and on its northern side was correct, the map of the old Survey to the contrary notwithstanding.

For there it was, a greenish-black, ugly monster of a mountain, looking like some shaggy buffalo seated on its haunches, its back to the glacial valley we were ascending, its head hidden by the great shoulders. An immense amphitheatre, walled in by a spur of the peak, lay at its southern base, a snow-covered lake filling the bottom, and it was partially encircled on the west and northwest by a chain of lesser lakes, from which leaped

---

6. The summit of Mt. Darwin is 13,831.

up tongues of Snow, that lay like white daggers struck into the black flesh of the mountain. Lower peaks of the same forbidding color were ranged in an irregular line that stretched many miles west. These formed that black wall which had hemmed in the basin of the Middle Fork, and Goddard was the pyramidal peak which rose from the centre of this wall. Camping at an altitude of 11,800 feet, we made ready for an early ascent.

The rising sun saw us already on our way, with full packs on our backs, for we meant that afternoon to continue our journey by passing eastward at the very base of the peak. The rippled surface of the snow-slopes was frozen hard, and we scarcely displaced a crystal in springing from ridge to ridge. The lakelets, too, were frozen deep, and we crossed them with perfect confidence. The altitude of the base of the peak was found to be 12,200 feet. An examination made the evening before had persuaded me to try a snow-tongue which led from a snow-field at the head of an ice-cascade, up a steep, narrow gorge or chute to the lower portion of the backbone of the mountain. Bonner consenting to this plan, we secured our packs in a crevasse under an immense fragment of rock, and taking lunch, camera, and all our instruments *except the aneroid,* climbed quickly to the top of the ice-cascade. Here the conviction was again forced upon us that the snow-tongue offered the best route of ascent, and up it we toiled. I should judge its angle of acclivity to have been about 45°, its width some thirty feet at the base, and five at the summit, and its length at least a quarter of a mile. When about half-way up, our need of an axe was quite pressing, for the surface was becoming so hard that it took several blows of the toe to pierce the crust and gain a footing. So we took to the cliffs on the left-hand side, and were soon on the backbone, which we found gentle of slope and comparatively easy to walk upon. An hour's walk, now over flinty blocks and fragments of all sizes, now over rock in place, brought us to the first summit, on which we built a monument and proceeded to take our observations.

When I discovered the absence of the barometer, I believe I was at that moment the most disgusted person in the State of California. Bonner refused me the consolation of a good kicking on the ground that his footing was too precarious, and during the four hours we remained on the peak I utterly refused to he comforted, even by the view, which was in many respects the finest I had ever beheld. Thank to my stupidity, the exact altitude is still to be determined. The old survey roughly estimated it at 14,000 feet, but as, levelling across to Mt. Darwin, our peak was found to be the higher, I feel confident that the mountain will ultimately be determined to be considerably over 14,000 feet high.[7]

From Mt. Goddard to the main crest at the Palisades the distance was from fifteen to twenty miles, and the intervening district was occupied by peaks, walls, and alpine gorges of great depth. Many of the peaks were but little lower than Mt. Goddard itself; and, on the whole, the width of the zone of crest is considerably greater here than anywhere else in the Sierra. The singular extension eastward of the axis of the range from Mt. Darwin is sufficient to account for this fact.

To the geologist, Mt. Goddard and its vicinity offers a most interesting and important field for study and speculation. As is true throughout all but the northern portion of the range, the igneous rocks—the lavas, basalts, and other volcanic materials—cannot be referred to volcanoes or visible vents in the vicinity of their occurrence, for there are none. They have doubtless been erupted through fissures in the granite and aqueous formations; but their position and relation to those rocks and to the metamorphic slates arid metamorphosed sedimentary rocks generally present many problems which trained minds will eventually concern themselves in solving. Mt. Goddard and the lower peaks which form an irregular wall westward are of slate, which, though really of many kinds and of many different colors, is of a greenish-black when seen in the mass. Silver, both in the free state and in combination, and a number of other metals and minerals are found in these slates. North of Mt. Goddard and these western peaks the granite appears, and to quite as great a height as the latter. To the south in the cañon, I noticed basaltic terraces sitting upon the reddish and altogether different kind of slate out of which the cañon has been eroded. South of the cañon the rock is granitic again. South of Goddard itself the wall of the amphitheatre, which is a spur of the mountain, changes insensibly from blackish slate to the purest gray granite. East of the peak, the divide between the King's and San Joaquin rivers similarly graduates into a material which, though showing in places the effects of great heat, is crystalline and indubitably granite. The crest to which the divide is joined is also granite, reddened, I think, by iron; and south of the divide from Goddard quite over to the Palisades lie a series of parallel gorges, separated by crested divides, the whole black

7. Mt. Goddard is 13,568.

"Snow Tunnel in the Enchanted Gorge." (Photograph by Theodore S. Solomons, 1895.) This is at the head of Disappearing Creek, just below Chasm. Lake. See Color Plate No. 5, taken at the same place in 1977.

as night, and, if a hasty examination did not deceive, formed of slate through which run dikes of a very old lava. The Palisades themselves are either of igneous material or of metamorphic slate. Thus we have granites, lavas, basalts, and slates overlying, underlying, and horizontally contiguous with one another, in quite obvious nonconformity with theory and precedent. That the granites in this region date back to the Jurassic period, and that the eruptions of the lavas are to be referred in every instance to the late Tertiary, is, I think, highly questionable.

Chasm Lake, between Scylla and Charybdis.

"Rotunda in the Enchanted Gorge." (Photograph by Theodore S. Solomons, 1895.) Scylla is at the left. See Color Plate No. 6 for another view up the Enchanted Gorge.

But whatever the story they tell to the geologist, these diversities of formation, adding as they do an element of contrast and variety, contribute not a little to the effectiveness of the picture, and invest the landscape with a heightened sublimity. One of these gorges to which I have alluded as leading on the southern side of the divide between the two rivers, is entitled to more than passing notice. Indeed, I do not know how more fittingly to conclude this brief description of the locality of Mt. Goddard than to give some account of the Enchanted Gorge.

We were caught in a storm while on Mt. Goddard, and were glad to camp at the highest clump of tamarack shrubbery we could find. This happened to be considerably above the big frozen lake, and ice and snow lay all about us. I have never passed a night in a higher altitude than this, nor do I care to, for we must have been nearly 13,500 feet high. We had no sooner built a fire than the snow began to fall, and though for a time it was nip and tuck between the two elements, our pitch-saturated logs conquered at last. In the morning we climbed round the southern base of the mountain, and made our way along the divide in a blinding storm, which becoming monotonous after six or eight hours, we determined to descend a deep gorge that had captured our admiration and aroused our curiosity when on the summit of Goddard. At half-past one this gorge lay directly south of us, and in an hour we had descended to its head, which we found was guarded by a nearly frozen lake, whose sheer, ice-smoothed walls arose on either side, up and up, seemingly into the very sky, their crowns two sharp black peaks of most majestic form. A Scylla and a Charybdis they seemed to us, as we stood at the margin of the lake and wondered how we might pass the dangerous portal.[8] By a little careful climbing we got around the lake, and stood at the head of the gorge. [See Color Plate No. 5.] Instead of the precipice we had feared to find, the narrow bottom was filled with snow, furnishing us a kind of turnpike, down which we fairly flew. Down, down, by sinuous curves, our road conducted us, as though into the bowels of the earth; for the walls, black, glinting, weird, rose a thousand and two thousand feet almost perpendicularly over our heads, and were lost in the storm-clouds that were discharging upon us a copious rain. For at least three miles we sped over the snow, when of a sudden the gorge widened into a kind of rotunda, the snow disappeared, and the stream which I expected to emerge from under it was conspicuous by its absence, nor could the roar of its subterranean flow be even faintly heard. Imagine a well a thousand feet wide and nearly twice as deep, its somewhat narrow bottom piled with fragments of rock, from the size of pebbles to that of buildings, the walls and floor of every hue that lends itself readily to a general effect of blackness, and the rotunda is pictured. Several torrents fell over the perpendicular western wall into a lake that had no visible outlet. [See Color Plate No. 6.]

8. Chasm Lake.

Bonner, at the left, and Solomons, in Kings River Canyon, 1895.
". . . hungry and tattered, but in superb physical condition."

After an hour's struggle over the gorge floor, the roughness of which defies description, we reached the lower end of the rotunda and the beginning of another shorter stretch of snow. The walls had now taken on the metallic lustre of many shades of bronze, the brilliancy of which was heightened by the polish imparted by the glacier which had formerly filled this deep gorge. The snow floor again giving place to monster rock fragments, again we struggled over the uneven surface; when, without warning, below a little moraine-like embankment, out gushed a great torrent of water, which, on reaching a part of the gorge so narrow that the snow yet filled it, burrowed underneath, darted out a hundred yards beyond, soon met another drift of snow under which it burrowed, as before, and in the middle of which it formed a lake with perpendicular banks of snow fully thirty feet in height, only to plunge again under the snow, this time leaving a roof so thin that my companion's feet pierced the crust, and he fell in up to his waist. With great coolness and dexterity, however, he extricated himself before I had more than grasped the situation. And so, till the fast-gathering gloom warned us to seek a camping-spot, we worked our way among the manifold wonders of that marvellous gorge. When finally we found trees on a kind of shelf, high above the stream, and, wearied with our day's toil, prepared to camp, the barometer registered a drop of nearly six thousand feet from the Goddard divide.

Next day we continued the descent of the gorge to its confluence with Goddard Creek, which from Mt. Goddard we had identified as heading in a number of lakes on the southeastern base of the mountain. Five miles below the confluence of the stream draining the Enchanted Gorge, Goddard Creek empties into the main Middle Fork of the King's River, twenty miles above Tehipitee Valley, the deepest "Yosemite" in the range. We explored and photographed this Middle Fork country and the Tehipitee, securing a number of excellent negatives, and then took the Granite Basin trail to our destination, the King's River Cañon, which we reached on July 28th, hungry and tattered, but in superb physical condition.

So accustomed had we become to our packs during the latter week of our trip, that it is no exaggeration to say that we had not felt the weight of the knapsacks, though when we reached our journey's end they weighed not less than twenty pounds apiece. The little expedition had been an entire success. In sixteen days we had covered fully three times as much territory as we could have hoped to explore had we travelled with a mule or burro. Yet my eyes had constantly been on the alert for passages practicable for animals; and to such good purpose had the quest been pursued that the Sierra Club will shortly place on file in its Club Rooms maps and descriptions which will enable the enterprising mountaineer to leave the Yosemite Valley with loaded animals, and to thread his way to the King's River Cañon through time very heart of the High Sierra.

The Grand Cañon
of the Tuolumne

R. M. Price

Originally published in the *Sierra Club Bulletin*, vol. 1, no. 1, January 1893

It was thought that a simple description of a trip from Soda Springs, in the Tuolumne Meadows, down through the grand cañon of the Tuolumne to Hetch Hetchy Valley, might prove interesting to the members of the SIERRA CLUB. The reader regrets, however, that his lack of geological and botanical knowledge renders it impossible far him to make this paper a scientific one, or anything more than a simple description, for this region presents a most interesting and fruitful field of study for both geologist and botanist. He trusts that the novel manner of traveling in the Sierras pursued by his companion and himself, and the fact that, up to the past summer, but one man had gone *through* the cañon may make this of some interest.[1]

In the middle of July, a fellow-member of the SIERRA CLUB, Mr. L. de F. Bartlett and myself, loaded down under rolls of blankets and knapsacks and haversacks containing our provisions, walked from Berenda, on the Southern Pacific, to Wawona, on the stage-road, thence on a trail by the way of Chilnooilny[2] creek and Givens' Ridge to Yosemite Valley, coming in by Glacier Point. Leaving the Valley July 27th, we struck out for the Tuolumne Meadows; but here work began, for a party to whom we had written to pack forty or fifty pounds of provisions to Soda Springs for us, had failed to get our message, and we were obliged to load ourselves down under packs weighing about forty-five pounds each,—no small weight to carry at an altitude of 10,000 feet. Our path lay over the old

---

1. Since reading the above paper the writer has learned that Mr. J. M. Hutchings, the first guardian of the Yosemite Valley, ascended Mount Ritter, and in 1875, descended the grand cañon of the Tuolumne.
2. One of several variant spellings of Chilnualna.

Mono trail by the way of Nevada Falls, Clouds' Rest and Cathedral Peak to the springs. From the Soda Springs, with six days' rations, we proceeded to Mounts Maclure and Ritter, which we ascended. This latter peak, over 13,000 feet high, and one of the most striking and sublime of the Sierras, has been ascended, as far as is known, but four times,—in the seventies by the President of this Club, Mr. Muir; in 1883, by Mr. Willard D. Johnson, at that time a topographer in the United States Geological Survey; on July 26th of this last summer by a party consisting of Messrs. Joseph LeConte, Jr., Theodore Solomons, and Sidney Peixotto; and on August 2d by our own small party.

We returned from Mount Ritter to Soda Springs, and after a run up that prime triangulation point of the United States Coast and Geodetic Survey, Mount Conness, prepared to descend through the Tuolumne cañon to Hetch Hetchy, notwithstanding statements of Clarence King and others that the cañon was impassable. In Professor Whitney's reports of the geological survey of California may be found this statement: "The river enters a cañon, which is about twenty miles long, and probably inaccessible through its entire length, at least we have never heard of its being explored, and it certainly cannot be entered from its head. Mr. King followed this cañon down as far as he could, to where the river precipitated itself down in a grand fall over a mass of rocks, so rounded on the edge, that it was *impossible* to approach near enough to look over into the chasm below, the walls on each side being too steep to be climbed." Our President, Mr. John Muir, was the only man who had passed entirely through the cañon up to the time when we made the descent. He had given us general directions how to proceed, and he had ended with the caution not to load ourselves down with blankets and provisions. This caution circumstances rendered it impossible to observe. We had hoped to find Mr. Lambert at his cabin at Soda Springs and engage him to pack our blankets and knapsacks to the Hetch Hetchy, or the Hog Ranch near Hetch Hetchy, so that we might not have to carry with us more than food enough for three or four days; but, on returning to the springs from Mount Conness, we found Lambert's place still deserted. The next morning came, but still no Lambert. Our time and food were so limited that we must either start immediately or give up the cañon altogether. To give it up would be a great disappointment, and, with our loads, unfortunately now not heavy with food, to attempt the descent of the cañon was not particularly inviting. Our provisions now consisted of a little bacon, six or seven pounds of flour, a cup of rice, sugar, a handful of cracked wheat, and a little tea and coffee. Anywhere in the immediate neighborhood of the appetites of two SIERRA CLUB tramps such a small quantity of food would not last long, and we were apprehensive lest it should give out before we could get through the cañon. But, stimulated by a desire for adventure and an eagerness to see the wonders of the cañon which had been described to us by Mr. Muir, we carefully packed our knapsacks, worked up our courage to the highest point, and started.

The grand cañon of the Tuolumne lies about fifteen miles due north of Yosemite and extends twenty miles in a westerly direction. During the glacial period a great glacier, probably one thousand feet thick, swept down from its sources around Lyell, Maclure, Dana, and Conness. Divided by Mount Hoffman and contiguous rocks to the east, part of this great glacier passed to the left grinding out the Tenaya cañon, and joining the larger glacier at work in Yosemite; the other and larger part passed to the right, eroding the Tuolumne cañon. The effects of this glacier as a polishing agent, notwithstanding the action of water and atmospheric agents of disintegration for ages, are still visible on the hard granite. In many places on the walls the polished granite reflects the sun like a mirror. The Tuolumne river, a stream nearly equal in size to the Merced, which flows through the Yosemite Valley, has its sources in the remnants of that glacial monster which cut out the cañon. Its bounding waters gradually quiet themselves in the Tuolumne Meadows to a placid stream, gathering force for their grand plunge into the cañon. Here, not peacefully, but bounding over precipices, dashing and foaming in numberless cascades, and plunging through sheer walled gorges, the stream threads its way through. Now and then it glides quietly through a diminutive meadow or rests in a crystal pool, as if it were accumulating energy for a fresh rush and plunge over the rocks. At the foot of the cliffs are great piles of talus, composed of huge boulders, probably loosened and thrown down from the cliffs above by some terrific post-glacial earthquake. At places there are immense boulders in the current of the stream, their rounded edges and polished surfaces evidencing a rolling, bounding, grinding down the river-bed, where they are now waiting for a heavy flood to start them again in their tumble down the cañon.

One mile of pleasant walking from the Soda Springs brought us to the head of the cañon; four more of easy clambering down the rocks by the Upper Falls and White Rapids and we reached the confluence of the

Virginia creek entering from the north,[3] and then we "struck it rough;" huge boulders to clamber over, almost impenetrable manzanita and chapparal (sic) to push our way through, and slippery, water-polished and glacier-polished rocks to scramble over. The roughness of the trip had not been exaggerated, but the beauty and grandeur of the falls and cascades, the sublimity of the cliffs, and the loveliness of the verdure in the cañon, fully repaid us for the hard work. When we stopped for lunch, a deep pool of crystal water attracted us, and we prepared to enjoy a refreshing dive and swim; but one plunge into that icy fluid was enough. Proceeding a short distance clown the cañon from the place where we had lunched we came to a rocky spur jutting down to the river's edge. Seeing that it would be almost impossible, if not entirely so, to pass around the point, we decided to attempt to clamber over it. After hard climbing we reached the top, only to find that the other side was almost perpendicular. This was probably the obstacle which had blocked Mr. King's further advance. Half way down, holding a small manzanita bush, was a narrow shelf to which a number of crevices led from the top of the spur. Twenty feet from the shelf, the talus reached to the perpendicular face of the rock. We must either descend or retrace our steps, to find in all probability no better place. Holding on with the ends of our fingers in a crevice of the rock we gradually worked our way down to the shelf, then, laying aside my knapsack, I tied the rope provided for such an emergency to my waist, and my companion having taken a twist around the manzanita bush, lowered me to the talus; next the knapsacks were lowered, and, finally, Bartlett fastened the rope to himself, took a twist about the bush and threw the other end to me. He then swung himself off the shelf, and, as I slowly payed out the rope, descended to my side. This was the first use we had made of our rope. Several times we had been sarcastically asked if we were going to lasso deer with it, and more than once we had been on the point of throwing it away; but were restrained from doing so by the thought that an emergency might come in which it would be useful.

Continuous scrambling from three o'clock in the afternoon till half-past six did not take us more than one and one-half miles down the cañon. Approaching night and a large, unnamed tributary coming in from

---

3. This is actually Conness Creek, where the Glen Aulin High Sierra Camp now is. Virginia Creek is farther on, below Waterwheel Falls.

Waterwheel Falls.

the north across our path stopped our progress for the day,[4] and, after as hearty a meal as our scant stock of provisions would permit, we spread our blankets and were sung to sleep by the music of the cascades.

The falls and cascades of the Tuolumne cañon are less majestic than some of the falls in the Yosemite, but they far excel those in Yosemite in variety of form and beauty, and they impress one much more forcibly with a feeling of their power. The peculiarities of several cascades struck us particularly. At one point the entire river, beaten into foam, rushes down a broad, polished surface of rock inclined at an angle of about forty-five degrees. It is the Silver Apron of the Merced, between Vernal and Nevada Falls, reproduced on a much grander scale.[5] At another point a depression in the rock caused the water of a cascade to be thrown vertically in the air in the form of and resembling an open feather fan.[6]

On the second morning, after such a sleep as only tired trampers enjoy in the crisp air of the mountains with naught but the star-lit sky for a tent, we crossed the before-mentioned tributary, jumping from rock to rock, stimulated by the feeling that, unless we were careful, we might take an undesired tumble in the water and roll among the boulders. The water-falls and cascades seen this day, with the exception of one, did not equal those seen on the previous day, but the verdure was becoming more luxuriant and the cliffs more sublime. This one cascade was another Silver Apron, even more beautiful and impressive than the one above described. An ideal camping-spot attracted our attention. It was a level place, shaded by a dense grove of giant cedars and yellow pines, carpeted by a thick mat of pine needles and ferns, close to where the river for a short distance rippled musically along. Late in the afternoon we reached the sheer walled gorge which Mr. Muir had told us we would find about half-way down the cañon. A glance showed the uselessness of attempting to continue near the bed of the river, so we took to the hills, clambered over a ridge about twelve hundred feet high, and at dark reached the river again just below the gorge. Here we found no ideal camping-spot, but, on the contrary, we had to be content with a bed of rocks inclined at a rather steep angle. How we wished that we could have made practical

---

4. Return Creek.
5. California Falls.
6. Waterwheel Falls.

Muir Gorge.

use of the camping-spot seen during the day. But after a few weeks' experience a Sierra tramper can sleep anywhere, and the next morning, notwithstanding our inhospitable berth, we arose refreshed and ready for
more hard work.

Looking back from some rising rocks a short distance below where we
had camped, we could see a perfect amphitheater, walled in by cliffs from
two thousand to three thousand feet high, apparently without a break, so
that we could not distinguish where the river entered. It was a most
imposing view. But time was precious and we could not linger long. Just
before noon, while leading the way, I attempted to make a long jump
from one boulder to another, between which lay a deep passage. Unfortunately, just as I leaped my pack overbalanced me. I reached the boulder,
but all in a heap and with a sprained ankle. To say the least, the prospect
was not encouraging,—eight or nine miles of the roughest mountain
scrambling before any food could be obtained. But necessity overcomes
many obstacles. My companion bound my ankle tightly with a bandana
handkerchief, and I managed to limp painfully along. Our fingers were
sore and bleeding from holding on to the rocks, our provisions would not
last more than two clays longer, and my ankle might at any time bring
me to a dead stop; that our spirits were depressed it is needless to say.
But as night approached we came to a strip of meadow which we thought
must be but a short distance from Hetch Hetchy, and we spread our
blankets with the consoling thought that early on the morrow we would
reach the valley.

The next day was one of continual disappointments. As we passed
each projecting ridge we looked ahead expectantly to see that massive
pile of rock in Hetch Hetchy, Sugar Loaf, loom up before us, but no
Sugar Loaf appeared. Though we had not seen a human being for ten
days we were not without company,—gnats, mosquitos, flies, several vari-
eties of ants, rattlesnakes, deer, and bear were about us in abundance. No
bear were visible, but there was unmistakable evidence of the presence of
numbers of them. We followed their trails for miles down the cañon as
plainly as if they had been made by a troop of cavalry. The noise of our
tramping through the brush gave them an opportunity of hiding before
they could be seen. Rattlesnakes were especially numerous, and we felt it
to be a moral obligation to kill them whenever they crossed our path. At
one time we were just about to spring on a boulder, when, on the exact
spot where we intended to jump, we saw a large rattler coiled ready to

spring. We disposed of Mr. Rattler before jumping. Several times this day we were obliged to use our rope in getting over difficult places. Late in the afternoon of the fourth day we concluded that we must be near Hetch Hetchy, and this time we were not disappointed, for Sugar Loaf came into view, and we knew that the valley was but a few miles below.

A few hours of comparatively easy walking, the next morning, and we had concluded our tramp through the grand cañon of the Tuolumne, glad that we were through with that kind of tramping, yet sorry to leave behind us the wonders of the cañon, which the roughness and difficulties of the trip had prevented us from fully enjoying.

The Descent of Tenaya Cañon

George Gibbs

Originally published in the *Sierra Club Bulletin*, vol. 3, no. 3, February 1901

On Monday, July 23, 1894, the writer and three friends were camped upon the shores of Lake Tenaya, twenty-odd miles by trail from the Yosemite Valley. We were at the close of a mountain tour which had occupied the whole of our college vacation. Leaving Fresno on the 29th of May, we had tramped across the Sierra, passing through King's River Cañon, and over Kearsarge Pass. Then we had explored the head-waters of the Kern; had spent four hours on the summit of Mt. Whitney; passed through Owen's Valley, until we camped at Casa Diablo. From here we again crossed the mountains by climbing the steep trail through Bloody Cañon. Now we were camping on the site of the old toll-house on Lake Tenaya.

We had been on the road some fifty-six days, and had tramped over 500 miles. Our trip had taken us into some of the grandest and wildest parts of the Sierra. Corbett, one of our party, and I wished, as a climax to the tour, to attempt a dangerous and exciting bit of mountaineering, and so decided upon the descent of Tenaya Cañon into Yosemite Valley. Neither of us knew anything about the cañon, though we had heard that Mr. Muir had successfully passed through it. Had we, before starting, known the extent of the difficulties to be met, we might have hesitated some time before undertaking the trip.

Lake Tenaya is a beautiful sheet of water situated at the head of the stream which supplies Mirror Lake below. To reach the Yosemite from here by the usual trail, one travels twenty-odd miles; by way of Tenaya Cañon the distance is eight. While Corbett and I made the attempt through the cañon, the other two of our party were to take our mules into the valley by the usual route, and all were to meet below at Mirror Lake.

At six in the morning we started, carrying with us a bite of lunch and about fifty feet of stout rope. We expected to reach the Yosemite by

noon,— the others intended to arrive in the valley at four in the afternoon,— so little did we realize what was before us! It took us fourteen
hours of the hardest and most trying work to cover the eight miles of
cañon.

Leaving Lake Tenaya, we followed along the right bank of the
stream. For a mile or two we made our way through thick underbrush and
over trunks of trees which lay all about the ground. We were congratulat-
ing ourselves on the easy work we were having, when we found that the
way was growing gradually steeper and the cañon narrower. The traveling
soon became very difficult. The glacier which had passed through the
cañon had left the walls and floor in places as smooth as glass. Suddenly
the way grew precipitous. There were no signs of brush, and the highly
polished rocks were very slippery. Ahead of us we heard the sound of falling waters, and knew that we were approaching a precipice. A precipice it
proved to be, and a frightfully steep one. We were puzzled, for if Mr. Muir
had gone down the cañon, he had certainly not descended the waterfall
before us.

Sliding down on my back thirty or forty feet along the smoothly polished rock surface, I barely succeeded in reaching a small projecting
ledge. To this I clung, and looking over saw that a single step would have
taken me over the edge of a perpendicular cliff hundreds of feet in height.
The sight appalled me. I started back to join Corbett. Then I realized
that, while there had been little difficulty in sliding down, to return was
another matter. Unaided, I could not do it. I shouted to Corbett. Fortunately he had the rope, and after two or three attempts threw me an end,
and with this help I was drawn up to the higher level where he stood. We
were at a loss as to the method of reaching the floor of this chasm before
us. Mr. Muir could never have gone down on the side of the stream
which I tried, neither could he have descended the bank directly across
the stream, for that, we found, was similar to the left side. The only thing
to do was to leave the stream and to attempt the descent from a point
about two hundred feet to the right. The wall here was broken by two or
three broad ledges and several narrower ones. Our only hope seemed to
be in dropping from ledge to ledge, by means of the rope, down the steep
wall on to the level below. This we finally accomplished, though it took
us three hours of climbing, sliding, lowering, dropping, and falling. We
would double the rope around some thick shrub or around a sharp-
pointed rock which protruded sufficiently, and then, gliding down on the

rope, would seek a footing at some point below. Thus, considerably exhausted, we came to the bottom. Here a plunge into a deep, cool pool refreshed us.

For a mile or more we now walked through underbrush or waded through the creek. Wet, tired, hungry, and a great deal less exuberant than in the morning, we trudged along, knowing that to go back now was impossible. With only four biscuits and a couple of cold rice-fritters in our pockets, the outlook was not cheerful.

It was now noon. Calculations showed that we had made about four miles. We must reach the Yosemite by night. The descent again grew steeper and steeper, and the walls of the cañon gradually narrowed, so that we were compelled to walk in the middle of the stream. The most exciting and dangerous incident of our descent now followed. The walls were not more than a hundred feet apart, and rose a thousand feet or more above us. The stream suddenly plunged into an extremely narrow gorge. We seemed to have reached the final jumping-off place. It was as impossible to climb out of the cañon as to go back, and to go straight ahead seemed out of the question. After a survey of the surrounding wall, we found only one solution to our difficulty. That was to make our way along a very narrow ledge on the right. This ledge, about two feet in its broadest places, sloped downwards toward its outer edge, constantly giving us the sensation, while moving along it, of slipping into the gorge below. Corbett thought that with the aid of the rope he might reach a ledge below, and while I secured and held the end, he lowered himself some distance down the side of the gorge. He was completely hidden from sight, and kept me in constant dread lest he should slip and be dashed against the granite rocks below. All at once the top of his head, followed by an extremely pale face, reappeared above the ledge. He had gotten down fairly well, but had found no good footing below, and had just been able to return by means of the rope. So to descend at this point was impossible, and it seemed as though nothing were left but to crawl farther along the ledge we were on—a very disagreeable alternative, as the ledge grew narrower at every step. We made a few yards on our hands and knees, and then came to a nearly perpendicular slope along which for a distance of thirty or forty feet ran a small ledge. It was about half the width of a man's shoe. Corbett started across, leaning against the wall and placing one foot directly before the other. Slowly, step by step, making each move with the greatest deliberation, he crossed, and finally with

a shout of joy reached a level spot beyond. It was now my turn, and, trying to forget the danger, I advanced, keeping my eyes always before me,
directed on the spot where my companion stood. In a few moments—a
period which seemed a hundred times longer—I joined him, with a
feeling of relief and pleasure that is hard to describe.

For a half-hour or more our descent continued to be a hard one. We
let each other down and pulled each other up over ledges and difficult
places, the rope seemingly indispensable. At last, about three o'clock, we
reached the bed of the stream once more. We then sat down to a lunch
and well-earned rest. We knew we were nearing Mirror Lake, because the
Half Dome, a guiding-point throughout the day, seemed now not very far
distant. The most dangerous portion of the trip was over; the remainder
was merely vexatious and tedious. It was a continuous climbing over
bowlder after bowlder. The brush and trees became so thick on the
sloping sides of the cañon as to drive us again and again into the stream,
compelling us to wade.

It was now about 6 P. M., and we were faint and tired. There seemed
no end to the bowlders, brush, and under-growth, and our arms and legs
ached from the repeated strains. We were on the left-hand side of the
stream and were walking along a grateful level stretch when it abruptly
ended in a fall of sixty or seventy feet. We did not want to turn back and
search for a means of getting around the fall, and so we looked for a place
near by. Standing on a projecting bowlder some yards to the right, we saw
close at hand a branch of a huge pine whose base was not far from the
foot of the fall. Corbett again took the lead, and after some hesitancy
swung himself upon the branch, which bent almost double under his
weight. He clung to it, dangling in mid air fifty feet above the ground.
Hand over hand he reached the main trunk, then slid quickly to the
ground. I followed him, and in a few moments our last difficulty had been
overcome.

It was growing late, and we knew the boys in the valley would be
anxious about our safety. We now came into a dense forest in which we
had to struggle through ferns and underbrush and where we were constantly stumbling over dead trunks of trees and creeping vines. It was not
until it was evening and completely dark that we finally emerged and
found ourselves before Mirror Lake. A few moments more and we joined
the other two, who welcomed us as if we were the dead come to life. For

once they were glad to see us, and to say that they were thankful—and we also, for that matter,—would be putting it mildly.

We learned from Mr. Clark, the Guardian of the valley, that Mr. Muir, and one other party, consisting of two men, had made the descent of the cañon. Our trip was the first for over twelve years.

If one loves excitement and peril, he may rest assured that he can find it in the trip we took. As an example of dangerous mountain-climbing, it will serve as one of the best; but neither Corbett nor I would wish any friend the doubtful pleasure of some of our experiences.

Plate 1. Middle Fork of the Kings River, between
Simpson Meadow and Palisade Creek. Page 15.

Plate 2. Columbine Peak and Knapsack Pass, from Dusy Basin. Page 16.

Plate 3. Milestone Mountain and Milestone Creek. Page 30.

Plate 4. Evolution Lake. Mounts Darwin and Spencer. Page 93.

Plate 5. Disappearing Creek, at the head of the Enchanted Gorge.
The photograph on page 99 was taken in the same place. Page 102.

Plate 6. Looking up the Enchanted Gorge. See the photograph
on Page 101 for a similar view. Page 102.

Plate 7. Triple Falls on Cartridge Creek. Page 152.

Plate 8. "In the middle of the afternoon we rested half an hour in the green grass on the margin of a beautiful lake with a charming little islet in it." Page 157. Nothing in this scene is named. The original route of the John Muir Trail went up Cartridge Creek, over Cartridge Pass, around this lake on the left, and down to the South Fork of the Kings River.

Plate 9. Arrow Peak and Bench Lake. Page 159.

Plate 10. Mount Stanford, from the summit of Gregorys Monument. Page 177.

Plate 11. Mount Humphreys and Muriel Lake. Page 195.

Plate 12. Marion Lake and Marion Peak. Page 216.

Plate 13. The Palisades, from Mather Pass. Palisade Lakes at the lower left. Page 219.

Plate 14. Amphitheater Lake. LeConte, Hutchinson, Moffitt, and Pike came down the tongue of snow from the pass, which is unnamed. The other side of the pass is a gradual slope down to the Dumbbell Lakes. Page 219.

Plate 15. Whaleback and Cloud Canyon. Page 230.

Plate 16. Colby Lake and Colby Pass. Page 232.

Explorations Among the Cañons North of the Tuolumne River.

Lieut. N. F. McClure

Originally published in the *Sierra Club Bulletin*, vol. 1, no. 5, January 1895

On August 18, 1894, I left the cavalry camp near Wawona, California, with a detachment of the Fourth U. S. Cavalry, consisting of twelve men and five pack-mules, with rations for twelve days, to scout for sheepmen, who were reported to be unusually thick in the vicinity of Tuolumne Meadows. On the afternoon of the second day I camped at that place. In the course of a conversation with Mr. Lambert, who resides there during the summer, I learned that he was in possession of a description of a route to Lake Eleanor by way of the cañons north of the Tuolumne River. At my request, he wrote this out in condensed form from a book which he had, the whole covering two-thirds of a sheet of legal-cap paper. This country was then unknown to me, and I had heard that it was one of excessive ruggedness, which a few sheep-herders and prospectors only had ever visited. I afterwards learned that First Sergeant Alvin Arndt, Troop "I," Fourth Cavalry, with a detachment of his troop, had crossed from Slide Cañon to Tiltill Valley in September, 1893, over a region of great roughness, and that he had found out from sheepmen that there was a route from Matterhorn Cañon to Hetch-Hetchy Valley, by keeping on the high ground between Rancheria Creek and the Tuolumne River.

Equipped with Mr. Lambert's directions and a copy of the map of the Sierra Club, I set forth on the morning of August 20th, on the Conness Trail. One mile northwest brought us to a small stream called Delaney Creek, and one mile and a quarter west of this we crossed Dingley Creek, where our trail forked. That to Mount Conness turned north, and was quite plain. The other, which I was to follow, was indicated in direction by an arrow pointing west; and, after searching about for a while, I discovered the blazes, beginning at a point about four hundred yards from the fork. In about a mile and a quarter we came to a large bare granite spot, over which the trail led; and a mile beyond this, to a bluff overlooking Conness Creek Cañon. A series of zigzags down this for three-fourths of a mile brought us to the stream below, Conness Creek, at the place where its left fork joins it, which latter is also called Alkali Creek. There was a meadow of good size here, and I availed myself of it by going into camp.

I had already sent a corporal and three men up the Conness Trail to look for sheep; and I now sent two men south on the same errand, while I, with three men, started up the west side of Alkali Creek on the trail of a pack-train which had turned back up that stream upon my approach, about an hour before. I suspected that the two men with it belonged to some party of sheep-herders, and that they were going back to warn some of their friends in charge of flocks near by.

The trail was plain, and, following rapidly up the creek for four miles, I reached a pretty meadow of eight or ten acres, upon which I found the enemy's pack-animals grazing. The two men were apparently asleep. I passed right on, as though not looking for them, and, in a half mile, crossed a grassy divide into the basin of a large stream which flows from Conness Mountain westward into Return Cañon. I scouted the upper part of this basin pretty thoroughly, and saw plenty of fresh "signs," but no sheep. Four hours found me again back with the pack-train of the sheepmen; but one of the packers had gone away on foot, in all probability to warn herders near by of our proximity. This suspicion was confirmed by the appearance of a dog about five hundred yards from us, which, as soon as it saw us, fled. Leaving one man in charge of our prisoner (for I now arrested the man), we searched the vicinity of the meadow for a radius of a mile, in the hope of finding sheep, but in vain. It was now getting late; so I made my prisoner pack up his train, and took him, his animals and his outfit back to my camp. There I found that my corporal had "bagged" three herders, and, from the animated conversation that now took place between his prisoners and mine, I saw that they were far from being strangers to one another. Next morning I sent a detachment up Alkali Creek, another to the scene of the capture of the three herders the day before, and a third, consisting of the corporal and two men, to take my four prisoners to Wawona. I accompanied the latter south over a pretty rough country to the Tioga road, which I struck at a point about three and one-half miles north of Lake Tenaya. I then returned alone by way of Mr. Lambert's to my camp.

On August 22d I started for Return Cañon, depending mostly on the "lay" of the country, since I could find but few traces left of the old Virginia Trail. I followed up Alkali Creek about two miles, and then struck almost due north, crossing the ridge between the two canons diagonally, and finally, after many tacks and zigzags, getting down into Return Cañon at the point where it receives the large tributary from the east,[1] whose upper basin I had explored two days before. Following up the main stream two miles, I suddenly came upon two good-sized flocks of sheep. The herders fled up into the rocks, and we were unable to capture them; so I had one or two shots fired to frighten them. I do not think that they have stopped running yet. We found two camps near by, with all the accouterments pertaining thereto; and these, together with four fine jacks, I secured and brought into my own camp, which I made on a meadow near by.

That afternoon my sergeant and I went up the cañon five miles and turned to the right through a saddle between two red peaks, which are part of the main chain of the Sierras. Right on top of the divide is Castle Lake,[2] a beautiful body of water, one-half mile long and very deep, fed by everlasting snow. This lake is the head waters of Green Creek, and is about one mile south of the north boundary of the reservation. At this time I saw no way of getting down into Green Creek Cañon. On August 23d I sent patrols from camp up and down Return Cañon. There were thousands of sheep running hither and thither, apparently abandoned by their herders. Fresh mutton was plentiful in our camp during the next few days. I ascended again to Castle Lake, and discovered a trail leading down Green Creek. Following this one-third of a mile, I discovered where the old Virginia Trail turned off sharp to the right up the hill for two hundreds yards to two small snow lakes, and then climbed for a half mile up a steep bluff to the divide between the head waters of Green Creek and those of Virginia Creek, from which divide the upper basin of the latter stream can be seen. By going about half a mile to the left of the

1. McCabe Creek.
2. Now named Summit Lake.

pass, on the ridge leading out to a large red mountain called Dunderberg
Peak, a fine view of Green Creek Cañon can be obtained. By ascending
the ridge dividing the head waters of Virginia Creek from those of Mill
Creek or Lundy Cañon, another good view is found. To the east is Mono
Lake. Three miles to the southeast is a large red peak, Mount Warren,
up whose steep sides, from a dark gorge below, a trail zigzagged, ascending
cliffs that seemed well-nigh impassable, and finally disappearing near the
top of the mountain. This trail was that from Lundy to Tioga, and it
passes over the very summit of Mount Warren, at an altitude of 12,000
feet.

     At my feet lay several little lakes fed by melting snowbanks, the
waters of which, finally uniting into a respectable stream, tumbled over
the rocks into a deep gorge, which I judged to be Lundy Cañon, and from
which the trail mentioned above started upward.

     On August 24th, I sent Sergeant Girdwood, with one man, to
Tuolumne Meadows to meet fresh supplies that I expected, while I, with
the remainder of the command, descended Return Cañon to the mouth
of Spiller (or Randall) Cañon. Turning up this and keeping on the
left-hand side of the stream, a stiff climb of a mile and a quarter brought
us to where the cañon was comparatively open, and about a mile beyond
this we found an old sheep corral. I afterward learned that there was a
route from this to Matterhorn Cañon, but did not look for one at this
time, as my directions from Mr. Lambert led me to believe that the only
passage-way was to he found at the extreme northern end of the cañon.
About five miles above the corral we came to a little lake, at the very
head of the stream, fed by a melting snowbank. A few yards above the
lake was the divide, beyond which lay Mono County, and a search of two
hours over this divide, and on both sides of it, failed to reveal any signs of
a way by which to leave the cañon with our animals. It was with the bit-
terest disappointment that I again turned my horse's head southward—for I felt that my directions having failed me here, I could no
longer depend upon them. After traveling three and one-half miles I
camped. One mile north of me was a high peak which has on its summit
three jagged spurs, which appear, as you advance up the cañon, like the
teeth of a gigantic circular saw, except that the left-hand one is the largest and the right-hand one smallest. After a good meal I felt better, and
was lying on my bedding, resting, when all at once, as my eyes were scan-
ning the side of the great backbone that separated me from Matterhorn

Cañon, I thought that I saw a place where a way to ascend might be found. Up I sprang and away I went to investigate. There was sparse timber scattered among the rocks, and I began to pick out a possible route; but it was all in vain. Each time I would come to some impassable obstacle and have to hunt for another path. I finally went up on top of the backbone and got a fine view of the surrounding country.

To the southwest, and about half a mile away, on a little plateau, probably over a thousand feet above Matterhorn Creek, lay a little lake surrounded by a small meadow. I now started along the ridge in a southwestern direction, keeping near the summit, and searching for a possible cleft or saddle through which animals might be taken. After going perhaps a quarter of a mile, I suddenly came upon the most remarkable natural pass that I ever beheld. A long, narrow cleft ran nearly east and west diagonally across the divide. It was about four hundred yards long, and considerable soil had collected in it, thus affording fine footing for horses. Investigating the west end of this, I soon discovered that I could get down to the little lake seen from above. It now remained to see whether I could find a practicable route from the east end of the pass to camp. I started for the bottom, hunting out a pathway as I went and marking it with little piles of stones; but I thought at the time that I should be obliged to build a trail over a few of the worst places. I returned to camp just at dusk, well pleased with my afternoon's work. Next morning we started bright and early, and after two hours of hard work reached the summit. As I had predicted, I had to build up pieces of trail in several places. I now left a man to watch for Sergeant Girdwood, whom I expected, and continued on down to the small lake, which was half a mile from the divide. There being a meadow here, I remarked to a soldier who was with me, a little in advance of the others, that it would be a good place to camp. I then went down alone for seven or eight hundred feet into the cañon, looking for a place to get the animals to the stream below. I confess that I did not like the outlook, as the slope was very great, and only a few inches of loose sand covered smooth granite rocks inclining at an angle of thirty degrees or more. I returned to the lake, and imagine my surprise to find the detachment in camp, horses unsaddled, mules unpacked, and the cook-fire blazing merrily away. The man to whom I had spoken about camping had taken my remark about its being a good camping-place in real earnest, and had told the others that my orders were to stay there until next clay. His name was Miller, and, naming the lake in honor of him,[3] I decided to remain there until the next morning. I spent the afternoon searching for a way of descent, and found one that turned to the left of the lake over a little ridge into a cañon, which it followed down about a mile in a southwestern direction to the bottom of the main cañon.

That evening my sergeant arrived with six more men, five fresh pack-mules, and eighty-five rations. I now had with me nine pack-mules (one having been sent back with the men who took the prisoners to Wawona), fifteen men, and about one hundred and fifty rations. Sergeant Girdwood had brought news of sheep in the vicinity of Bloody Cañon; so I decided to divide my party. Next morning I took seven men, the five

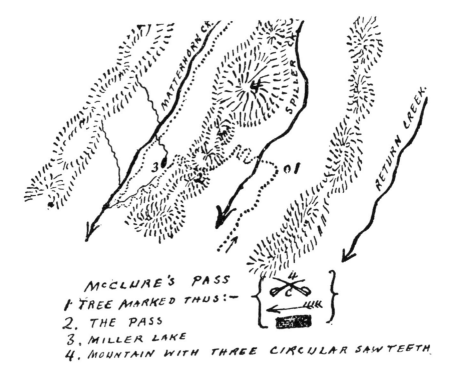

McCLURE'S PASS
1 TREE MARKED THUS :—
2. THE PASS
3. MILLER LAKE
4. MOUNTAIN WITH THREE CIRCULAR SAW TEETH.

---

3. This is the true Miller Lake—in reality just an unnamed pond on the
    Matterhorn Peak 7.5' quadrangle. The name "Miller Lake" is incorrectly
    applied to a lake on the *Falls Ridge* quadrangle.

mules and the seven horses that were best shod, and about eighty rations, and sent the sergeant with the remainder of the command to Bloody Cañon. A mile of zigzagging down the path that I had selected the day before brought me to Matterhorn Creek, up which I turned with high hopes. The route now led for five miles through little meadows on each side of the stream, until a comparatively low saddle was seen to the left of us and near the head of the cañon. Investigating this, I found it was a natural pass.[4] The scenery here was truly sublime. I doubt if any part of the main chain of the Sierras presents a greater ruggedness than that portion along whose slopes Matterhorn and Slide Cañon Creeks find their sources. Going through the saddle, our route now lay over a little glacier down to the stream starting from its foot.[5] We were here on the head waters of Rancheria Creek; but I did not know it at the time.[6] This stream rises among a number of glaciers (the one we crossed being one of these), and for a number of miles is called Slide Cañon. Later it becomes Deep Cañon Creek, and still beyond this Rancheria Creek, leaping into the upper end of Hetch-Hetchy Valley as a stream of considerable size.

After traveling three and one-half miles down the cañon, I came to the most wonderful natural object that I ever beheld. A vast granite cliff, two thousand feet in height, had literally tumbled from the bluff on the right-hand side of the stream with such force that it had not only made a mighty dam across the cañon, but many large stones had rolled far up on the opposite side. As it fell it had evidently broken into blocks, which were now seen of almost every size, piled one upon another in the wildest confusion. The smaller particles had settled between the crevices, leaving great holes among the larger blocks, some of which weighed many tons. To look at it, one might think that it had occurred but yesterday; but it was, in all probability, ages ago, as the ground just above the slide is two hundred feet or more higher than that just below, showing that earth has accumulated on the upper side for many years. Above the slide was a very small lake and a meadow of five acres, and I concluded to camp here.

---

4. Burro Pass.
5. Piute Creek.
6. This is not correct. Piute Creek is in a separate watershed; it flows into the Tuolumne River at Pate Valley. Deep Canyon is on Breeze Creek, a tributary of Rancheria Creek, which flows into the Tuolumne at Hetch Hetchy.

The flocks of sheep were near by, and I gave the herders warning not to come farther down, as I believed the line of the north boundary of the Park to be about where I was.

That afternoon I scouted down stream four miles to a place where the walls of the cañon closed in on the stream. There was a waterfall here of probably one hundred feet, and I could not get my horses farther. After returning to camp, one of the herders came to me, and I explained to him that I would let him "go in peace" if he would show me the way to Jack Main's Cañon. He said that the only man who knew the way had decamped upon my approach, and was now hidden. I told him to hunt the fellow up and, after a search (real or pretended) of three hours, be was found. He was a very willing man—very different from the average Portuguese or Basque sheepman—and would have been an invaluable guide had he not had a serious impediment of speech. This, combined with his strong foreign accent, made much of his talk unintelligible to me. He said that he knew the way to Jack Main's Cañon; but I could not find out whether he knew of either Lake Vernon or Lake Eleanor, as he seemed not to recognize these names. August 28th we started, our guide in the lead; and, working up the hillside to the left of the great slide, we were enabled, after going about one-third of a mile, to get down again into the cañon.

About a mile and a half below the slide, my guide suddenly turned sharp to the right and began to work up what seemed to be, from below, an impassable cliff; the rocks being bare and steep, with here and there a few scattered tamarack trees and bunches of willows. After going up perhaps a hundred feet, the trail suddenly turns into a seam running up the side of the bluff in the direction of the head of the main cañon. This seam, or inclined ledge, can scarcely be noticed from below; but it is in reality about forty feet wide, and has caught enough soil and debris to make it quite good footing. We led our horses up this place, as is always my custom in a rough country. A stiff climb of a mile, and we came out upon a plateau where there was quite a meadow, and I think there was a small lake a few hundred yards further on in the midst of the meadow. When I speak of the trail here, I really refer to a sheep walk, with once in a great while a pile of stones to mark the route. There was no well-defined pathway; and one going over this country must travel more or less by the great cañons, which correspond, in a rough way, to the streets of a mighty city. This is the case all the way from Alkali Creek to Jack

FROM SLIDE TO KERRICK CAÑON
1. PASS INTO KERRICK.   2 ROCK ISLAND LAKE.
3 & 4. TWIN CAÑONS.   5 MEADOW AND LITTLE LAKE
6. THE SEAM OR LEDGE   7 THE GREAT SLIDE
8. LAKE AND MEADOW   9,10 &11 THE FORKS OF KERRICK
    CAÑON   12 BUTTE TO RIGHT OF TRAIL

Main's Cañon. We passed along the southern edge of the meadow, and then bore directly toward the south side of an irregular butte about a mile away. We went close to the foot of this, keeping it on our right, and soon came down into a little cañon, which we crossed. Then we passed over the ridge and down into a second cañon very similar to the preceding one, and running nearly parallel with it. These two cañons I named "The Twin Cañons." They are each about three miles long, and unite probably a mile below where I crossed them, and then join Rock Cañon, a mile beyond.[7] Leaving the second of "The Twins," we crossed another small divide, from which we could see a large lake, a mile in length. A stream headed three miles above this, and flowing down into and through the lake, finally disappeared to the southward in a narrow cañon which appeared to join Kerrick Cañon several miles below.[8] I named the stream Rock Creek, and the lake Rock Island Lake, from a large granite island that was visible near the northern end. A descent of a few hundred yards brought us to the lake, and, following up the east bank of this a short distance, we forded the stream coming in at the northern end, and, turning up the cañon, soon came to a saddle to the left of us on the ridge dividing Rock Cañon from the next to the west. Passing through this gap we were in Kerrick Cañon, near its head waters.[9] The main stream is formed by three branches uniting near together. We followed down the east fork for a mile or more, and then up the west fork for a mile and a half, which brought us out on the main crest of the Sierras. Here one can obtain a fine view of the upper basin of what I thought to be Robinson Creek, in Mono County. A lake a mile long, and fifteen hundred feet below, drained into this stream.

The west fork of Kerrick Creek, which we had just left, lies to the south, while to the west is the east fork of Thompson Creek, down which our route now led for a mile and a quarter. The main stream, which is on the south side of the crest of the Sierras, is formed by the uniting of two branches; and we now turned up the western one. About a half mile further this stream subdivides into two brooks, and the trail goes right up the point between the two for about three-fourths of a mile and then turns sharp to the left above a small lake two hundred yards to the left of our path. A few hundred yards farther and we were in a pass on the main crest of the Sierra Nevada, and a portion of Mono County, which we were now for the first time to enter, lay before us. Looking to the west across this, one could see two extremely rough cañons coming together about five miles to the northwest. One of these headed at our feet, and contained half a dozen little lakes, while the other headed about three

---

7. These two small canyons are at the head of Crazy Mule Gulch.
8. Rock Creek flows into Piute Creek, not Kerrick.
9. This locale is at the headwaters of Rancheria Creek, which flows through Kerrick Canyon.

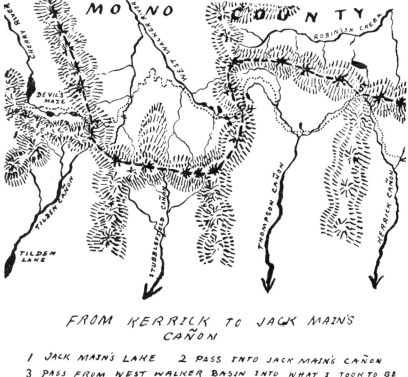

FROM KERRICK TO JACK MAIN'S
CAÑON

1 JACK MAIN'S LAKE   2 PASS INTO JACK MAIN'S CAÑON
3 PASS FROM WEST WALKER BASIN INTO WHAT I TOOK TO BE
CHERRY RIVER BASIN.   4 PASS FROM THOMPSON CAÑON TO WEST
WALKER BASIN.   5 PASS FROM KERRICK TO THOMPSON CAÑON

miles in an air line to the west. Between the two a long, rugged granite point shot out from the main crest. My first impression in looking across this region was that it would be impossible to get animals over to a gap high up on the main crest beyond the second cañon, which our guide now pointed out to us as being the pass by which we were to return to the southwestern slopes of the Sierras in Tuolumne County. To our left, as we looked toward this pass, was the main range, studded with high, jagged peaks and curving gradually around like an enormous amphitheater, until it reached the saddle through which we were to go, and then extending miles to the northwest. Many snowbanks, and even glaciers, lay along the northern slopes, and from these hundreds of rivulets trickled and tumbled into the two main cañons, cutting the declivities in the most fantastic manner into innumerable arroyos and minor cañons, and making the terrane one of extreme roughness for animal travel. We followed down the east cañon past the little lakes for two miles, and then left the stream and began to work gradually over and up the rocky point above mentioned, picking our way slowly amongst the boulders and ravines, with an occasional rock pile here and there to mark the route. We finally got into the west cañon, and, traveling up this for a mile, came to a high cascade. Here we turned to the right and worked up the side of the ridge in a westerly direction, leaving the falls behind us. Two low places, a few hundred yards apart, were now seen to the front, and, after a very rough climb of perhaps half a mile, we passed through the left of these, and were in Tuolumne County and again on the south side of the main crest.[10] Al! of the travel in Mono County was very rough; and it is my belief that I here crossed the head waters of West Walker River, but I am not sure.[11] We were now, I think, at the source of Cherry River. To the left of us, as we faced west, a long black ridge, almost as rugged as the main range and nearly as high, extended to the west as far as we could see; and our guide, who was to leave us here, pointed out to me a low place in this ridge which was about three miles away, and was the pass leading into the head of Jack Main's Cañon. Three lakes lay between us and the pass, which we were two hours in reaching; and long before we got there I wished that I had kept our guide a little longer. It looked so easy when we started; but we wound around and around among jagged volcanic rocks, now and then coming to a perpendicular wall ten or fifteen feet high, and having to retrace our steps. I called this little piece of trail the "Devil' s Maze." My recollection is that we passed to the right of the first and second lakes and to the left of the third and largest,[12] from which we turned sharp to the left, and, going through the pass,[13] were in Jack Main's Cañon. Half a mile below us lay a large, long lake, which is called Jack Main' s Lake.[14] It was almost dark when we got down to this, and I immediately camped. Grazing here was poor, and there had evidently been thousands of sheep about. In fact, there were two flocks visible from my camp. To add to our discomfort, a thunder shower set in

10. Not correct. They didn't cross the county line until the next pass.
11. He did indeed cross the headwaters of the West Walker River.
12. Lakes Helen, Ruth, and Stella.
13. Dorothy Lake Pass.
14. Now named Dorothy Lake.

and gave us something of a wetting. We were now on the head waters of Fall River,[15] which flows southwest through Lake Vernon and finally leaps over the bluff into lower Hetch-Hetchy, making one fall at low water, but dividing at high water and making two.[16]

Next day I marched six miles down stream, on the right-hand side, to good grass, and camped. At this point there is a large, round peak on the left of, and rising about two thousand feet above, the river;[17] and the stream here widens out into a hole three hundred yards long, fifty wide, and very deep. During this day the march had taken us through another of the great wonders of this region, namely, the "Dead Forest." From Jack Main's Lake to the enlargement of the river, the cañon is very broad, and covered with tamarack trees, almost every one of which is dead. The reason for this unusual freak of nature I do not know.

In the afternoon I ascended the high peak, and from its summit obtained a magnificent view. The main cañon was visible from a point two miles below its head to a large lake eight miles away, which I afterwards found to be Lake Vernon. To the northeast were the rugged spurs to the north of which I had passed the day before while traveling in Mono County, and between me and them was a cañon, probably five miles in length, at the lower end of which lay a lake, one and one-half miles long and one-half mile wide. This was Tilden Lake, and the stream flowing into it was Tilden Cañon Creek, which left the lake at the foot of the mountain on which I stood, and curved around its base, falling into Jack Main's Cañon, in a series of cataracts, a half mile below. To the east of the lake, a long ridge[18] extended from the main crest in a southwesterly direction to a large butte, or mountain, east of Lake Vernon, which I afterwards found was Mount Gibson. A high ridge, very rugged and steep, divided Jack Main and Tilden Cañons, while another extended along the west side of the former cañon until it finally ended in the high ground west of Lake Vernon. Almost west of me, on a plateau probably eight hundred feet above the main cañon, and two miles away, lay another large and, apparently, very shallow lake. I had a compass with me, and

---

15. Falls Creek.
16. Wapama Falls.
17. Chittenden Peak.
18. Macomb Ridge.

took many bearings; so that these objects are pretty accurately located. When I returned to camp, one of my men, Branigan, who had been down the trail for four miles, reported that, about two miles below, the bluffs closed in on the river, and the traveling became extremely rough. He also reported that the main stream disappeared into the ground about four miles below. I did not believe this at the time, thinking him mistaken, but found afterwards that the river did in reality pass through a tunnel for a distance of three or four hundred yards. I was sorry that my limited time did not allow of my making a thorough examination of this wonderful curiosity; and I hope that some of the readers of this will he able to visit this tunnel in the near future, and give us a complete description of it.

On August 30th we marched two miles, through meadows, down the river, and then reached a point where it was pretty rough. A mile below this, I crossed the stream to the east side, hunting for better ground; and, in half a mile, came to a lake, the size of Lake Vernon, hidden away in a cove in the wall of the gorge, and draining into the river, which flows about one hundred yards away.[19] I was obliged to re-cross to the west side just below the lake; and, to any one traveling this route, I will say that it is best never to cross the river after once leaving Jack Main's Lake, at the head of the cañon, but to keep on the west side. Three or four small lakes were passed during the next eight miles. This part of the route was extremely tedious, and thoroughly tried the patience of all. The river winds like a snake down the gorge, making numerous horseshoe bends. At almost every western curve a rocky point, ending in a "jump-off" came down to the stream; and lying in each corresponding eastern bend would be a small meadow, interspersed with tamarack and willows. The trail generally led across these meadows, and over the rocky points; and it was at the latter places that we had the greatest difficulty in following it. A few scattering piles of stones would sometimes mark it, but we depended mainly on the horse-dung, which occurred at frequent intervals. This was due to the travel over the trail, and also to the fact that some rancher had a good many horses scattered along the river, arid these, in traveling from one meadow to another, made use of the only practicable route, viz., the trail. In many places the travel was so rough that it seemed impossible to pass, but the rough granite rocks gave good footing to the animals, and

---

19. Wilma Lake.

we arrived in sight of what I took to be the meadow north of Lake
Vernon, without injury to a single horse or mule. By climbing up the side
of the cañon two hundred yards, I could see the lake about a mile to the
south. From this point the river plunged, in a series of cataracts, to the
low ground above the lake, and we could follow it no further.

How to get out of the cañon was a problem that at first startled me,
as I saw in it visions of taking the back track; but a solution was found in
a narrow gorge to our right, which joined the main cañon at this point.
Up this a trail led, but it was so badly washed and so thickly overgrown
with brushwood that it took us two hours to make it passable. Ascending
this gorge for half a mile, we soon came out on the ridge to the west of

VICINITY OF LAKE VERNON

"Rattlesnake Lake" is actually Branigan Lake, named by McClure himself.
"The Beehive" is the cabin at Lake Vernon.

Lake Vernon,[20] and following this a little west of south brought us in two miles to the McGill-Vernon Trail at a point about three miles southwest of the lake. Two miles nearly west on this trail took us to "The Beehive," a fenced meadow belonging to McGill, into which we turned our tired stock after making camp.

Next day we proceeded five miles southwest to McGill's, where I again camped. In the afternoon I visited Lake Eleanor, four miles to the northwest, returning before night to my camp. The ranch belongs to Mr. Miguel D. Errera, but his American friends have corrupted *Miguel* into *McGill* and by that name is his house known. Trails lead from this point to Lake Vernon, Lake Eleanor, Hetch-Hetchy, and the Hog Ranch, via Poopenaut Valley. I took the last of these on September 1st, and camped at Ackerson's. September 2d I proceeded to the Yosemite Valley, and the 3d found me again in Wawona, after an absence of seventeen days and a most enjoyable trip in the mountains. In conclusion, I will say that almost every sheep-herder has a different name for each of the great cañons north of the Tuolumne River, and this may prove in future a stumbling-block to those wishing to visit this region. *One should never forget that the name he hears spoken may be associated in the mind of his interlocutor with a totally different place front what is in his own mind.* In a map which I am preparing of this part of the National Park, I hope to remove much of the confusion existing on this subject, by naming the most prominent features.

From Jack Main's Cañon to where I left the Fall River, north of Lake Vernon, there is more or less of a trail; but if one keep always on the west side in coming down, he will be able to get through, though not without hard work. From Tuolumne Meadows to Lake Eleanor there is generally no trouble in finding grazing. All the cañons south of the main chain of the Sierras have been hollowed out broad and deep near their heads, by the pressure of great ice fields, and here are found beautiful meadows. Probably, at no point in the world can the glacial action of the ages past be so well studied as in these numerous valleys. I have been told that there is a good route from what I have called Thompson Cañon to Tiltill Valley. This would be a better journey for any one desiring to remain within the Park limits than the one which I describe in this paper. There

---

20. Moraine Ridge.

are also the two routes to which I referred in the beginning of this narrative as having been discovered by First Sergeant Alvin Arndt, Troop "I," Fourth Cavalry.

On the trail which I followed, that part from Rock Island Lake to the mountain which I climbed in Jack Main's Cañon, is probably outside the limits of the Yosemite National Park.

The best time to visit this region is probably the month of August.

Three Days with Mt. King

Bolton Coit Brown
Originally published in the *Sierra Club Bulletin*, vol. 1, no. 7, January 1896

On the 24th of June [1895], Mr. A. B. Clark and I left Palo Alto for the High Sierra, about the head-waters of King's River. The 25th we spent in fitting out at Fresno, and early on the morning of the 26th walked out of town, with six weeks' provisions, two saddle-horses, and a pack-mule. We were obliged to walk, for our animals were so small that they were well loaded even without us. That night we camped among the forks of the river a mile or two beyond Centreville. Next morning we crossed the bridge over the '76 Canal—where the ford used to be,—and the sunrise found us passing between two small but fine mountains that jut into the wide plain and form the true advance-posts of the Sierra. These on the map are Mt. Tcho-e-tum-ne and Mt. Campbell. In a day and a half we reached the Sequoia Mills, and from thence, over an easy trail, in three days reached the lower end of King's River Cañon.

After a day here, we moved up nine miles to the head of the cañon, and established there a sort of headquarters from which to make excursions into the surrounding country. Here we remained for some days, enjoying the scenery, catching trout in the river—the most beautiful of rivers,—lying under the trees along its banks, taking little walks, making sketches, and chasing after runaway animals,—varying these Arcadian pursuits by stiffer jaunts up the wild walls that shut us in, one day even going up and making sketches from the top of Avalanche Peak.

Having never been in that region before, I fell to studying the map, and that with such diligence as presently to develop in me a strong desire to see what was up Paradise River.[1] When this became irresistible, I early one morning buckled on my knapsack, and telling Clark I should not be gone over three days, started for the gap in the cañon walls where the river comes through. I took the regular trail to the ford where you cross

---

1. South Fork of the Kings River.

to go up Bubb's Creek; but not crossing it, turned to the left, and kept on along the bank, through bushes and rocks, and presently came upon traces of a disused trail. Followed with difficulty, the old blazes led for some hundreds of yards along between the talus to the left and the tangle of vegetation on the river flat to the right, then turned to the right, across the wreck of an old sheep bridge over a dark, mud-bottomed pool, and then directly into the jungle of the river bottom. Tall cottonwoods shut out the sky, and intricate bushes shut out the cottonwoods, and I went wallowing through a rank growth of big-leaved plants, wet with dew, and very beautiful in the cool morning,—bracken shoulder-high, and columbine clear above it, and here and there tall tiger-lilies. At last I came out upon the river again, and was led along its edge through a small open meadow, into and through a fine park-like grove of oaks; but after this came unlimited fallen rock, in which the trail ended, and I just fought my way along as best I might.

A mile or two further on these fallen rocks make the river into an almost continuous series of roaring cascades, that continue, more or less, almost up to Paradise Valley. It is as difficult as useless to specify the finest parts. It is all splendid, and there is sufficient volume of water to give real dignity and impressiveness. Along the edge the water merely slaps and spatters, but in the middle a thundering chaos jars the very foundations of the mountains. At one place the cañon widens a little, the trees fall back, and just at the head of this opening roars a tremendous fall, the highest on the river, wherein the water is battered so fine and shot so far that it blows away into the woods, and the whole cañon-side is a-reek with its wetness. Walking there is like walking in the rain; the fall itself is almost invisible in its own mist, and the big rocks by it loom fiat and gray when the spray drifts aside.

Having added to my already dew-soaked garments sufficient of this fall spray, good not only to look at and move about in, but also to breathe your lungs full of, 1 climbed up along the very edge of the fall, holding myself from a slip on the polished rocks by the tips of the outreaching branches. The climbing is rough, but nowhere really difficult; and though it gives you plenty of exercise and a general sense of great accomplishment, yet, practically, there is not the least real danger.

At about ten o' clock I rose over a vast talus-pile of gigantic rocks, and before me lay Paradise Valley, a widening of the cañon that has permitted a floor of earth to form, perhaps half a mile wide by three or four long, through which the ever-beautiful river winds among its groves of pine and aspen, while the great rock walls soar to giddy depths in the blue sky, where dazzling clouds float and gleam beyond the gray peaks. It is rather less attractive when you get into it, for it is a veritable nest of the sheepman—and his sheep. Still, it is delightful, especially the upper part, where the river tumbles in big cascades, and makes rapids and deep-green swirling pools, with bits of white foam on them, and the valley floor is not earth, but glacier-carved granite.

At its head the valley divides into two gorges, the main one bearing slightly to the left, and furnishing about half of its water supply, while the other and smaller cañon runs off to the right. Ignoring the trail that goes up the latter, and clambering instead along the rocks by the water, I began the ascent, having in mind to cross the stream, scale the right wall at a convenient place, and then work back among the heights for Mt. King and Mt. Gardner. Having absolutely no information, I had to find it all out for myself—which I count a good part of the interest. After several vain attempts to cross the torrent, a bridge appeared in the shape of a large log, that carried me over dry-shod, indeed, but plunged me directly into a mass of tough manzanita bushes, where I was nearly torn to pieces before reaching the steep and comparatively bare rocks above.

Here appeared the first snow. Some fragmentary banks I walked on, and in the gorge below, about a quarter of a mile above where I had crossed, I could see a fine typical snow bridge. It was a simple and perfect arch, fifteen feet thick, gracefully spanning the stream for perhaps forty yards, and on both sides spreading up the slopes its great white, sweeping wings.

Away above and to the left the wall was divided by a notch, through which poured a stream from the regions above, and at this notch I aimed. But I never reached it, for in an hour the rocky face of the mountain became so smooth and steep, and the ledges to climb on so few and so narrow, that I was fairly stuck, and compelled to back down to a point whence a new start could be made up toward the right. In this direction I knew, from having seen its drainage stream from the gorge below, that there must be another notch, and beyond the notch a basin. An hour or two brought me round a spur, facing—unfortunately far below me, for I had climbed too high before discovering it—the usual rock-walled basin, a mile or two across, amongst whose few trees I must evidently pass the night, for even then the sun had set. So I hastened unwillingly—for one hates to go down when making an ascent,—and by a long diagonal across

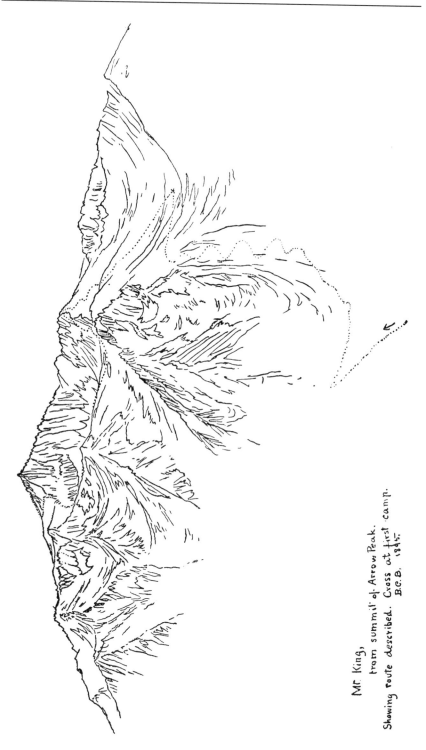

Mt King,
from summit of Arrow Peak.
Showing route described. Cross at first camp.
B.C.B. 1845.

the cliff face, landed just at dusk on the quaking sods of the melancholy little stream that gurgled its tortuous way about among the blackened logs which, thanks to the sheep industry, constituted the chief timber.

A careful search presently discovered an excellent sleeping-place in the shape of a cave-like hollow under a huge bowlder. This I improved by walling up its ends with stones and covering the rock floor deep with pine and willow twigs. Then, after dragging together enough wood for an all-night fire, and eating, amid a hard fight with the mosquitoes, a lunch of bread and dried peaches, I crawled into my den, like any other animal. Though without blankets, yet, by feeding the fire anew every hour, I kept off excessive cold. One of the times that I arose I waited and saw a memorable sight—the moon rise over the wild, snow-splashed crests of the High Sierra. First came the paling of the stars, then the glow behind the mountain wall, then a spark—one sharp fire-tip on its vast black rim,—then steadily—

> "Not slower than majesty moves for a mean and a measure
> Of motion; not faster than dateless Olympian leisure
> Might pace with unblown ample garments from pleasure to
>   pleasure,"—[2]

the mountain sinks, and the moon climbs, its radiance touching with silver the rivulet below, chalking one side of every rock, and flooding with its weird light wide ranges of lonely mountains far away in the north and east-strange and wild, solemn and beautiful, in the utter silence of the mountain midnight.

At last stars, moon, and the night itself grew pale, and the dawn had come. A hasty toilet, some bread and peaches and a drink of water, and I set off toward a lower place in the south-eastern wall, intending, if it should prove possible, to get upon its top and follow it to the summit of Mt. King. Ledges, covered here and there with tufts and patches of sodden grass, not long free from the snow, then masses of fallen rock, with an occasional oasis of hard-frozen snow, good to walk on for a change—these formed the way. In three or four hours I reached the highest point on the ridge. But the glow of satisfaction that should attend such arrivals, in this case received instant check, for as my head rose over the last rock —behold, another deep and wide basin, even larger than the one I had

---

2. "Sunrise," from *Hymns of the Marshes*, 1880, by Sidney Lanier.

just climbed out of! It contained much snow and some partially thawed-out lakes, but not a tree, nor even a single bush, in its whole lonely expanse. In this inhospitable gulf of granite and snow I must have passed the night, had I succeeded in reaching the first-attempted notch on the day before.

Seeing no alternative, I worked off diagonally down the rocky slope, then across a wide snow-field, and so, just at the lower edge of this, reached the highest of the lakes. It was still partly choked up with snow, and the surface was yet filmed with ice from last night's freeze. Sitting at its edge to sketch, I was astonished to find mosquitoes, and in the water—frogs!

I was now at the very base of the last grand peak, that rose cold and grim and glorious from its snow-encumbered base. According to my best judgment, after a careful scrutiny, the wisest way—in fact, the only way—to attack it was to try for the edge of the ridge to the left. All the rest was sheer palisades, where even the snow could not cling, but lay in broad, sweeping buttresses along their base. So, with much panting and many a pause—for the altitude began to tell,—I ascended a long snow-field, and then, with a stiff scramble, got myself upon the edge of the desired ridge. This I followed hopefully toward the summit (making the sketch at the head of this article by the way), until it became obvious that between me and the top were precipices impossible to scale. To the right, was an absolute chasm; the precipice from the summit down into it was as good as vertical, and somewhere from one to two thousand feet deep. To the left was a similar basin; but between it and the top came a flattish place, just steep enough to hold the snow, and, accordingly, having upon it a wide snow-field (seen at the left in the sketch). Beyond this rose a wall like the one I was on, except that it seemed to offer a chance to reach the summit by going up it. With some qualms, I started across the snow. It was very steep, and being without ice-ax wherewith to dig secure steps, or alpenstock to control myself with in case of a slide, I naturally kept a keen eye on certain sharp rocks protruding from the snow several hundred feet below, just about where I should go to, if I did slip. But by facing the mountain and going sidewise, kicking my toes as deep as possible into the soft surface of the snow, I got over without mishap, and breathed easier. Then, by good fortune, I found what seemed the only pass from the snow to the top of the cliff. Having safely ascended this, I began to clamber up the last few hundred feet. The wall was not wide,—to the right a reasonable precipice, with the snow-field below; but to the left, dropping sheer down from the edges of my shoes, an abyss of air, awful to look into, and requiring some nerve to keep steady on its very brink. This whole side of the ridge, sweeping forward and becoming the whole side of the main peak, seemed fairly *concave*, it was so steep. A stone dropped over took eight seconds to reach anything.

When the climbing becomes really delicate, a knapsack always worries me. It has a bad way—mine has—of scaring me by hitting or touching something, or making me think it is going to hit or touch something, just where a touch might put your center of gravity outside your base; and then—anyway, I feel better without one. So here I laid mine aside, for the work was now simply gymnastics. Soon even my pocket-flask bothered so that it also had to be put aside, that I might hug closer to the rock. Finally the thing got so narrow that I dared not crawl round to the right of each rock, for fear of falling into the right abyss, nor to the left, for fear of the still more fearful left abyss; so I had either to go back or to hoist myself accurately over the top of each successive rock; for now the way had narrowed to practically one series of big, flat rocks, set on edge at right angles to the line of travel, and with space enough between them for a man. I could just reach their sharp tops when I stood between two. Here I proceeded, by hooking my fingers over the top and drawing myself up, and bending over until I balanced upon the pit of my stomach, then making a half-turn on that pivot, like a compass needle, and slowly letting myself down the other side.

A person who does not climb often imagines that one who does is a reckless mortal, whose life luck alone preserves. In his mind's eye he sees him prancing gaily along giddy heights, with a straw in his teeth, skipping freely from cliff to cliff, with two chances to one to miss his footing and tumble over a frightful precipice at almost any time. As a matter of fact, however, it is probable that really serious climbing makes one more unceasingly and acutely careful than any occupation you can easily think of. When every foothold and handhold must be separately found and judged, while in the depths below certain and instant death awaits the first slip—no! average human nature is not careless then. I, at any rate, grow quite ecstatically careful—the intense nervous stimulus and tension, combined with the absolute steadiness and poise required, being exactly one of the chief delights of the sport. I am sure several men with pike-poles could not have got me off that ridge.

But it was all in vain. Presently loomed above me a vertical cliff fifty feet high—smooth as the side of a house. Only wings could go up there. From that moment my case was hopeless. I could see all of two of the three sides of the mountain, and they seemed to be both alike inaccessible. My only possible chance lay in the third, and as yet unseen, side of the mighty pyramid, on one edge of which I was perched. But that could only be reached by going far back down the mountain and circling half round it—a good day's work in itself and therefore quite out of the question with the time at my disposal. Even then it was well along in the afternoon, and I had climbed, without eating, since the early morning lunch. Food was low, and by to-morrow night I must be at the camp in King's River Cañon. The summit was only one or two hundred feet above me; so the view was nearly as good where I was. So, considering everything, I ceased further effort, and gave myself up to the wonders of the mighty panorama beneath and around me.

The whole drainage system of the South Fork spread out like a map, and all the splendid mountains away off north and east of Paradise Valley, where the map shows nothing, were beautiful exceedingly, as the shadows of vast fields of floating clouds slid over them, bringing out now this one and now that, and revealing far more fully their real forms than sunshine or shadow alone ever can. Far to the north-east I could see a fine group of shining lakes that seemed to be the head-waters of the South Fork. One seemed very large, even from my great distance. I dreamed of great expeditions throughout all that new region; and, strange to say, a few weeks later one of them actually came to pass.

With a longing look at the granite spire towering so still there in the deep blue, yet seeming almost to reel as I gazed, I put my back to it, retraced my way, secured my abandoned property, and hit off down the crest. I did not, however, retrace my morning's route; but, instead of getting down and crossing the steep snow, which was really dangerous, I followed down the ridge for half an hour, making then a difficult descent to a lower part of the same great snow-field. It being late and the snow soft, I ran, going half-knee-deep at every jump, until my wearied legs collapsed, and I came all in a heap on my head in the snow. Recovering, I plunged on, and finished half a mile below in a slide down a long steep slope, ending just at the edge of a little glacial lake—dark, and green, and silent These deep, solitary lakes always give me, in an especial way, a sense of undisturbedness and complete isolation—for which I love them.

This one was particularly charming. The vertical rocks that walled it on its mountain side dropped sheer down and out of sight in its still depths, while beside them, and forming part of its rim, swept the tail of the vast snow-field I had slid down. Opposite the snow was a characteristic glacier-polished ridge a few feet high, in the angles of which writhed little stunted pines. A hundred yards below lay another much larger and equally lovely body of water—this, also, partly edged with snow. Climbing down and crossing the outlet, my way led over wet rocks and boggy places, and soon among small flowers and grass in patches among the rocks,—down. down, hundreds of feet, reaching at last the largest lake of all—one that might take itself quite seriously, being perhaps two miles in circumference. Following the edge of this round to its outlet, I found trees, and decided to spend the night, being very weary. But after a cup of hot chocolate and a few mouthfuls of food, I seemed quite restored; and not liking the general feel of the place, I again set out, following the stream, with much running and jumping, making better speed than at any time yet, and dropped down the steep northern face of the mountain,—rocks, ledges, bushes, trees, and green velvet bogs alternating.

Signs of sheep began to appear, and by the time I reached King's River it was evident that a camp must be near. And, sure enough, a mile below, I ran into a flock of sheep, herded by one solitary mortal. He was a typical French peasant,—blue blouse outside his trousers, big shoes, stick, and shepherd-dog. He did not know a word of English, and I was too tired to think of even one in French. His pot, a-boiling, had a savory smell, and without ado I dropped my knapsack near it, pillowed my head thereupon, and never moved for an hour, while the man folded his sheep. Then, by a certain process, I secured an informal invitation to stay to tea. Afterwards, I made a good bed of juniper twigs, and as I was lugging wood for an all-night fire, here came my shepherd with such a tattered and dilapidated old blanket, which he quite insisted on my taking, giving me to understand that a bundle visible down under his tree contained one for him. In the morning I observed the bundle, and thought it had not been opened, and my heart was touched. So, between the fire and the blanket, the night wore away, though I got little sleep. As I lay there alone in the cold of the early dawn, full of far-away dreams as I watched the soft dawn-gray above the solemn mountains, there came a shout from the shepherd: "Hi! hi! Coffee!" Looking round to his camp, some distance away, there he was, waving his hand at me and at the coffee-pot.

He had no need to keep it up long. We sat opposite by the coffee, with one of those huge grindstone loaves of bread between us. Small ceremony we observed. He put an empty tin cup before me, which I filled, and, following his example, opened my big clasp-knife, slashed off handy-sized hunks of bread, and we ate in silent content. Then he took his stick, and went towards his sheep, crying: "Hi! hi!" while I strapped on my burden, and struck down the cañon, following the sound of the rushing water.

In less than two hours I came to the snow bridge already mentioned. I got down under it, and wet me in its drippings. I had a mind to make a sketch there in the dim light, but an unpleasant consciousness of the weight of unsupported snow over my head sent me outside, where I did make a sort of a sketch. From underneath, the bridge was one wide, sweeping main arch, the surface being made up of small hollows little vaults, like the roof a Gothic cathedral,—from the angles of which the water ran in streams. It was also upheld by rounded columns of snow extending down from the main roof, and resting each upon the top of a big bowlder. It seemed very singular, and at first inexplicable. But I think the cause must be that along the lines of greatest thrust, which, of course, must meet resisting points, like tops of bowlders, the snow is most compact, and therefore slowest to thaw; so that the warm air eats away around these compressed parts first, leaving them as supports just where support is needed. The result was a beautiful vaulted roof, supported on snow columns resting on stone bases. The stream tumbled into the snow cave in a noisy waterfall, swept along the dripping tunnel with ripple and plash, and then out into the daylight below with another crashing fall. The willows underneath were turning yellow, and the buds just beginning to swell.

Without incident, I reached and traversed Paradise Valley. At its lower end, I climbed out over piles of enormous rocks, then down the wild gorge, through lovely beds of tall grasses and perfect flowers—no sheep had been there,— through jungles of prickly oaks, over dusty slopes that filled my shoes with stones, along tunnel-like paths through the tangled undergrowth by the river—bear-paths, with some alarmingly fresh tracks,—and so on, down and down, past the roaring cataracts, near sunset; and then, by hard pushing, arrived in camp just as he cool of the evening was putting the lizards to sleep, and the twilight made me stumble on the trail.

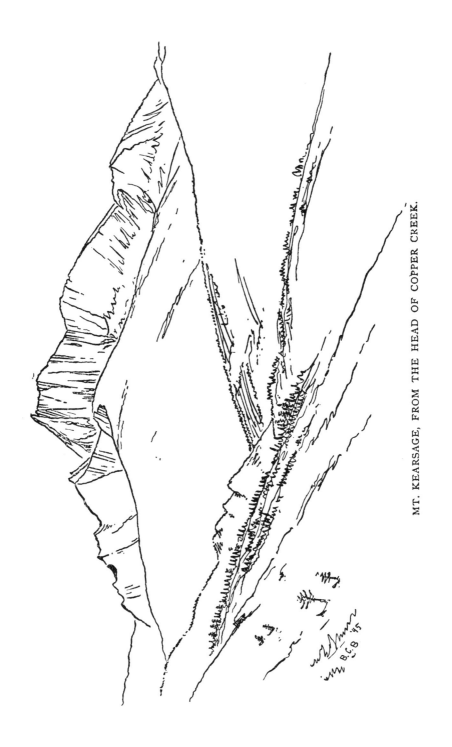

MT. KEARSAGE, FROM THE HEAD OF COPPER CREEK.

A Trip About the Headwaters of the South and Middle Forks of King's River.

Bolton Coit Brown

Originally published in the *Sierra Club Bulletin*, vol. 1, no. 8, May 1896

One morning, near the end of July, I left camp at the head of King's River Cañon, and, with my few remaining rations packed upon a little black mule, went zigzag up the dusty trail to the left of Copper Creek. By eleven o'clock I reached Robert Woods' sheep corral, from whence Mt. Brewer loomed up so majestically that I decided to camp and devote the afternoon to drawing it. Next morning, notwithstanding that I had carefully hobbled him, the mule was gone, and that so effectually, that it was three hours late before we finally got started. Then I mistook the directions that had been given me, turned off the trail and headed straight up to the left, in a wild attempt to climb directly over that wall of the cañon, putting in three more hours of hard work before I became assured of my mistakes But, at last, I backed down, crossed the bottom of the gorge, and climbed a little ridge just beyond, where, running along its top, was the trail—obvious to man and beast. A mile farther up, while Jack paused for breath, I made the opposite sketch of what I took to be Mt. Kearsarge.

Late in the afternoon we got up to the pass over the left wall at the head of Copper Creek, where the elevation seemed about 10,000 feet [10,347]; the wind blew cold, and the last of the trees were still in the company of snow-banks. I camped on the very crest just beside the trail in a little velvety meadow, and, putting a pail of snow to melt, for there was no water, I sat on the edge and hung my feet over, while I made still another drawing of Mt. Brewer and his neighbors.

The view is a grand panorama of all the mountains from the Kaweahs to Kearsarge; and over all the central portion, where Mt. Brewer dominates, there towered and slowly and silently boiled and drifted, one vast cumulus cloud. Its height was stupendous; it seemed to reach miles straight up into the sky, From its flat base, just combing itself among the tops of the peaks, to its highest battlement, must have been 20,000 feet.

Beyond this pass the trail drops over a rough ledge down into the wide, desolate granite basin from which it takes its name—the Granite Basin Trail. There are two or three lakes, and numberless little pools and rivulets of most crystal-clear water between emerald beds of close turf, all starry with wee fragrant white violets. One follows, in a general way, the base of the right (eastern) wall, meandering about among the few trees and the very many rocks. The trail is rather blind in places, and useless besides, so that the best way would be to travel straight for the lowest notch in the wall to the northwest, where the trail again becomes actual and useful.

At midday we climbed out over this pass and rested on the summit, the divide between the South and Middle Forks.[1] Passing over slushy snowbanks, deep mud and wet rock, the trail led down a small cañon, skirting, one after another, lush green meadows cut into strange geographies by the stream's meanderings. At one place I tried to get Jack to go across the stream, and a difference in our opinions resulted in his collapsing in two feet of water. Whereupon, I was compelled to frustrate his obvious attempt at suicide by holding his head out of water with one hand, while with the other I cut off and threw ashore the dripping pack. Things were in a bad way, and I knew by the look in his eye that Jack fondly expected we should have to stay there until the next morning. But there was very shortly an interesting array of wet clothes, blankets, groceries arid sketches spread on the top of a big flat rock to dry in the sun and wind; and then, by the help of a rousing fire, I hurried things so successfully that, in about two hours, the mule, much to his disgust, was again packed and footing his reluctant way toward other adventures.

About two miles below the pass we spent the night. A short distance beyond our camping-place the trail bears to the right and along the eastern face of the cañon wall. After a little it bears still further to the right,

---

1. Granite Pass, 10,673.

then crosses a stream and turns back to the left again, in this way getting around an inaccessible fork of the main cañon. Immediately after crossing the stream just mentioned, you pass through a beautiful meadow with timothy grass in it, and a sheep corral at its lower end. From the corral you work to the right, up a bare stony slope, and come out upon a wide park-like plateau covered with pines. When you have crossed and arrived at the northern edge of this, you get a fine view of the main crest to the northeast, and of all the mountains beyond the Middle Fork, clear round to the blue foothills in the west. From this table-land the trail zigzags sharply down several thousand feet, reaching the Middle Fork about a mile below the mouth of Goddard Creek.[2]

Here I spent several days, exploring, climbing, and sketching. The finest thing in the vicinity is Mt. Woodworth, situated in the crotch between Goddard Creek and the river. Against the herders' advice, I went straight up the southwestern spur, and above this followed along the base of the jagged spires that bound the mountain's southern face. The summit, which seemed about 12,000 feet high [12,219], I reached at noon, after a most delightful ascent. I saw the crest of Mt. Goddard, and from it, sweeping round to the east, a wilderness of savage ridges over-topped at the sky-line by the awful crags of the Saw-Tooth Mountains.[3] This region is undoubtedly the wildest and roughest part of the whole Sierra Nevada range. From all accounts, it has never been explored. Even the sheepmen do not go there, because there is no grass. I made a drawing of the highest peak in the main crest, and, in honor of Dr. Jordan, called it Mt. Jordan.[4] Upon seeing this drawing, Mr. LeConte recognized the peak, and said that observations upon it from other high points showed it to be over 14,000 feet high [14,242].

The descent—along the eastern edge of the southern face of the mountain—was even more enchanting than the ascent. From the summit pinnacle, in the cracks of which I lay for two hours, sketching, and munching bread, and which I believe I was the first to visit, I scrambled a hundred yards to the east, and treated myself to a good shuddering look

---

2. At Simpson Meadow.
3. The Palisades.
4. North Palisade. The name "Mount Jordan" was later applied to a peak on the Kings-Kern Divide.

'Mt Jordan, Principal peak of the Saw Tooth Mts. Its location on the Sierra Club map is about at the intersection of lines drawn north from Paradise Valley and west from the Owens River Smelting Works. Drawn from the summit of Mt Woodworth, by B. C. Brown, Aug.t 1895

over the edge into the abysses between the terrible black spires that make that side of the mountain top. Some of these appear in the Mt. Jordan drawing. The rock does not seem to be granite, but breaks in flattish fragments, that ring musically when struck. Then came a long run down the steep slope of broken rock, followed by a glorious standing slide of half a mile on an unbroken ribbon of snow not fifty feet wide. When the snow became water, I took to the bank, arid walked among the dainty flowers springing from the ruddy soil—the moss-pink, the Mariposa lily, and many others whose names I do not know, though they were not the less beautiful for that. A little farther down, the sparse and polished shafts of the grasses, bent with the weight of their plumy heads, make a misty veil, through which the bright castilleja gleams like a flame. Here and there, over the steep concave of the sun-warmed mountain side, stand storm-scarred junipers; their mighty trunks bright cinnamon-red, and six to seven feet through, set their huge talons immovably into the rock crevices, and hold up in the afternoon sunshine dense masses of sweet-smelling foliage, whispering gently in the mountain airs. Such trees, such rocks, such flowers, such vasty gulfs of air above, below, and around; such wealth of warm sunshine; such a paradise of sunny solitude sweeping aloft far into the sky's deepest blue—these and the intoxication of the air at ten thousand feet, the sublime beauty of the remote ranges of snowy peaks, the silver thread of the river winding through the blue haze thousands of feet below—these, and many other sweet influences, stirred in me a deeper sense of the *heavenliness* of the mountains and a deeper joy in them than was ever mine before.

All the next day I tried to get Jack up to these heavenly highlands to camp there, but in vain. We missed our dinners, got wet in a thunder-shower, and had to return at last. Jack had another adventure, in rolling down a steep, dusty chute. I held to his rope, and did my best to stop him, but he was too heavy,—over and over he went, all curled up to facilitate the process,—I think he liked it, and cheerfully would have gone this way to the foot of the mountain. I jumped along, and, as we passed a little pine, I swerved and brought the rope across it. But it was too small,—it checked things an instant, then bent, slid up under my arm, I hung on like grim death, but under it slipped; and over and over, Jack continued to roll. But I did get him stopped at last, and then came an interesting time trying to remove the pack so gently as not to start him again. This finally accomplished, I got him on his feet—he turned two somersaults in the act—and, by digging tracks with my own heels for him to step in, worked him out of the chute into the surrounding thicket of scrubby manzanita and repacked him. And lashing a demoralized heterogenous pack upon a monumentally stupid mule, airily poised upon a slope like a Gothic roof, amidst a perfect mat of stiff bushes that catch every rope every time you throw it,—this, gentle reader, tries the temper of the best of men. Thereafter I devoted my exclusive attention to getting down to the river before dark, and succeeded in doing it.

Along the south bank of the river is a trail, which, after a day's rest, I set out to follow. Having tramped about five miles and crossed one or two minor creeks, I reached the mouth of Cartridge Creek—a large tributary coming down from the east. It is bridged by a log, a few rods beyond which is a recently built but untenanted miner's cabin. Passing this, the trail turns to the right and ascends the side of the cañon; there I left it, and worked off to the left parallel to the river, intending to follow it as far as possible towards the Saw-Tooth Mountains. But within a mile the country became quite impassable for the animal, whereupon I faced about and started upwards to the left to find, if it existed, the trail I had abandoned; or, failing this, to follow up the northern bank of Cartridge Creek without it. Presently I came upon and explored the deserted mine that belonged to the cabin below, and discovered that it was to this, and not elsewhere, that the abandoned trail led. From the mine a scramble down the slope to the right brought me again to Cartridge Creek. Up we clambered—the mule snatching bits of weeds and I chewing the inner bark of the pine to keep down hunger. There were just enough monuments and old blazes to show that some one had been that way before. Pasture, there was none until near nightfall, when, far up the stony slope to the left, there appeared a small patch of green color. Unloading the outfit beneath two gigantic spruce trees, I led Jack up to the green patch, and miserably insufficient we found it. But it was better than rocks, so I left him there.

Next morning, after an hour's travel, we passed a sheep corral; and a mile or two above it a considerable stream coming in from the left,— tumbling down the cliff in a fine waterfall. Beyond this tributary another comes down from the right, and just here is a large waterfall—a thundering cataract, fifty or a hundred feet high and very picturesque. [See Color Plate No. 7.] The ascent is to the left of this. By following a herder's tracks I found the one spot where an animal could be gotten up. (I digress to remark that Jack was a mighty poor mountain mule. Of

Looking up the canyon of Cartridge Creek.
The route described is to the left (north) of the central mountain, then to the right, passing around behind it over what I have called Red Rock Pass, which is on the divide between the Middle and the South Fork of the King's River. B.C.B. 1895.

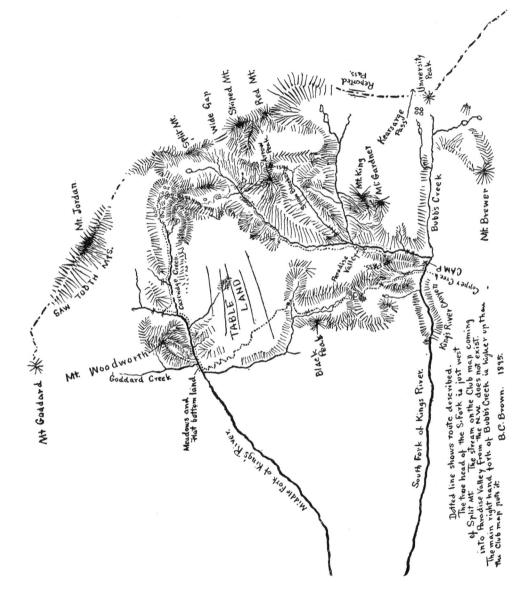

Mt Goddard

SAW TOOTH MTS.

Mt. Jordan

Split Mt.

Wide Gap

Striped Mt.

Red Mt.

Reported Pass.

University Peak

Arrow Peak

Cartridge Pass

Kearsarge Pass

Mt. King

Mt. Gardner

Bubbs Creek

Mt. Brewer

Cartridge Creek

TABLE LAND

Paradise Valley

CAMP

Copper Creek

Kings River Canyon

Mt. Woodworth

Goddard Creek

Black Peak

Meadows and flat bottom land

Middle Fork of Kings River.

South Fork of Kings River.

Dotted line shows route described.
The true head of the S.Fork is just west
of Split Mt. The stream on the Club map coming
into Paradise Valley from the N.W. does not exist.
The main right hand fork of Bubbs Creek is higher up than
the Club map puts it.
                                        B.C. Brown. 1895.

course he would say that I was a mighty poor mountain muleteer,—and while admitting some lack in mule technique, yet it certainly remains true that Jack would not attempt many places where I tried to lead him, which he could certainly have done; and would himself attempt, and fail at, places where I should never have dreamed of leading anything less than a South American condor.) When about half way up the pass to the left of the falls, over he went, turning two complete back somersaults that landed him in a gracefully recumbent and pathetically human attitude. This necessitated his being unpacked,— for once down he is immovable until the pack is off—and my carrying the load myself to the flat above. Afterwards, I built a series of steps and laboriously coaxed him up them one at a time. A mile above the falls we halted for rest and a bite, and I made the opposite sketch of the view up the cañon. [Page 153.]

About five o'clock I camped for the night upon a charming knoll of shining granite, glacier-polished,—just across the stream from which grew plenty of feed. The timber line was near, and sweeping snow-fields patched the rocky walls of the mountains about and even below my little encampment. From some scrubby mountain pines near by I got bristly boughs—which Jack dragged to where I wanted them—and I built a good bed, resting, like an eagle's nest, upon the bare polished granite. Next came the cheery fire; and then, after a bath in the icy stream, I was pre-pared to enjoy the situation to the full, basking in the sun and studying the view down the cañon; for, softened as it was into a sort of mountain dreamland—a vision of the Delectable Mountains—in the warm haze of the afternoon sunshine, it was as grand and as beautiful a scene as ever my eyes beheld.

There being now no longer any sign of trail or track, I set off the next morning before sunrise, without the mule, making a wide scout, to see what came next. After climbing up beyond a long series of cascades, I ascended the central peak,—shown in the sketch,—for an outlook. Even from there the way was doubtful, and I came down the southern side, and went some way up that gorge before I found out that it was a pocket. Turning, I came back along the northern edge of a fine, deep lake, whose blue expanse reflected still the dazzling snow that rimmed its other side, Just below the outlet appeared old traces of mules, upon which hint I began to work out a route back to camp, and in a couple of hours had a carefully picked and monumented trail all the way.

About noon Jack and I moved on again. We crossed the creek, passed up the southern side some distance, and then recrossed just above a little grove of pines, one of the trunks of which bears upon its eastern side the letters P. R.—Pretty Rough, I thought. With only one or two serious rows in getting Jack over my trail, I reached the edge of the big basin that lies to the north, and swings round to the east, of the central peak in the sketch. Pushing on through this, among innumerable pools, over polished rock, velvet grass patches, dried mud, wet mud and snowbanks, we got well up towards the eastern edge before evening. The spot was ringed about with a seemingly impassable wall of granite mountains, and it began to look as though I had got to the end of my travels in that direction. There was no timber, and no grass that a mule could bite close enough to feed upon. Leaving Jack amidst a wilderness of huge boulders and rock ledges, I ran off to look for a pass, feed, a camping spot, or anything else of interest. Away to the eastward there seemed a motion among the boulders,—looking sharply, there was no mistaking—it was a man! leaping along over the rocks. I ran to him, and found a French shepherd sitting on a rock, with his stick and his dog, watching his sheep. I had already made up my mind to try a certain place in the southern wall for a way over, and was glad to have my judgment confirmed by his pointing to the same spot as a pass. It can be distinguished by the slightly reddish stain in the rocks near its top. I now hunted up the mule and led him back a mile or more to feed and wood, where we camped for the night; and a freezing cold night it was. Before the sun was three hours high on the following morning we had gotten up the impossible-looking pass and paused in the snowy saddle above,—some 11,000 feet high. I called it Red Pass;[5] and it is the divide between the basins of the South and Middle Forks. Leaving the mule, I clambered out to the left up the edge of the crest we were upon to where it joins another in a small peak. This peak proved to be part of the first ridge, to the west of the main crest.

Turning now to the south, along the edge of this sharp ridge; I headed for a fine spiry peak that it rose into within half a mile of where I was.[6] Soon the steepness and narrowness forced me to drop down to the right—the left was sheer precipice—cross the curiously fluted western

---

5. Cartridge Pass, over 11,680.
6. Mt. Ruskin.

face and make the ascent by the southern spur. This I succeeded in accomplishing, but only after a few minutes of the most aerial and dangerous climbing that I ever happened to attempt.

To the east—at the bottom of a thousand-foot precipice—lay the basin of lakes and snow-banks in which the north prong of the South Fork takes its rise. Within sight I counted twenty-six blue lakes. After building a small monument and leaving a note, I began to climb down. I dreaded, yet I would not have missed it for anything. The problem was to get down the crevices between huge, almost vertical, prisms of granite. Facing outward, and thus necessarily looking into the awful gulf of air above which I was poised, I pressed the opposite walls with my hands, and so, inch by inch, let myself down. Sometimes it was not a crevice,— but, worse yet, an edge that must be descended. The weather-worn rocks are very rough, and studded with bits of sharp crystals and the projecting edges of little lines of quartz,—and those formed the steps in my ladder. I suppose an inch or two of solid rock is as safe as a yard or two—but somehow you don't feel just the same about it.

After an absence of three hours I again felt the familiar backward tug of Jack at the end of his lead-rope, as we took up what they call in South Africa the "spoor" of the last herder that had gone over Red Pass, and wound along down the rocks.

In the middle of the afternoon we rested half an hour in the green grass on the margin of a beautiful lake with a charming little islet in it. **[See Color Plate No. 8.]** An hour after leaving this I made the accompanying sketch of the noble peak which we had been working toward since leaving the pass. By nightfall, after a long day, full of the things delightful to the heart of the true mountaineer, we camped by a boggy meadow on the river where there was a little stockade and some herders' outfits.

All day I had watched this big mountain, so grandly simple and typical in form, that now loomed directly above me to the southwest. Of course, I wanted to climb it, but my feet were almost literally on the ground, rations were low and the future unknown. It worried me a good deal, but just before falling asleep I decided that it would be foolish to attempt it, and that I would not. In the night I awoke and saw its snowy slopes gleaming serenely in the moonlight. At daybreak it was still there—it called to me at breakfast, its rocky pinnacles beckoned me, its soaring summit challenged me. I could stand it no longer and hurriedly swallowing the last of my coffee, I threw prudence to the winds, flung

Arrow Peak,
from the north. B. C. B.

some sketching materials and things in the knapsack, stuck the ice-axe in my belt and was away through the pines and boulders, over the roaring stream, through labyrinths of fallen timber and dashing water and nodding, many-colored columbine, almost on the run for sheer joy of that mountain and the delight of climbing up it. There seemed just three possibilities of reaching the top—which were, by its three main spurs that unite at its apex and spread out to form its base. In the drawing they are the right hand outline of the mountain, its left hand outline and the central angle. All are very steep and in parts a mere row of balanced pinnacles dividing two precipices. I chose the central one and went straight up it from base to crest—an exceedingly simple ascent, yet very good exercise and most of it serious climbing. More than once the ridge narrowed to an actual edge which I had to straddle and hitch along. With the strong handle of the ice-axe, made of a wagon-spoke, I tilted off its poise a two-ton cube of rock,—Crunch! *Crash!* BOOM!—the awful thunderous roaring down the horrid throat of the crevice—a far, growling rattle and a smell of brimstone;—it was a huge success. A sharp rock cut the bare sole of my foot, but not deeply. Twice I stopped to sketch—once making the one here given as Wide Gap.[7] About midday I clambered up the last and summit rock—some 13,000 feet high [12,958]—and swept my eyes around. It was perfect. The whole Sierra Nevada range seemed spread before me, a sea of wildest mountain crests, splashed with snow, basking in the clear sunshine and veiled in a tender blue haze. A sense of profound peace came over me. It was so still I heard only the ringing in my ears. [See Color Plate No. 9.]

To the northeast above the head of the cañon (the left prong of the South Fork, which I should call the real South Fork) was a wide opening in the main crest,—an interval two or three miles long with a bare sweeping surface broad enough to build a city on. I called it Wide Gap. It seemed an obvious, and on the west, at least, an easily reached pass. But of its other side I cannot speak, for lack of food and shoes prevented my crossing it. To the north of this gap the crest rises into a huge mountain with a double summit—seen at the left in the sketch—which I called Split Mountain. Corresponding to this on the south it throws up to a vast

---

7.   Taboose Pass. The view is looking northeast, not northwest as it says in the caption on the following page.

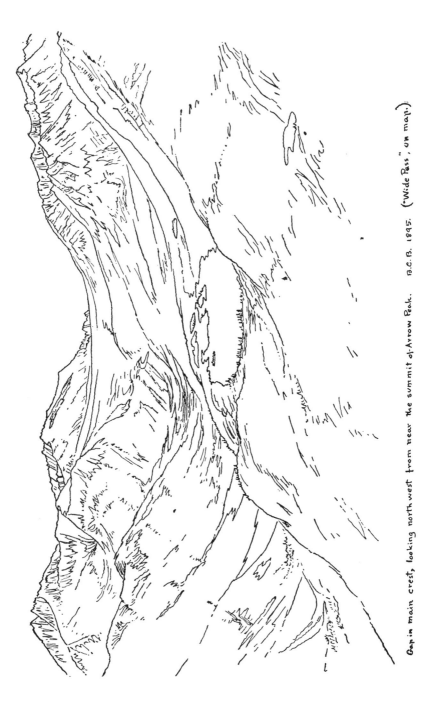

Gap in main crest, looking north west from near the summit of Arrow Peak. B.C.B. 1895. ("Wide Pass", on map.)

height a ragged mass that divides broadly into three main parts. That nearest the pass is strikingly barred across its steep craggy summit with light streaks. As this is an unusually marked case of this peculiarity and as it seems well occasionally to have a mountain whose name bears some relation to its visible character, I called it Striped Mountain. The next summit south of this is higher yet and remarkable for being entirely of a deep rusty-red color. I therefore called it Red Mountain. The spur running from between these two out to the west is much paler in color—suggesting ashes—and I called it White Mountain. From Arrow Peak there were thirty-two blue lakes in sight. It was from here that I made the sketch of Mt. King that appeared in the January BULLETIN.

In descending, I followed the southern surface of the eastern spur in search of a rumored pass through that wall; and within a mile found signs where sheep had sometime been driven over. But the actual opening in the rocky barrier—a few yards wide—was blocked by fifteen feet of snow, with an almost vertical face on the side where I must approach it with the mule. Had I got over this pass I should have gone right down the southern side of these mountains, and landed at or very near the head of Paradise Valley. As it was, however, I at once abandoned all idea of getting Jack over that ridge, and descended to the camp. Arriving some time before dark, I packed up and moved a couple of miles down the gorge before night,—this to avoid the mosquitoes, which had made the first night a misery.

The next day was given to a flying trip, without the mule, down the cañon several miles, to look for a route that way out into Paradise Valley, from which there exists a trail to King's River Cañon. The place was frightfully rough, but it was that or nothing, for rations were already too low to permit of a return as I had come. In the morning, then, we set out early, and, by unceasing industry until evening, and at expense of much skin from poor Jack's legs, got over perhaps three miles. The next day was even worse; we made less distance and the mule sustained several rolling falls. I could not help these, much as I regretted them. I regretted them, because they hurt the mule somewhat, and racked his constitution—also that of the pack,—and because always I had to unpack him before he would try to get up. He had only a hundred pounds to start with, and to-day I carried twenty-five of that on my own back. Once, as we picked our way along the top of the stream-bank across a kind of semi-vertical bog, his footing slid from under him and he rolled toward the precipice.

As he started, I instinctively freed myself from the lead-rope and flung it after him. Over the edge he went—turning a complete somersault in the air and striking on his back on the smooth bedrock in the edge of the stream. He fell ten or twenty feet, and should have been killed; yet, strange to say, when I removed the pack, and applied the proper means, he scrambled to his feet, seemingly quite as much amazed as I was at his continued existence.

All along here the water shoots swiftly down over polished rocks. As it was necessary to get Jack over, and I had never tried just such a crossing, I first began to experiment upon the force of the water in the glassy slide by stepping out into it. It spouted about my legs, and then, before I knew it, began to shove me down stream—in fact, to wash me away! I could not turn round, and so, in far less time than it takes to tell it, I did the only thing left to do—make a rush straight *across*—dashing through the swiftest of it, and so out safe on the other side. It was the most hair-raising experience of the whole summer, and I confess that for a minute thereafter my nerves felt queer. I decidedly declined to go back in the same way, but went far above and crossed in a quieter spot.

For a long time Jack stood in the margin, with a water-fountain spouting from each leg—stubbornly refusing to go across; but in the end, by much yelling and throwing of things at him, he was persuaded, and went. Again crossing far above, I returned and escorted him several hundred yards down the river, sometimes along its edge and sometimes mid-thigh-deep in the icy water, exploring among the boulders with my feet from one foaming pool to another. Returning then, I ascended and brought down the pack. Parts of that cañon I traversed seven times. As I came staggering back under a hundred pounds of dripping paraphernalia, Jack's nose was deep in a bunch of green grass. Perhaps I imagined it, but there seemed a gleam of humor in his patient eye as I labored by over the rocks, looking for a place where it would be possible again to lead a packed mule.

And so, in such ways, we fared on—and at night some miles of this sort of going were still between us and Paradise Valley.

In the morning the mule was quite lame, food low, and traveling next to impossible. I went off alone, and tramped and studied that cañon from wall to wall for hours, finally deciding to try to pass along the very base of the cliffs at the top of the talus, several hundred feet above the stream. Carefully I chose every step of the way, and marked it all with stones,—

that is, the three-quarters of a mile that I explored. Then I packed the animal and started him, but it was no go. We had not made a hundred yards when he keeled over, and began turning back somersaults down the slope. That settled his fate. I cut off the load, got him on his feet, and headed back towards the grass. Opening up the pack I selected what I thought I could carry, cut some harness from the pack-saddle, and loaded myself for a forced march to my old camp in King's River Cañon.[8]

Being in perfect training I made excellent time, and by one o'clock had struggled through several miles of rocks and manzanita jungle and reached the head of Paradise Valley. Traversing this with only a few moments' stop to eat dried peaches and granula, I climbed a couple of thousand feet over the western wall, made a mistake at the crest, and rushed off two miles northward and up several hundred feet when I should not, discovered the error, and turned and ran diagonally down across the western face of the spur and reached Copper Creek, below Woods' corral, shortly before sunset. Thence, by trail, I plunged down two or three thousand feet, to the floor of King's River Cañon, and then a mile up it to my old camp, where I had an extra horse and a cache of food—arriving just at dark, after an absence of more than two weeks.

I never did a harder day's work than that last. After working many hours to get the mule out—then at eleven I started with a thirty-pound load and went as fast as I could clamber and trot for eight hours, I ate a light supper and lay down. At dawn, arose and cooked beans. At nine I ate them. Then I went two miles after my horse. At ten I had a bath. I put on a pair of rubber-soled tennis shoes, and by twelve o'clock had the horse packed and was headed for Fresno,—a hundred miles away. Two nights of the following four I was prevented from getting much sleep, yet in spite of this, such is the marvelous effect of six weeks in the High Sierra, we reached the '76 Canal at five o'clock of the third day—having come since morning thirty miles without strain,—and at eleven o'clock the next forenoon we walked into Fresno. I was shockingly ragged and sunburned and dusty, but I had had a glorious vacation, had grown ten years younger and "felt like a fighting-cock" as sporty men say.

---

8. The going is so difficult in this part of the South Fork that even now there is still no trail there.

Wanderings in the High Sierra Between Mt. King and Mt. Williamson

Bolton Coit Brown

Originally published in the *Sierra Club Bulletin* in two parts:
vol. 2, no. 1, January 1897, and vol. 2, no. 2, May 1897

On the 12th of June, 1896, my wife and I packed our mules, and set out from Sanger for the High Sierra. We spent the first night two miles beyond Centreville, to the delight of the mosquitoes, and the next three at the "Road Camp," four miles from Millwood.[1] We slept one night at Round Meadows; and at Bearskin Meadows,—a delightful place, remained twenty-four hours. From Burton's Meadows, where we camped three days, we made an expedition, and climbed Finger Rock, so noticeable a feature from Bearskin Meadows. We also gave half a day to a rewarding scramble out north, to the top of the walls that shut in the King's River; and the mountains afford nothing finer than the scenery we enjoyed. Moving deliberately on, we stayed five days at Horse Corral Meadows, and tramped to the summit of the glaciated point, a mile north; and another day ascended the peak south of the Meadow, crossing from it eastward, along the connecting ridge, to Lookout Mountain. The view, especially of the Roaring River basin, Mt. Brewer, and the Kaweahs, was very grand. That day it rained hard while we were out, and our camp was, naturally, soaked. Again, we trudged to the southeast two or three miles, then northeast and up Grand Lookout, from which the wonderful view of the cañon and beyond into the great Sierra wilderness, with filmy

---

1. Millwood was a lumber camp and sawmill built in 1889 by the Kings River Lumber Company. It was at the head of a 54-mile-long flume that carried logs to Sanger. The site is about a mile west of Sequoia Lake.

rain and black clouds, and lighter regions picturesquely contrasting, we shall never forget. One might well put in a whole summer hereabouts. In our case, as it was, two weeks slipped away before we reached the cañon.

The evening we arrived it stormed, and John Fox hospitably sheltered us over night in his cabin. The next day we went on, and camped in the upper end of the cañon, where for some days we simply idled about and enjoyed ourselves. One morning the tracks on the ground showed that a bear had paid us a visit. Doubtless through fright at this same bear, the little pack-mule Peggotty ran away from the others and got lost. We trailed her through the jungle to the river's edge, but a diligent search for a mile along the other shore failed to discover where she came out; so we mourned her as drowned. However, she turned up all right afterwards, miles down the river, though how she got there is a mystery to this hour.

The saddle-mule we named Grasshopper, because he always jumped over the bad places in the trail. He seemed to be a right-minded mule, and we liked him. Having planned to see the Charlotta [Charlotte] Lake country, we put a pack on him,—Satan, the other pack-mule, being too uncertain, and Peggotty so very small—and I started through the ford on the mare. In midstream, at a sudden cry from Lucy, I looked over my shoulder just in time to see poor Grasshopper swept by the powerful current off the ford into the deeps below. Instantly, I turned his lead-rope once round the saddle-horn and held as hard as I dared, while, with just the top of his pack and his head showing, he wallowed and struggled for his life to keep from being sucked under the big log-jam forty feet below. But the river was high and ran like a millrace, and I had to let his rope go, for fear he would pull my animal and me into the deep water also. He struck the jam just as the mare landed, and I sprang and ran for the logs. Meantime he continued to make a splendid, and to my vast surprise, a successful fight; by the sheer power of his swimming, he was actually holding his own against the heavy onset of the river. With his submerged pack reeling drunkenly in the current, he looked like a sinking steamer, and for a moment it was an even chance whether or not he would be sucked under, to drown among the black snags beneath the jam. But now, just as he had got his head turned towards the side he started from, he suddenly stopped paddling, when, of course, the current pressed him tight against the face of the jam. There must have been a submerged log holding his legs, for he did not go under, though he made no effort, being momentarily exhausted. I hurried, but before I could get there Lucy, from the other side, had clambered out over the driftwood to him, secured his lead-rope, and by pulling and encouraging him, succeeded in getting him ashore.

And now while we waited for the wet pack to dry, there began a rain which continued for two days. At the end of this time we loaded Peggotty, and, joining forces with Mr. Le Conte's party, which came along just then, we all crossed together without mishap. Two days' travel brought us up to the valley south of Mt. Gardiner, where, ten thousand feet high, we camped in the rain under a lean-to of poplar branches. The second day I climbed Mt. Gardiner.[2] Lucy did not go. Upon the mountain, I had the pleasure of again meeting Mr. Le Conte and several members of his party.

We moved on, and at 10,700 feet established ourselves on a little promontory beyond Lake Charlotta. It was raining; so we built a rude shelter of logs and sticks; and it served us very well for a week. One day we went up the red peak south of the lake (12,000 feet),[3] and practiced mountaineering by following along the jagged crest just above the Cathedral Spires, looking down 4000 feet into Bubb's Cañon. A fine thunder-storm, growling over in the Mt. Williamson region, sent electricity at us. The invisible something passed with tingling prickles and a thin, squeaky, crackling sound through our outstretched finger-tips; and Lucy's front hair streamed out towards the storm, like the pictures in the high-school books on physics, and "buzzed," as she said.

Our provisions having run out, I took Peggy back to the cañon for more, making the trip down in four hours. On the morrow, accompanied by Dr. Wood and Dr. Little of Stanford, I brought back a hundred pounds of groceries. We arrived just at dark, and Lucy, who had been alone two days and a night, was right glad to see us. Next day we visited

---

2. The drawing on page 70 is a sketch of the northern face of Mt. Gardiner. The name of Mt. Kearsarge under it is a mistake. It is perfectly easy to ascend, except the last spur (the top spike in the sketch), which involves a crawl along a knife-edge, above the precipices there shown, and is not altogether easy. Mr. Le Conte and I, however, rather to our own surprise, succeeded in getting there. Indeed, Mr. Le Conte even carried a camera, set up his tripod on the dizzy pinnacle, and took a series of beautiful views. We were, apparently, the first to make the ascent.

3. Mount Bago, 11,868.

Kearsarge Pass (12,000 feet), and climbed the peak (13,300 feet) immediately north of it.[4] At another time we explored with especial delight a
chain of lonely, snowy tarns, hidden in the wild mountains north of Lake
Charlotta. We also climbed the small peak (12,000 feet) southeast of the
lake. Moving still higher up, we camped at the timber-line above Bullfrog
Lake, whence we ascended University Peak (13,990 feet) [13,362]. The
next day we went a-fishing, with unlimited success; the biggest trout we
caught measured fifteen inches by the tape.

From here we traveled down the Rhoda Creek trail and up the south
fork of Bubb's Creek—which suppose we call South Cañon. I think the
less this painful name of Bubb's is spread around the mountains, the
better. Camping on East Lake in South Cañon, we set out early one
morning, and at about eight o' clock had reached the summit of Mt.
Brewer (13,886 feet) [13,570]. On the way down we developed a scheme
for leaving Peggotty, and going ourselves over the King's-Kern Divide to
climb Mt. Williamson. Though Lucy had never before been in the mountains, yet already she had become so hardy and skillful a climber that I
hesitated at nothing on her account. After much discussion as to whether
we had rations enough, we decided to risk it and start the next morning.

Having baked up all the flour into eatables, we packed it on our
backs, and headed up South Cañon. A mile above East Lake the stream
forks, and, following the eastern branch, we soon reached a round, beautiful lake. This we named Castilleja Lake, the castilleja blossoms being
especially perfect and brilliant upon its shores.[5] From here we passed
directly up the immense gorge to the south, and climbing the wall at its
head, found ourselves on the crest of the King's-Kern Divide, looking
straight down Kern Cañon.[6] It had rained all the morning, and was now
so misty that not a peak was visible; we, therefore, had to go pretty much
by guess. We traveled southeast through an immense labyrinth of lakes,
ponds, pools, and puddles, having crossed which we came round the
southern end of the last lake against the eastern basin-wall, shaped just

---

4. Kearsarge Pass is about 11,800. The peak north of the pass, Mt. Gould,
   is 13,005.
5. This name has never been on USGS maps. The lake is 0.7 miles
   east-northeast of the north end of Lake Reflection.
6. Appropriately named Lucys Foot Pass.

like South America, and climbed into a low, rounded saddle beyond. Now we were on the back of a long red spur, which, from the big mountain on the north, extends some miles to the south. As the clouds and rain still hid all the peaks, we knew nothing better to do than to follow the back of this red spur southward to its termination in a high plateau overlooking the rugged, broken region at the beginning of Kern Cañon. Descending from the plateau, we tramped eastward along the timber-line, past several small lakes; and at last, as night was approaching, and we had only the vaguest notion of where we were, we prepared to bivouac.

The elevation must have been more than 11,000 feet; and a cold, steady rainstorm was blowing, with no signs of improvement. We had neither blankets nor even coats, and no tools with which to make a hut, and as there were no caves, nor even a protecting ledge, we said nothing at all about the matter. Lucy, bending over to shelter them with her back, handed me dry matches, wherewith, however, I failed to get a fire, because everything was too wet to light. With an ax, or even a big knife, it might have been done; but, as it was, we gave it up. But now, rather than lie all night there on the rocks in the storm, we determined to go back a mile to where we had seen a burning log, probably left by some herder. On the way, however, we came across a big log which looked rather promising, and, to our great joy, we actually fired it up. Then we piled on so much wood that it became a roaring furnace which drove us back and back, and scorched the bag of provisions, and made us so hot and steamy that we were veritable pillars of cloud. But still it rained.

Darkness came on, and by the time we had finished our lunch, we were so tired that we just lay down among the dripping stones, and, even while the storm beat upon our sun-burned faces, fell asleep. But such slumbers are very intermittent, and we never passed more than a few minutes without waking, and probably hunting out a new place to lie on, or, at least, turning the frozen, wet side to the fire, and the roasted side to the wind and rain. About three, the rain ceased to fall, and not long thereafter, as we munched our breakfast in the dawn, the storm-clouds broke and fled away and hid themselves among the snowy fastnesses of the Kaweahs; and the sunrise came so glorious that we were repaid over and over for all the dreary night.

Leaving the timber, we tramped up for a mile, to get a general outlook, but remained still uncertain where Mt. Williamson was. At last we

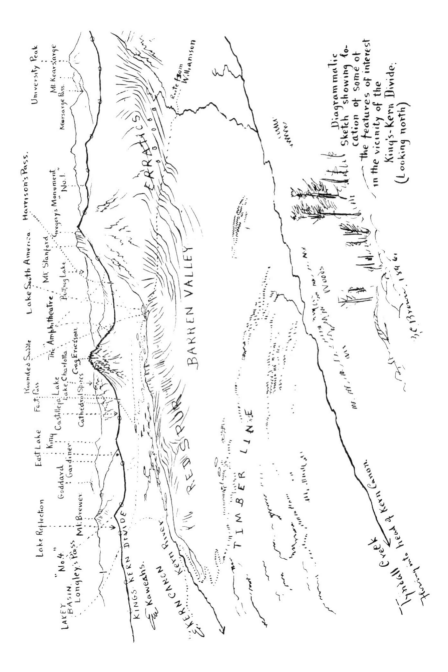

Diagrammatic Sketch showing location of some of the features of interest in the vicinity of the Kings-Kern Divide. (Looking north)

decided to try climbing the mountain two miles north of us, a splendid, rough peak, apparently about 14,000 feet high.

Lucy was not at all used up by our twenty-four hours of hardship and exposure, and would not hear of returning to camp without climbing something. But, as it turned out, this mountain, though fine, was not Mt. Williamson; for, when we had gone some hundreds of feet up it, the rugged mass of Williamson appeared, unmistakable, miles away to the southeast. At once abandoning our contemplated ascent, we backed down and hurried across the basin at the head of Tyndall Creek to the wide, high saddle sweeping between Mt. Tyndall and the peak northeast of it.[7] This great saddle, which is a part of the Main Crest, we crossed before eight o'clock; and clambered down into the beautiful and amazingly wild and rough Alpine bowl that fills the triangle between Williamson, Tyndall, and Barnard.[8]

Mt. Williamson, which is not on the Main Crest, but to the east of it, towered in the morning light, dark, massive, and bristling—a stupendous pile and a most impressive sight. Its shape may be likened to that of a house, with gables east and west. Having crossed the bowl, we attacked the mountain by climbing up two or three hundred feet over a small, reddish slide at its extreme northwestern angle. Thence we followed a previously selected diagonal upwards across the western end of the house, and gained a small notch near the eaves on the southwestern corner.

The climb to this perch, though not especially dangerous, was exceedingly rough, and very impressive because of the vast heights above, that seemed almost to overhang us, and the vast depths below, that we

---

On the Sketch-Map on the facing page:
I.–Foot Pass is Lucys Foot Pass, named for Lucy Fletcher Brown
L.–Wide pass over the main crest is Shepherd Pass.
S.–"No. 4" is Mt. Jordan.
V.–Crag Ericsson is Mt. Ericsson.
g.–"No. 1" is Junction Peak.

---

7. Shepherd Pass.
8. They went southeast from Shepherd Pass into Williamson Bowl between Tyndall and Williamson, where Lake Helen of Troy is.

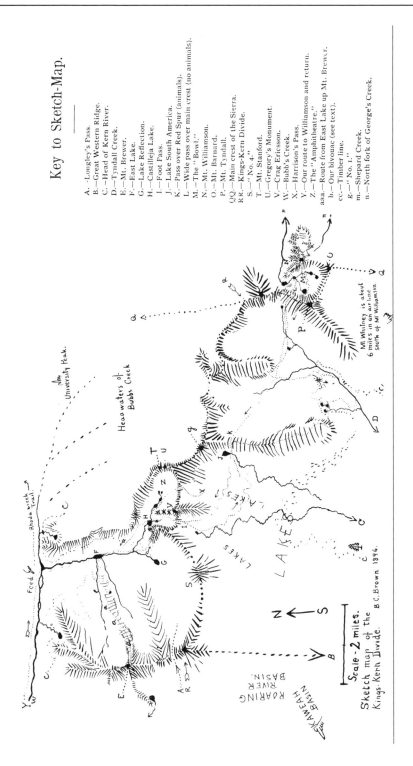

Key to Sketch-Map.

A.—Longley's Pass.
B.—Great Western Ridge.
C.—Head of Kern River.
D.—Tyndall Creek.
E.—Mt. Brewer.
F.—East Lake.
G.—Lake Reflection.
H.—Castilleja Lake.
I.—Foot Pass.
J.—Lake South America.
K.—Pass over Red Spur (animals).
L.—Wide pass over main crest (no animals).
M.—The "Bowl."
N.—Mt. Williamson.
O.—Mt. Barnard.
P.—Mt. Tyndall.
QQ.—Main crest of the Sierra.
RR.—Kings-Kern Divide.
S.—"No. 4."
T.—Mt. Stanford.
U.—Gregory's Monument.
V.—Crag Ericsson.
W.—Bubb's Creek.
X.—Harrison's Pass.
Y.—Our route to Williamson and return.
Z.—The "Amphitheatre."
aaa.—Route from East Lake up Mt. Brewer.
b.—Our bivouac (see text).
cc.—Timber line.
g.—"No. 1."
m.—Shepard Creek.
n.—North fork of George's Creek.

Sketch map of the
Kings-Kern Divide.   B. C. Brown 1896.

Scale - 2 miles.

seemed almost to overhang. Looking through the notch, we saw the southern face of the peak—a wilderness of vertical crags and gullies, seemingly impassable. Yet the hope of finding there a line of ascent carried us out among them, where, after some really ticklish cliff work, we got upon the lowest seat of a bottomless amphitheatre with very high and steep sides. Wallowing up to the top of a big snow-bank, we managed to squirm from it on to the next ledge; thence we edged up a crack to the one above, whose smooth slope was ascended by sitting down and shoving ourselves up backwards with the palms of our hands. The next step we reached by cross-bracing ourselves against the sides of a vertical crack; everything the gymnasium ever taught us, and several things it neglected, now came in play. Eventually, up the bottom of a narrow, steep chûte, over patches of snow and ice, with plenty of all-over climbing, we got up the highest and steepest part of the southern wall of the peak—through the eaves, as it were,— and upon the more moderate slope of the roof. From here to the ridge-pole, and thence westward to the summit at its end, was easy.

By noon we had conquered our mountain and stood 14,448 [14,375] feet above sea-level, Naturally, the view is something to he experienced rather than described. Everything in that part of the world is in sight. Gazing off into the immense pale distances of mountain and plain, where it seemed as if one saw away into Colorado to the east and Mexico to the south, we marveled at that magic of atmosphere and light and distance which could transform mere flat earth and barren mountain into these enchanting visions of ravishing beauty. Flocks of gentle clouds floated in white multitudes beneath us, while their violet shadows dappled the mountain ranges and the tawny desert. Owens Valley, hardly five miles away, lay ten thousand feet below. Scores of miles to the south, that great inland sea, Owens Lake, stretched its vast surface of heavenly blue; and, wide as it is, so great was our height, that whole topographies of mountain ranges and wide plains beyond it lay piled up into the sky in level layers, and lost themselves along the immensely remote and hazy horizon. About us, and visibly beneath, stood the compact host of silent, beautiful, restful mountains; snow-spotted, cloud-shadowed, sun-lighted, chancing always, yet each in his place changeless since the dawn of primeval time.

The summit, if I remember rightly, held records of three ascents, of which one was made fifteen years ago. I think they were all from the plains of Inyo County to the east. Perhaps we were the first to reach it from the west. On the return we fully monumented our route as far as the notch in the southwestern corner; and beyond this left a few marks down along the western face. Among such a multitude of crags and crannies there may be many ways of possible ascent; but from all that we saw, both going and returning, they would seem to he rather scarce, and not easy to find in a limited time. Two friends of ours, who attempted it a few days later from the same side, failed to make the summit through going up a chûte, the head of which turned out to be a cul-de-sac from which they could not climb out.

Reaching the bottom of the bowl in the middle of the afternoon, we crossed it and climbed out over a steep snowfield close under the awful precipices of Tyndall's eastern face. It would be easy to ascend Mt. Tyndall by its northern angle. We talked, in a joking way, of doing it then and there as we passed; and Lucy declared her ability to compass it and get back to timber before dark. Probably we could have done it, ascending in two hours and descending in one; but we refrained. Our labors were beginning to tell on us, our shoes were worn to tattered wrecks, and, besides, we feared the storm had raised East Lake so high as to cover the grass where Peggotty was tied. Therefore, although it had taken us a day to get from camp to the point where we now were, we determined to try to return that night. And we did it,— though we had to run part of the way. We tried hard, but failed to make the pass over the divide by sunset, and, arriving just at nightfall, had to go rattling down its steep northern gullies, all wet and slippery, in the dark. Thence, through a mile or two of the usual glacial piles of huge blocks, relieved by an occasional pallid snow-field, we descended without accident; and, leaving Castilleja Lake on our left, worked through the granite ledges into the dark pine-woods below. Down through these, by our sense of general direction, we stumbled and slid; and finally, at about ten o'clock, reached the camp at East Lake. That day we tramped and climbed, at speed, for fifteen hours, during the last six or seven of which we had not paused for two consecutive minutes. The lake had risen two feet, and quite covered Peggotty's poor little grass; but some wandering mountaineer had come to her rescue and tethered her on the feed above. Next day we returned to King's River Cañon, where we found most of our stock all right; but Satan had run away again—fallen in love with a herder's outfit, and followed it over into the Middle Fork basin, as we afterwards heard.

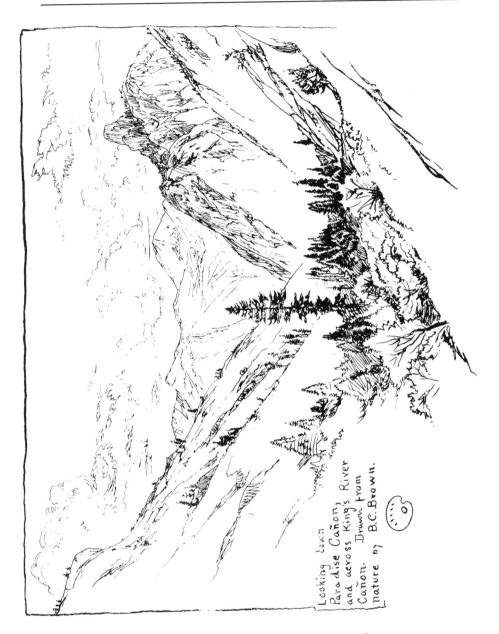

Looking down
Paradise Cañon,
and across King's River
Cañon. Drawn from
nature by B.C.Brown.

Having roughed it for three weeks, we now proposed to give ourselves the fun of making a really proper camp. We selected a beautiful
spot among a grove of white oaks, twenty minutes above the ford in Paradise Valley, and proceeded to camp as you ought to camp. We made a
fine table of a remarkable granite slab, with seats to match, and a shelf to
hold the water pail. Also, we built a wonderful stone stove, with a patent

draught, which worked as no camp stove ever worked before. Then we
made a beautiful wood-pile with the sticks all of a size and of just the
right kind. We made a kind of leaf-covered roof over the bed, after which
no rain fell. We arranged a place to wash dishes, and one to take baths in
at the river, and put a regular cut-out trail down to them. We constructed an "elevator" with platform and rope, by which to hoist the eatables into the trees, out of reach of campers' horses and of bears. For, in
this cañon, according to an old fellow with a rifle whom we met one day,
"you can get a bear-fight most any time." And indeed, shortly before our
advent, a party of ten from the Stanford Camp, two miles below, mostly
ladies, wearing big hats with mosquito netting over them, took a stroll up
here, and some three hundred yards above came face to face with a grizzly
bear. He was described as "belt high," coming along the trail toward
them, swinging his head from side to side. For the story's sake, it is too
bad the bear merely turned around and went back up the trail. Professor
Kellogg, who was leading the procession, pronounced it a grizzly, and
John Fox says he knew there was one up there somewhere. He thinks it is
the last one, and speaks lightly of him as "Old Club-foot." But Fox can
afford to be flippant about bears; he used to be a professional hunter of
them, and long ago he, with his partner, killed two hundred and thirty-six
grizzlies in the Rocky Mountains. But at last a grizzly got his partner, and
Fox exchanged the Rockies for an abode in the Sierra. He has been there
seventeen years now; says he likes it better than he does anything else,
and proposes to "stay with it."

For some time, Lucy and I had wished to capture a desirable mountain, and name it after Stanford University; and so, when somebody left a
Sierra Club cylinder down at the Stanford Camp, I brought it up and we
proposed to plant it. Owing to a slight accident in camp, Lucy was feeling
under the weather, and to make the trip less fatiguing, we next morning
saddled Grasshopper and the mare, and rode up Bubb's Cañon, and then
through South Cañon to East lake. The trail beyond to Castilleja Lake—
if one may call it a trail—is extremely steep, and I did not regret the time
I had spent looking over 200 mules for the ones with the strongest hind
legs. I went on before, the train followed—three of them, for Peggy had
insisted on tagging along for company's sake—and Lucy was rear guard to
prevent their turning back. At the timber-line, I went on alone to search
out a route among the polished granite mountain-ribs to the lake. This

found, the beasts came through all right, and we camped two hours before sunset.

In the morning, we gathered up from the stiff frosty grass the ropes of our chilled animals, and succeeded in leading them up to the top of the face of the immense terminal moraine that blocks the mouth of the gorge just south of the lake. Here, thick with good feed, was a charming little meadow, into the middle of which we dragged large rocks—there being no trees or bushes—and thereunto anchored the stock.

This gorge—the same we had traversed on the Mt. Williamson trip— we now ascended; and having clambered up the cliffs at its head, turned eastward, and began to climb the adjacent steep and craggy peak. Working slightly to the north, we soon reached the top of the eastern wall, and looked over into an appalling gulf; from one to two thousand feet deep. Facing now southeast, we scrambled on, up among the wild pinnacles, and at noon gained the summit crag. The elevation seemed about 13,600 feet [13,608], and the view, especially to the south down the long and peculiarly straight cañon of the Kern, and to the southeast toward the Williamson-Tyndall group, and southwest to the beautiful, snowy Kaweahs, was extremely interesting and wonderfully beautiful. As it seemed that we were the first to make this ascent, we built a monument and left a record, naming it, in honor of Capt. John Ericsson, and in recognition of its extremely craggy character, Crag Ericsson

The reason we did not name it Mt. Stanford was because from its top we could see that the next mountain to the east was considerably higher, and therefore we kept this name for it. Working cautiously down the bottoms of deep and almost vertical crevices in the eastern face of Crag Ericsson, we landed on the edge of the divide and followed it eastward, Presently we came upon three stones built together, marking the head of Harrison's Pass. According to my notion, it will hardly be a popular pass until a windlass and cable are put at its head. Beyond this we ascended a great slope of big, tumbled rocks, and at its top, just where you can first look over into the deep, snowy gulf to the northeast, we found another monument. Its single record showed it to have been made two years before by Warren Gregory and his companions.[9]

---

9. Named Gregorys Monument, altitude over 13,920.

It now became apparent that the summit of this peak is the sharp edge of a thin wall, or curtain of rock, of vast height, and precipitous upon both sides. This knife-edge runs north and south; it may be a thousand feet long, sags a hundred feet in the middle, and rises into a point at each end. These ends are very nearly the same height, and the above-mentioned monument was at the southern point. But we thought the northern one was a little higher, as it was certainly the natural termination of the promontory, and decided to put the club cylinder there, if possible. Though she had climbed steadily for nine hours, Lucy had not felt quite herself all day, and so now, when I cautioned her that the passage along the soaring knife-edge, with its 2000-foot precipices on either side, might prove trying to both nerves and muscles, she wisely decided not to attempt it. After arranging to meet at a particular lake in the amphitheatre below, which she was to reach by following down the edge of the southwestern precipice, and descending Harrison's Pass, and I by descending the peak upon its northern side, and dropping over into the amphitheatre from the north, Lucy started back, and I slowly let myself over a smooth rock, and began to work out on the knife-edge, along the top of the wall. In twenty minutes I had accomplished it, and, across the depths beneath us, exchanged shouts with Lucy, now but a moving speck among the rocks. The altitude is probably not far from fourteen thousand feet [13,963]. A bird like an eagle, soaring grandly far beneath, saw me or heard my shouts, and circled slowly up to my level; and then higher, and higher, till lost in the depths of the dark violet sky above. Fourteen thousand feet was nothing to him. **[See Color Plate No. 10.]**

I built a monument and left in it the Club Register, No. 14, with the name Mt. Stanford upon it. The idea of descending northward I abandoned because of the complicated masses of pinnacles, gulleys, and precipices in that quarter, which would delay me too long; and started to go back the same way I came, intending to follow down Lucy's route. But an apparently practicable chute, just where the knife-edge joins the northern peak, tempted me into trying, instead, the descent of the western face. I managed to get down about a thousand feet, and was then stopped by a sheer precipice. However, after climbing back up the chute some distance, it proved possible to work southward from gulley to gulley, and in this way I gradually descended to the cliff-base, and went flying down a steep snow-slope, and out over half a mile of talus blocks to the rock-encompassed pool where Lucy had for some time been awaiting me.

An hour before sunset we reached Castilleja Lake, and next morning rode down six thousand feet to our permanent camp in Paradise Valley,—and a rough old ride it was.

But we had not been there very long when I began to hanker for another try at Mt. King, which I had tried last year, but had not succeeded in climbing. One evening I suggested to Lucy that I rise very early the next day and endeavor to get to the summit of Mt. King, and return before night. She replied, "I wish you would; and I hope you will get to the top. I would a great deal rather that you should do it than anybody else." After that, what could I do but go?

So in the morning, about an hour after sunrise,—which was at least two hours later than it should have been,—I took a lunch and a forty-foot rope and started out. Lucy came with me to the river bank, and the old mare ferried me over. Realizing that there was not a second to waste, I at once put on full steam and hustled through tangles of bushes, and trees, and jumbles of fallen rocks at a great rate. All the raspberry bushes had been recently pawed over, and the ripe berries had been eaten, so I fully expected to see a bear, but none appeared. However, in a way, I had a bear as guide; for I followed the tracks of one up the gulley of the second tributary from the east, gaining thus the wider cañon above. The first section of this cañon is painfully long, and its floor is exceedingly rough. At its head I ascended a steep slope, two or three hundred feet high, alongside of a series of cascades. From the top of this rise, exactly centering the picture between the cañon walls, there appeared a sharp, hard peak, which I knew must be the edgewise view of Mt. King. It looked very far away, and seemed as though it would take at least the rest of the day to reach its base, let alone climbing it. How ever, I kept on going, and tore through the exasperating jungle of interlocked manzanita bushes and crooked poplars, "regardless." Finally I got above this, and hurrying up grassy slopes and rocky knolls, at last left the timber altogether, and ran a couple of miles to the head of a long couloir that terminates against a southern spur of Mt. King. At about half after eleven I sat a few minutes and lunched by the very last green spot Then I went directly up the steep southern face of the peak, until, some five hundred feet be low the summit, I could look over its eastern shoulder—a look which quite gave me a qualm—it being absolutely sheer for more than a thousand feet beneath. Working across to the western edge, I looked over that precipice, and it was deeper still. These two walls approached each other, and where they met is the summit. Near the top the rocks got steeper and became more like vertical cliffs. At last I could climb no higher unaided.[10]

Poised on a narrow ledge, I noosed the rope and lassoed a horn of rock projecting over the edge of the smooth-faced precipice overhead. But a pull on the rope toppled the rock bodily over, nearly hitting me, who could not dodge. So I took out the noose, and having tied a big knot in the rope-end, threw it repeatedly until this caught in a crack, when I climbed the rope. I did not dally with the job either, for every second I was afraid the knot would pull through the crack. A few yards above, the operation had to be repeated, and before the summit was reached, it was repeated several times. The ugliest place of all was exactly at the last rock, only a few feet below the top. With great caution, and as much deliberation as I had used speed below, I finally looped the rope over an all-too-slight projection, along the upper edge of the side face of the topmost block, and compelled myself to put one foot in it and lift myself, and so stand, dangling in that precarious sling, until I could get my arms on the top and squirm over,

This summit is more like that of the spire of Strassburg (sic) Cathedral (550 feet) where I once stood, than any other peak I ever climbed. It is a true spire of rock, an up-tossed corner at the meeting of three great mountain walls. It is about thirteen thousand two hundred feet high [12,905], stands somewhat isolated, and commands a glorious view. It is accessible only at the place where I went up, and only with a rope at that. The top of the summit-block slopes northwest, is about fifteen feet across, and as smooth as a cobblestone. If you fall off one side, you will be killed in the vicinity; if you fall off any of the other sides, you will be pulverized in the remote nadir beneath.

---

10. Upon this steep southern face of the peak, I kept running across the fresh track of some animal like a large sheep or deer. He seemed to be going up ahead of me, the track was so fresh. And I saw no returning track, though I passed quite across the territory over which the animal must come down. These tracks went well up toward this extreme summit, and into higher or wilder places than I ever saw sheep or deer tracks. But on my descent, I found the tracks going down again. Is it possible that I had scared up a bighorn, which started up the peak for safety, but being followed, stood behind some crag while I passed on up to the top, and then came out and ran down?

About half-past one I roped myself down again, spider-wise, from this airy pedestal; and having left a row of monuments as far as the green spot where I had lunched, scampered away down the long couloir, jumping bowlders, pools, and streams in the highest spirits. I continued to run wherever the surface did not make it absolutely impossible, hurried in the tail of the afternoon across what seemed like miles and miles of chaotic masses of big talus blocks, then, in the deepening shadows, down the throat of the narrow gorge where the stream dashes, in the twilight over massive bowlders in titanic heaps along the base of the Paradise Valley walls; then, in the dark, across the rushing river I went, foolhardily, mid-thigh deep; and then, rustling through the fallen white oak leaves, I sighted the gleam of Lucy's fire, and in a moment more,—was home.

That ended our mountaineering for the summer. We remained some days longer in the cañon; indeed, we stayed until, notwithstanding that we had had three mule loads of provisions, we were actually starved out. The streams had gone down two thirds, and where six weeks before we had washed the dishes, tall plants grew. The grass plumes held ripened seeds, and in the jungle swamps, tiger lily and columbine had given place to golden rod. As we listened to the music and watched the green swirls of our beloved river, golden leaves—autumns first—glided by. Then we remembered that life is not all play, and knew the time had come for us to leave this noblest of playgrounds. And so we went, with sincere regret, and many pledges to return, down through the wild beauty of the long cañon, up the steep trail, and out over the rolling, forest-clad foothills, toward the yellow plains, sixty miles away.

Exploration of the East Creek Amphitheater

Cornelius Beach Bradley

Originally published in the *Sierra Club Bulletin*, vol. 2, no. 5, January 1899

A visit to the Southern Sierra had long been a cherished wish
of mine, postponed, however, of necessity year by year, until its fulfill-
ment seemed almost hopeless. But at last all obstacles were removed by
an invitation to join a party of friends making their first trip in that region
—Mr. and Mrs. Robert M. Price, Miss Lalla Harris, and Mr. Joseph
Shinn. Leaving Niles on the morning of June 25th [1898], we reached
Sanger the same afternoon, and Millwood, at the end of the wagon-road,
on the next day. Here we found our "jacks" awaiting us, and next morning, the 27th, we began our actual tramp. Three short marches brought
us to King's Cañon, where we spent two days. Eleven days were spent
among the various branches of Bubb's Creek. On July 11th, we struggled
over the King's and Kern Divide by way of Harrison's Pass, and four days
later we stood on the summit of Mt. Whitney. From this point began our
homeward journey, via the Hockett and Jordan trails; and on the 22d we
once more struck a wagon-road on the Tule River, and our 200-mile
tramp was ended.

Aside from the complete change and the quickening both of body
and spirit, which are the prime motives of all such expeditions, we had
proposed to ourselves three definite objects of effort: the exploration of
the great amphitheater at the head of the eastern arm of Bubb's Creek,
the ascent of Mt. Whitney, and a reconnaissance of the upper basin of
Roaring River by way of some pass in the neighborhood of Milestone
Mountain. But our time was strictly limited—too limited, as it proved, for
the execution of so extended a program and for much wayside pleasuring
too. Our trip was therefore a strenuous one. On eight days only out of the
twenty-seven, were we not actually packed up and on the march; and five
out of the eight were spent, either by some or by all of the party, in climbing or in exploring, which was quite as arduous as the marching. To say

nothing of Mt. Whitney, five of the great peaks of the amphitheater at the head of Bubb's Creek were climbed,— three of them for the first time,—and a sixth, also new, was almost conquered. when a blinding thunderstorm, with hail and rain, rendered further progress too hazardous to be thought of. We had, of course, the usual experiences with animals and packs, and the inevitable perplexities about directions and trails in a region where trails are, so to speak, conspicuously obscure or altogether absent. But, thanks to the excellent management of our leaders, and thanks to the excellent foresight of our commissariat, we escaped not merely all untoward and disabling accidents, but almost everything that

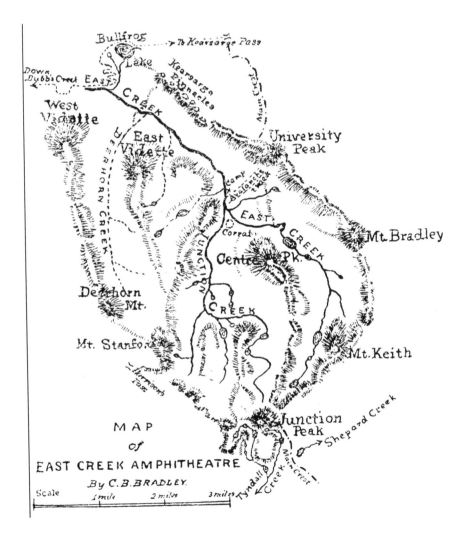

MAP
of
EAST CREEK AMPHITHEATRE
By C.B.BRADLEY.

could really be called hardship—Harrison's Pass alone excepted. We all came through—horse, foot, and dragoons—in prime condition.

After leaving the Cañon, our first attack was upon the unexplored eastern branch of Bubb's Creek, which, for convenience of designation, it is proposed to call East Creek. Its valley is really the continuation of the main Bubb's Creek valley beyond the confluence of its south fork, or South Creek, as Professor Brown suggests that it be called. Its lower portion, as far as the junction of Kearsarge Creek, is well known, being traversed by a trail to Bullfrog Lake, intersecting there the main Kearsarge trail via Lake Charlotte. But beyond Kearsarge Creek there is no record of any exploration, save that of sheep-herders. We found it an open U-shaped valley, with an unbroken rock-wall on its northern side, forming at first the jagged ridge known as the Kearsarge Pinnacles, and further on sweeping up into the great peaks of the main divide, beginning with University Peak and ending with Mt. Keith. On the southern side there is no continuous wall, but instead, a series of bold promontories, the ends of long walls or buttresses running up into the King's and Kern Divide, some miles away to the south. Two of these promontories, standing guard, as it were, the one at the entrance to the valley and the other just within it, form a striking pair, and we named them the Videttes. A third, standing more detached, and in the very center of the mighty cirque at the head of the valley, we named Center Peak.[1]

It was late in the afternoon of July 3d when we left the trail to Bullfrog Lake, and entered upon *terra incognita.* Finding good open country all along on the north side of the stream, we pushed on some two miles up the valley, and camped beside a bleak little meadow directly abreast of University Peak. Just beyond our camp was a great avalanche track, where some fifty or seventy-five years ago a great snow-field, breaking loose from its moorings far up on the slopes of the peak and plunging down the mountain-side, had swept quite across the valley and dashed part way up the slope on the other side. Its track was perhaps 600 yards wide, and as clean-cut as the swath of a scythe. Within it every tree was prostrated, and their rotting trunks—lying all one way on the open bottom, or heaped in a confused windrow at. the very end, where the crest

---

1. Bradley's "East Creek Amphitheatre" is Center Basin. The creek that flows from the basin to Bubbs Creek has no name.

Center Basin. Center Peak at the right.

of the wave recoiled from the opposite slope—were eloquent witnesses to the terrific force of the avalanche. A similar track, but older and less conspicuous, we had passed perhaps a mile below. Both form striking gray bands across the valley, visible miles away from any commanding point of view.

Next morning reconnaissance was made in various directions; but a storm presently burst upon us, and the rest of the day we had to spend, for the most part, huddled together under such meager shelter as we could improvise. But the clouds broke away before sunset, and, thanks to the endless resources of the ladies, while everything was still dripping about us, we sat down to a Fourth-of-July dinner long to be remembered —with daintily cooked viands and abundant good cheer, as well as with appropriate toasts and speeches. We could not know for some three weeks yet what actually was doing at Santiago and elsewhere on that fateful Fourth, but the uncertainty only gave an added touch of pathos to the sentiments.

On the 5th we resumed our work of exploration. One of us was detailed to keep camp; three were to climb an unknown peak on the main crest, next beyond University Peak; while to me fell the easier task of climbing Center Peak and of mapping the stream which heads beyond it in Junction Peak. Both ascents were entirely successful; each party built a cairn and left therein a record of the ascent. But unfortunately I was not on hand to save the other party from the serious indiscretion of naming their peak Mt. Bradley. I protest that I had done nothing to deserve such treatment at their hands, nor had there been either tacit consent or even contributory negligence on my part; for my views on the naming of mountains have been publicly and emphatically expressed. And, worst of all, there seems now no way to remedy the mischief, unless it be by making the ascent myself some time, and stealing the record!—a device which somehow did not occur to me at the moment.

Next day we all set out together to climb Mt. Keith, the peak next beyond the last, singled out and named some years ago, but never as yet ascended, so far as we could learn. After two hours of leisurely walk up the open valley we reached its foot, and two hours later we stood on its summit—the highest peak in all the Bubb's Creek circuit, with only Whitney, Shasta, and two or three others overtopping it in all California. The day was fine, and the view superb. All the nearer world seemed spread out like a map at our feet, while cast, west, north, and south, as far as eye could reach, rolled a billowy sea of mountain peaks, streaked and tipped with snow-foam. A cairn was built, and in it was deposited one of our two Sierra Club register-boxes, with names, date, and record of this, the first ascent. To climb Junction Peak was all that now remained to complete our conquest of this portion of the Sierra crest, and for that climb we had reserved our second register-box. But my reconnaissance of the day before, and the view still nearer at hand from the summit of

Center Basin from Junction Pass. The prominent peak is Mount Bradley,
and to its left the Center Basin Crags. The half-frozen lake in the
foreground is at 12,090 feet.

Keith, had convinced us that it was not to be climbed by either of the faces in view from the north. Yet it might perhaps be climbed from the south after we had crossed the divide.

And a few days later two of us, pushing on from Harrison's Pass, did try it by way of the high quadrate mesa embraced between the arms of Tyndall Creek.[2] But just at the farther end of the mesa, where it drops away to a splintered and crumbling knife-edge leading up to the main peak. the thunderstorm to which reference has already been made burst upon us. So, after sheltering ourselves awhile among the rocks from the fury of the hail, we were content to clamber down again in safety, and tramp some miles in the rain to the appointed rendezvous with our friends. Meanwhile Mr. Price, remaining behind at the pass, had climbed Mt. Stanford, being the only person, so far as the record shows, to reach the cairn built by Professor Brown in 1896. All others had ventured no farther than Gregory's monument.

But to return to our camp on East Creek. Although our exploration of the valley was by no means complete, since it covered little more than the great amphitheater at its head, nevertheless it was felt that we must push on. Still, University Peak was too temptingly near at hand to be left without a visit. So, while two of us broke camp and took the pack-train around by trail to Bullfrog Lake, the other three took the more direct route right over the peak, rejoining us in camp at about 6 P. M.

The rest of our trip may be more briefly dismissed. After crossing the King's and Kern Divide, it became evident that the time still remaining at our disposal would not suffice for the whole of our program. Either Mt. Whitney or Roaring River must be left out. A careful reconnaissance for some miles along the Kern River failed to reveal the promised trail or opening leading over into the Roaring River basin. We could not be sure that there was any practicable pass at all. So, considering that a bird in the hand is worth two in the bush, we decided on the Whitney trip. The return by the southern route was but the inevitable result of abandoning the Roaring River scheme.

In general, the country immediately south of the divide seemed to us much less beautiful and interesting than the Bubb's Creek basin. It was a region of vast spaces with little in them; bleak sandy deserts, boggy moors

---

2. Diamond Mesa.

without shrub or tree, dreary miles of moraines. Even the forests on the hillsides had a ghastly look; for the tiny, short needles of the Balfour pine cannot cover, or even soften, the nakedness of the ground. The reddish-brown trunks rise stark and stiff out of white granite rocks or sand. The Balfour pine itself; however, is a striking tree, with more variety of individual character and form, with more piquancy of carriage than almost any pine we had ever seen. Then there is a peculiarity of texture in much of the granite of this region, which causes it to weather in strange spiry and flamboyant forms, quite unlike the splintering into angular blocks along the Bubb' s Creek crests. A striking example is seen in the fantastic conical spires which dot the northern roof-like slope of Mt. Tyndall. The topmost layer of all, however, as seen on the summit of Mt. Whitney, is a fine massive, enduring rock, split indeed by frost into immense blocks, but not crumbling into sand. And it is doubtless to this enduring quality of the rock that Mt Whitney owes its pre-eminence.

The country grew more interesting again as we neared the Kern River; and from there on we were in a region populous with campers from the Inyo and San Joaquin Valleys. The upper—and larger—Kern Lake we found to be only a meadow, flooded not very long ago by a fall of rock which dammed up the river. The lake is an unsightly thing; dead trees are rotting in stagnant water, and the bed is fast filling up with silt. It will not be long before it is meadow again. On the Kern we had the only two adventures of the trip—the capture of our best fish, a five-pound river-trout, and the narrow escape of one of our party from the claws of an angry mother bear.

The Tule River, which we struck below Nelson's (just off the southern edge of the Club map), was in its way one of the most beautiful things we had seen. Though flowing through open foot-hill country clothed only with chaparral and scrub, the water was crystal-clear from its mountain springs, and the bed of the stream was of clean white granite rock *in situ,* sculptured into a succession of deep oblong pools; arid over the smooth lip of each the water fell in charming cascades, or chutes, into the pool below— a string of emeralds on a silver chain.

Among the many things one would like to have done on such a trip, I may mention two or three which we should still wish to do were we ever again in that region. We should like to have another chance to climb

Junction Peak, and to ascertain the truth about a reported pass in the second gap to the west of that peak.[3] We should like to complete our map by exploring to their heads all the southern tributaries of East Creek, especially Deerhorn Creek.[4] We should like to carry a few live trout from Bubb's Creek to plant in East Lake and Lake Reflection. And, more than all these, we should like to find ourselves with a fortnight to spare about the head-waters of Roaring River.

---

3. Forester Pass. The John Muir Trail was built across this pass in 1931, thus eliminating the former route via Center Basin, Junction Pass, The Pothole, and Shepherd Pass.
4. Vidette Creek.

The Basin of the South Fork of the San Joaquin River

Joseph N. Le Conte

Originally published in the *Sierra Club Bulletin*, vol. 2, no. 5, January 1899

That portion of the Sierra Nevada Range drained by the South Fork of the San Joaquin and the Middle Fork of King's River may well be called the heart of the High Sierra. Although the summit peaks do not rise to quite such an elevation as do some at the source of the Kern, still the mountains are so much more rugged, the cañons so much deeper and more numerous than in the southerly region, that the peculiarly savage type of High Sierra scenery seems to reach its culmination here.

Our information bearing on the San Joaquin Sierra is almost entirely due to Mr. Theo. S. Solomons, who visited the region during three summers, and explored nearly two-thirds of the great basin of the South Fork. His work, which is incorporated in the last edition of the Sierra Club map, is remarkably accurate, considering the extent of the country covered and the few instruments at his disposal. By referring to the map, it will be seen that the South Fork of the San Joaquin River heads at Mt. Goddard and flows north-west nearly parallel to the main crest for a distance of forty miles, where it joins with the Middle Fork, makes an abrupt turn to the west, and flows through a deep transverse cañon to the California plain. This stream is fed by four main tributaries from the east. The first and largest is Mono Creek, which enters about twelve miles above the junction of the principal forks, and drains the crest from the Red Slate group to Mt. Abbott.[1] The second, Bear Creek, joins the South Fork five miles above. Ten miles farther the North Branch enters through

---

1. The correct spelling of the name is "Abbot."

a very deep cañon and drains a vast area about the foot of Mt. Humphreys. And last is the Middle Branch, heading back to the Goddard Divide. South of this divide are the sources of the Middle Fork of King's River. This region is the roughest and most inaccessible in the whole range, and has not as yet been mapped, even in the most general way.

It was my good fortune last spring to be able to make arrangements with Mr. C. L. Cory for an extended trip through the upper San Joaquin country, with particular reference to the unmapped region about Mt. Humphreys. Our plan was to follow the South Fork to its source, making side excursions to the main crest by way of the large tributaries, and thus run a rough chain of triangulation between the highest peaks from Mt. Ritter to Mt. Whitney. If time permitted, we hoped to push across the King's River basin, and thus make that magnificent and wild cross-country trip from Yosemite to the King's River Cañon.

The start was made from Wawona, on June 16th [1898]. As we did not expect to be able to replenish our stock of provisions during the next six weeks, we took two pack-animals with us. We entered the mountains by the same route as that followed by Mr. Solomons, namely, over the Mammoth Trail to the Jackass Meadows, across the Middle Fork of the San Joaquin at Miller's sheep-bridge, and thence by the Miller and Lux trail to its crossing at Mono Creek. The trail up to this point runs through the forest belt of the Middle Sierra, and it was covered without difficulty by noon of June 21st. Here we left the main trail and started up the creek to make our first acquaintance with the summits. Throughout its lower course Mono Creek flows through a wide, level valley covered with reddish sandy soil and a sparse growth of timber. Higher up it comes clown through a magnificent cañon, whose walls rise to a height of 2,000 feet above the stream. The southern wall is especially fine, and at intervals side-gorges break through it, forming deep recesses, about whose heads are the snowy summits of the Abbott group, nearly 14,000 feet in elevation. A rough trail led up the left bank, and scarcity of feed for our animals drove us far up the cañon, nearly to the fourth recess, before we camped, at 7:30 P. M., at an elevation of 9,100 feet.

The Abbott group appeared the most inviting, but we wished, if possible, to get a station nearer Mt. Ritter; so we decided on Red Slate Peak for our first climb. By five the next morning we were off with camera, plane-table, and lunch, and took our way up the first stream entering Mono Creek from the north. After a couple of hours' steady climbing, we came in sight of a splendid jagged peak, which appeared to be the one we were seeking. In order to reach its base, we were obliged to climb out upon the main crest of the range at an elevation of 11,500 feet. From this point we saw that Red Slate Peak was far beyond, and that the nearer one was evidently that called Red-and-White Peak on the map. This latter, though not so high as Red Slate, is a far more imposing object; but it appeared to be entirely inaccessible from the south. So it was without any great feelings of regret that we turned our attention to the more distant mountain. We were now forced to descend the eastern slope of the range for nearly 2,000 feet into a deep cañon, most of the way lying over hard-frozen snow-fields. Once at the bottom, it was an easy matter to skirt the southern spurs of Red-and-White Peak and make our way into a snow-filled cañon that led up to the Red Slate. We crossed long stretches of snow, around the margin of several frozen lakes, and at last reached the foot of the mountain and started up its southern flank. From this point the ascent is quite easy, although the jagged fragments of slate are even more trying to the patience than to the shoes. We reached the top by noon, after seven hours' steady climbing. There was no monument or sign of any sort to show that an ascent had ever been made before.[2]

The view from the summit is one of the very finest that the High Sierra affords, and was the most truly Alpine we saw during the whole trip. Toward the north the crest retains its rugged character for a distance of ten miles only, beyond which it breaks down in the neighborhood of the Mammoth Pass. But to the south the mountains were piled up in indescribable confusion, over an unnamed and almost unknown wilderness. Rising above the sweeping snow-fields were a few giants of the range which we were able to recognize—Mt. Abbott and Mt. Gabb, at the head of the Mono Creek recesses; the Seven Gables, on Bear Creek; still farther to the south, the spiry summit of Mt. Humphreys; and farthest of all, old Mt. Goddard, which lifted its head high above its neighbors. To the west was the great basin of Fish Creek, and close by the pinnacles of the Red-and-White group; while far to the north we could recognize our old

2. From his description, LeConte apparently went up Hopkins Creek, over Hopkins Pass and down to Big McGee Lake, then followed the route taken by the modern McGee Trail to the vicinity of McGee Pass, and climbed Red Slate from there.

friends of the Yosemite region—Lyell, Ritter, Dana, and Conness. By noon the sky was thickly overcast, and a cold wind made it very difficult to do any map-work; but by 1:30 P. M. we had succeeded fairly well and started down.

At five in the evening we reached camp, only to find to our dismay that one of our pack-animals was dead—probably poisoned by eating laurel. This accident cost us four days' delay, during which time we lived with a party of hospitable sheep-men till we could replace our jack, "Dewey," with a rare mule, "Dynamite."

The loss of time prevented an attempt at Mt. Abbott, so we started out again on June 27th, crossed the divide between Mono and Bear Creeks, and descended by a terribly rough route, and without a trail, into the cañon of the latter.[3] Once in the bottom, there was no more trouble, and we made our way up the cañon to the foot of the Seven Gables, camping a second time at 9,100 feet. On the morning of the 29th, the Seven Gables was ascended. Though over 13,000 feet in elevation, the ascent is made without the slightest difficulty; in fact, we reached the top by 8:45 A. M. Now for the first time we obtained a clear view of Mt. Humphreys, about nine miles away in an air-line. One glance at it showed that its summit was difficult, if not impossible, of access. We could see that this mountain formed the culminating point of a long knife-edge on the main crest. The western side was a sheer precipice for certainly 1,000 feet; and with our knowledge of the eastern slopes of High Sierra peaks, we knew that that side was at least as bad, if not worse. So there was only one possible route to the summit, and that was along the knife-edge itself, although it was gashed down in many places by deep clefts. Furthermore, the region to the west of it was one of peculiar ruggedness, and it seemed as though we could not get our animals within a day's march of the mountain from any direction. The day was a perfect one, and we remained on the summit for hours, gazing at the wonderful panorama. By four o'clock we started down, and returned to "Mosquito Camp" all too soon.

During the next two days we made our way back to Mono Creek, and again took the Miller and Lux trail up the South Fork of the San Joaquin to Lost Valley or the Blaney [Blayney] Meadows. This is a Yosemite-like

---

3. The route pioneered by Theodore Solomons in 1894.

valley about four miles below the junction of the North Branch and the
South Fork, and here is located the main camp of the sheep-men, whose
range extends over the whole region drained by the upper South Fork.
At a fine hot spring we found the camp, and in the evening one of the
pack-trains came in. From the packer we learned that the cañon of the
North Branch was utterly impassable for animals, but that it might be
possible to reach Mt. Humphreys by keeping on the high ridges to the
north of the cañon. So, at noon of July 2d, we climbed 3,000 feet out of
the South Fork Cañon, and camped at an elevation of 10,550 feet, just
below the top of the ridge.[4] A magnificent panorama was now spread out
before us. We were in the angle between the tremendous cañons of the
Main South Fork and the North Branch, each 3,000 feet deep. The former, in a perfect maze of tributary gorges, headed back to Mt. Goddard
and the wilderness of peaks to the east of it. The latter was directly
beneath us, but the bottom of the cañon could not be seen, as the summits of the northern wall rose so high as to be projected against the
southern, which rose precipice upon precipice far above us into the
region of snow. Farther up we could see the silvery thread of the stream.
The whole course of the cañon could be followed to the point where it
forked into two almost equal branches encircling Mt. Humphreys. The
last of the sunset rays shone upon this great mountain, rising like a
golden spire out of the deep shadow. Even at a distance of ten miles its
great height could be appreciated, for not a peak within a radius of eight
miles even approached it in altitude.

It is needless to relate the experiences of the next two days, for they
consisted of nothing more than a series of fruitless attempts to get eastward across a plateau scored with deep transverse canons. So we returned
to the hot-spring camp in despair, and decided to abandon the attempt of
getting our pack-animals any nearer.

So, early on the morning of July 6th, we packed our knapsacks with
food for three days, took a light feather quilt apiece, the plane-table,
aneroid, and Sierra Club register-box, but left behind from force of necessity the camera. Thus equipped, we took our way up the South Fork
cañon as far as the North Branch, crossed this latter on a log bridge, and

4. Apparently they went up Senger Creek from Blayney Meadow, and then
    could not discern a route eastward from there.

started up its cañon.[5] Any one who has traveled one of these great canons without a trail will understand what the work of the next three hours
was like. It was breaking through thick brush, climbing over or between
huge bowlders of the talus slope, or scaling rocky promontories which
projected into the stream. By 10 A. M. we reached the forks of the river,
and found the traveling easier as we took our way up the south tributary.
Finally we climbed out of the cañon by its north side, and made our way
over a desolate moraine-strewn plateau to the last storm-beaten tree,
where we threw down our packs for a camp at an elevation of 11,000 feet,
at the very foot of Mt. Humphreys. **[See Color Plate No. 11.]**

It would be impossible to describe our feelings as we stood at last in
the presence of this great mountain, so utterly different from any other in
the Sierra. It stood alone, a solitary pinnacle of rock, rising 3,000 feet
above a wide, desolate plain. Not a tree nor a vestige of vegetation was in
sight, nor was there even a trimming of snow to relieve its savageness of
aspect. The western side appeared to be a sheer precipice for 1,500 feet.
That the whole ridge was a knife-edge we could tell by the myriad of tiny
fringing columns projected against the sky. On the north the rocks fell in
a clear sweep 500 feet from the summit to the knife-edge, and in the
other direction, after a gradual slope for a short distance, there was
another break of 1,000 feet to the southern knife-edge. The eastern side
we could not see, but there could be no doubt that it also was a precipice.
At first there seemed to be no possible way of getting to the top. We sat
for hours in silence, gazing at the mighty shaft, and as the sun sank
behind us we watched the shadows creep amongst the crags. Then we
became aware of a gorge up the southern wall, which the shadows threw
into relief; but even with the aid of our telescope, it seemed a hopeless
task to ascend it.

By five next morning we set out across the wilderness of old moraines
toward the mountain. Soon the sun rose, but its warmth did not reach us,
for the mountain cast its shadow far out over the plateau; but golden
streamers of light crowned the summit like a glorious aureole. We
reached the foot of the debris pile in a couple of hours. It was not over
500 feet high, and soon we were upon the rocky front. We made our way
without great difficulty up a rugged gorge to the crest of the southern

---

5. Going up Piute Canyon.

knife-edge, where the warm sunlight poured in through a cleft in the ragged wall. From here we could see the awful precipice on the eastern side, a granite wall 2,000 feet high, as smooth as the face of El Capitan. Our ridge rose in a vertical edge for hundreds of feet, offering not a single foothold. So after basking a while in the sunshine, we made our way to the little gully which had been seen from below. This ran transversely up the western face, and our hopes rose when we approached it, as the way seemed clear for several hundred feet. But these hopes were of short duration, for we soon encountered steep slopes covered with clear ice, which could not be ascended without either rope or ice-ax. I think a climber, properly equipped, might easily pass this place; and perhaps early in the season, when the gorge is filled with snow, one might ascend by its aid. But whether this would eventually lead to the summit is by no means certain. The little gorge crossed the main ridge, and seemed to run out into nothing on the face of the great eastern precipice. After pushing even beyond what seemed safe, we descended to the foot of the western cliff, and cautiously worked our way around its base, thus finally gaining the top of the northern knife-edge at the point where the summit rises vertically above it. No one could possibly ascend the mountain from this side, and we could again see the eastern wall. So we climbed along the crest northerly to the top of a little pinnacle, and lay down in full view of the summit, which looked down upon and defied us. What would we not have given for our camera at that moment! If it had only been possible to bring away a photograph—a suggestion of that wonderful sight, that spire of granite over five hundred feet high, not two hundred feet wide where we stood, and whose sides continued on a thousand feet below! I have never felt so impressed, so utterly overpowered, by the presence of a great mountain as when standing amongst the crags of Mt. Humphreys looking up that smooth wall to its airy summit, and again down ten thousand feet into the depths of the Owen's Valley.

We built a monument where we stood and deposited therein the Sierra Club register-box, which I trust will some day be taken on to the summit. The aneroid read 13,550 feet, and on careful comparison on return to camp of the height still remaining with that already covered, we judged that the mountain was a trifle over 14,000 feet [13,986]. This is probably very nearly correct, as Mt. Humphreys overtops everything north of the Palisades. The descent to the talus was slow but not difficult, and camp was reached by one o' clock. After lunch we shouldered our knapsacks and went down as far as the forks of the stream, camping for the night at the more reasonable elevation of 9,300 feet.[6]

By ten o'clock next morning we returned to the hot spring. During the morning it rained hard, but cleared off in the night; and finding the weather fairly settled by noon, we started with our outfit up the cañon of the South Fork on July 8th. The trail was rather obscure, though not very rough, and the cañon was truly magnificent. The west side was a fine rocky wall for a distance of many miles, over which the tributaries from that direction plunged in a succession of cataracts. By evening our trail crossed the river, and we camped in a grassy flat on the further side, near the junction of the Middle Branch.[7] This last large tributary enters between two bold, rocky buttresses, and forms a fall of considerable height. Its cañon looked inviting, but we had already wasted too much time in the North Branch country, and so pushed on up the main stream, reaching the base of Mt. Goddard by noon of the 10th.

The South Fork of the San Joaquin heads in a wide, grassy valley, very much like the upper Tuolumne meadows, but hemmed in on both sides by snowy ranges of mountains. One can ride a horse without the slightest difficulty quite to the foot of Mt. Goddard; but there his journey must end, for there is no possible way of taking animals across the Goddard Divide, or, even if it could be crossed, of descending the rocky gorges leading down to the King's River below.

We camped near the timber-line and rested in the afternoon while watching the cirrus clouds drifting about. In the morning the whole sky was heavily overcast, but we had decided to wait no longer for this uncertain High Sierra weather, and so made our way across the intervening meadow-land to the foot of the mountain. The ascent of Mt. Goddard is accomplished without the least difficulty. It is very much such a climb as Mt. Dana affords, for the whole mountain is covered with loose fragments of slate. The view from the summit is unquestionably the most extensive to he found in the High Sierra. Every prominent point of the crest can he seen from Mt. Conness to Mt. Whitney, a distance of one hundred and twelve miles in an air-line. That portion of the crest from Mt. Humphreys to the Palisades is especially fine, all the higher peaks about the latter

---

6. Hutchinson Meadow.
7. Evolution Creek.

averaging over 14,000 feet. The upper tributaries of the King's River flow in deep parallel gorges, separated by high, jagged divides. The cañons of Goddard and Disappearing Creeks are amongst the deepest, descending over 8,000 feet in a comparatively few miles. The aneroid reading on Mt. Goddard was 13,500 [13,568] feet.

From this point we could clearly see that our route to the south was blocked, unless we should abandon our outfit and proceed on foot. We had been told on several occasions of a certain Baird trail, which crossed from the San Joaquin over to the North Fork of the King's at some point to the north-west of Goddard. From our elevated position we were sure we could see the point at which it crossed the high divide, and after some hesitation decided to make an attempt to follow it. So we took careful note of the intervening country, frying to impress on our memories the prominent landmarks, till, warned by the gathering thunderstorm, we were obliged to pack up our things and return to camp about noon. The following morning found us on the march by five o'clock. We retraced our steps a mile or so down the South Fork to the point where North Goddard Creek enters it. Here a wide bench runs diagonally up the west wall of the cañon, and, as we had hoped, we found the remnants of an old trail. This we followed carefully for nearly two miles; but in spite of all our efforts, we lost all trace of it in a wide meadow some thousand feet above the river cañon. We would not retreat, however, till every attempt to cross the divide had failed, and so decided to push on without a trail. The gap at the head of the meadow was evidently impassable. The next one to the north proved to be even worse; but after two or three hours' scrambling over the ridges to the south we finally came upon a pass to the north of Red Mountain that seemed a little better. I climbed to the crest of the divide to pick out a possible way, but found no sign of a trail, and the pass was fearfully rough. It seemed a great risk to take our animals up; but the great basin of the North Fork of King's River, dotted with lakes and meadows, looked so inviting that I marked out the best way with "monuments" and returned to the packs. My companion reported that a lower pass was to the south of Red Mountain, but as the one ahead was at least passable, we decided to try it. Every Sierra climber who departs from the beaten paths will understand what the experience of the next few hours was; so I will not describe the process of building trails across talus-slopes nor of boosting mules up steep slopes of sand. But we finally reached the top without serious accident, and, thinking our troubles over, tied our four-footed companions in misery to a couple of bowlders, while we ascended Red Mountain to get a better view of the country to the south.[8] But we little knew what was ahead; for the descent to the lake basin below was even worse than the climb. It was nearly three o' clock before we finally pulled up upon the shore of a little lake, after ten hours of the hardest work of our trip. We rested at the lake the remainder of the day, and next morning started across the basin of the North Fork of King's River. There was no trail, of course, and the route was very rough, but by the best sort of luck we made our way down into the cañon of the North Fork, and over another high divide to the headwaters of Crown Creek, which flows into the Middle Fork of King' s River at Tehipite Valley. This stream was followed without difficulty, till late in the evening we ran across a well-marked trail.

There was no more trouble after this. On the morning of July 14th we followed the trail to Collins's Meadow, and from there descended into the Tehipite Valley. The wonders of this magnificent cañon have seldom been exaggerated. The only real exception seems to me to be in the estimated height of the great dome, which is certainly not over 3,000 feet, probably a little less,—far different from 5,200 feet, as sometimes claimed. In the cañon we found some campers, with whom we traveled for the next two days over that most villainous of trails up the river cañon to Simpson Meadow. Here we left them and took the Granite Basin trail over the great divide between the main forks of the King's River. From our camp in Copper Creek basin we made a last climb to the summit of Goat Mountain, took a farewell view out over the glorious Alps through which we had been traveling, and on the afternoon of July 19th descended by the familiar Copper Creek trail to our old stamping-grounds of the King's River Cañon.

---

8. Hell For Sure Pass, just south of Red Mountain, is the route of the modern trail across what is now named LeConte Divide.

Another Paradise

Bolton Coit Brown
Originally published in the *Sierra Club Bulletin*, vol. 3, no. 2, May 1900

Mr. Muir once remarked that the poorest mountaineers always have the most adventures. In the light of this, we can look back upon our two months' trip (1899) and please our pride by noting the absence of falls, predicaments, or disasters. Thoreau says,—and Lucy and I agree with him,—that "a man sits as many risks as he runs." Applying this to our two-year-old daughter, we put her on a burro, and whither we went she went also. And she enjoyed it all—grew rosy, hearty, and hardy, just as big folks do in the mountains. She did not so much as bump her head all summer, and except for the time a rattlesnake slid too close to her, and once when an owl tried to drag her out of her little nest and fly away with her, she had no disagreeable experiences whatever. Our camping was of the simplest—no tents, stoves, or other superfluities. The child lived mostly on malted milk, chocolate, and "trout fish." I verily believe she injured the fishing by her consumption of these last.

Our route was from Sanger, via Millwood and the "old trail" to King's River Cañon, up Bubbs' Creek,[1] past the mouth of South Cañon, and so up to Bullfrog Lake. Half a mile above the lake, a small stream flows into its inlet from the north. Upon this stream, two hundred yards above the point where the Independence Trail crosses it, at an altitude of over 11,000 feet, we camped for three weeks.

During this time I made several exploring trips into the basin next north of the Bullfrog Lake Basin. Notwithstanding its nearness to a well-known trail, the inaccessibility of this country has kept it almost unknown, and, so far as I know, quite unvisited, until this summer. It

---

1. Mrs. Brown suggests that this stream be called *Bubbling* Creek. Why not? Let Bubbs have the trail—perhaps he made that; but why should his unfortunate cognomen include this glorious mountain stream? Would it not be more fitting if we went up Bubbs' *Trail;* and went a-fishing in *Bubbling creek?*

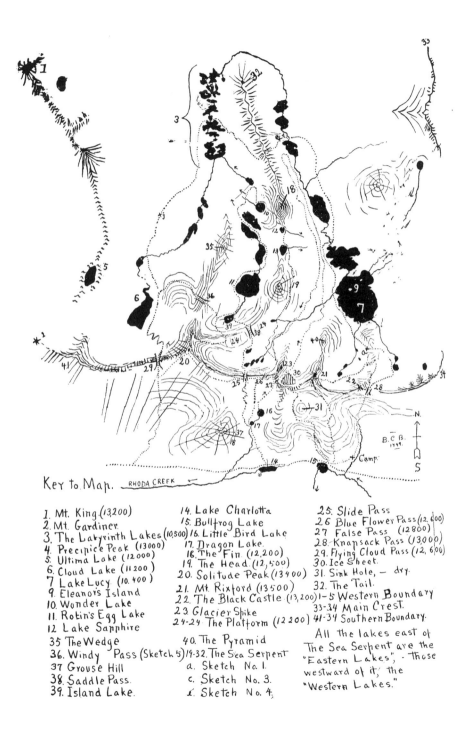

Key to Map. RHODA CREEK

1. Mt. King (13,200)
2. Mt. Gardiner.
3. The Labyrinth Lakes (10,500)
4. Precipice Peak (13000)
5. Ultima Lake (12000)
6. Cloud Lake (11200)
7. Lake Lucy. (10.400)
9. Eleanor's Island
10. Wonder Lake
11. Robin's Egg Lake
12. Lake Sapphire
35. The Wedge
36. Windy Pass (Sketch 5)
37. Grouse Hill
38. Saddle Pass.
39. Island Lake.

14. Lake Charlotta
15. Bullfrog Lake
16. Little Bird Lake
17. Dragon Lake.
18. The Fin (12,200)
19. The Head (12,500)
20. Solitude Peak (13400)
21. Mt. Rixford (13500)
22. The Black Castle (13,200)
23. Glacier Spike
24-24. The Platform (12200)
40. The Pyramid
19-32. The Sea Serpent
a. Sketch No. 1.
c. Sketch No. 3.
✗. Sketch No. 4.

25. Slide Pass
26 Blue Flower Pass (12,600)
27 False Pass (12800)
28. Knapsack Pass (13000)
29. Flying Cloud Pass (12,600)
30. Ice Sheet.
31. Sink Hole, — dry.
32. The Tail.
1-5 Western Boundary
33-34 Main Crest.
41-34 Southern Boundary.

All the lakes east of
The Sea Serpent are the
"Eastern Lakes", - those
westward of it; the
"Western Lakes."

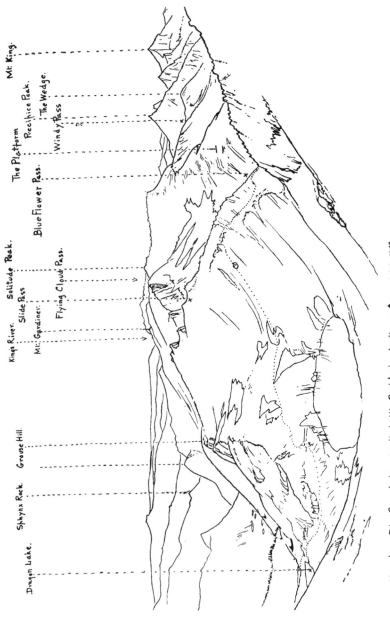

View from False Pass looking West;— Little Bird Lake in the centre.   R.C.A. 1899.

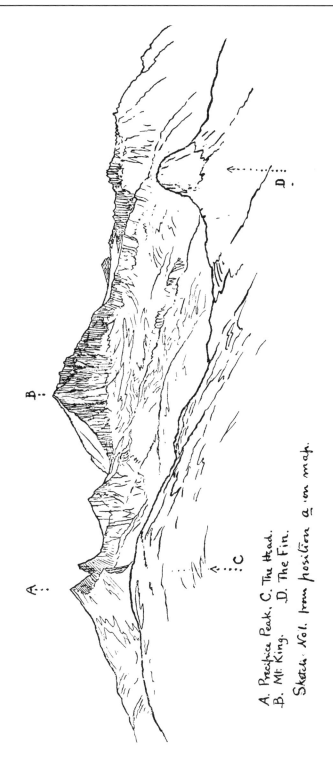

A. Precipice Peak. C. The Head.
B. Mt King. D. The Fin.
Sketch Vol. from position a. on map.

Notes on the sketch map on page 201.

Brown applied names right and left; many of them have not survived. On modern topo maps, none of the individual lakes in Sixty Lakes Basin is named. Brown's map accords quite well with the modern maps, but to assist you with identification the following are given their present names.

3. The Labyrinth Lakes—Sixty Lakes Basin.

7. Lake Lucy—the upper Rae Lake.

20. Solitude Peak—west of Glen Pass, unnamed.

26. Blue Flower Pass—Glen Pass,

contains from twenty-five to fifty square miles, is about as wide as it is long, and, after I had gone all over it, I put it down as distinctly the finest and completest epitome of Sierra scenery I had seen. Whatever makes the charm and the peculiar character of the High Sierra is here in typical perfection—peaks, walls, precipices, snow-fields, table-lands, gorges, ice-smoothed rocks, willow-bowered cascades, mountain-pines, colum-bine, and many other blossoms, perfect and extensive meadows, and lakes—ah, the *lakes!*—in every variety, form, and position—fifty of them if there is one, and streams, from the tinkling, flower-spattering, grass-hidden rill to the hoarse bowlder-rolling torrents. These latter—one day when I was there—sounded like an artillery-battle as they plunged their storm-swollen volumes of yellow flood down the mountain-sides. Surely that day the mountains said, as one did to Thoreau, "Here comes one of our friends; let us get up a good storm to welcome him." Hour after hour wind-driven torrents of rain and hail came down. The ground was grayed with ice-pebbles. The lake-surfaces roared and hissed under their beating. Blinding lightning-flash and tremendous detonations of thunder-crash, peal on peal and roll on roll, filled that mighty bowl with the grandeur of elemental tumult.

This day I was out fourteen hours, and, despite the storm, cooked two hot meals. I arose at half-past two, and at the crack of dawn left camp for Flying Cloud Pass. My route is dotted on the map. I traveled very slowly,— merely wandered, in fact,—lying under rocks at the heavi-est storm-gusts, working out bits of trail, making in the less fierce moments dripping sketch-notes of the scenery, and so on until late in the afternoon, when the breaking storm found me toiling up the northern wall of the southern ridge. Reaching the summit just at sunset I saw from

Sketch 2.
Flying Cloud Pass.
Solitude Peak to the left.
Cloud Lake below. Looking South.

B.C.B.

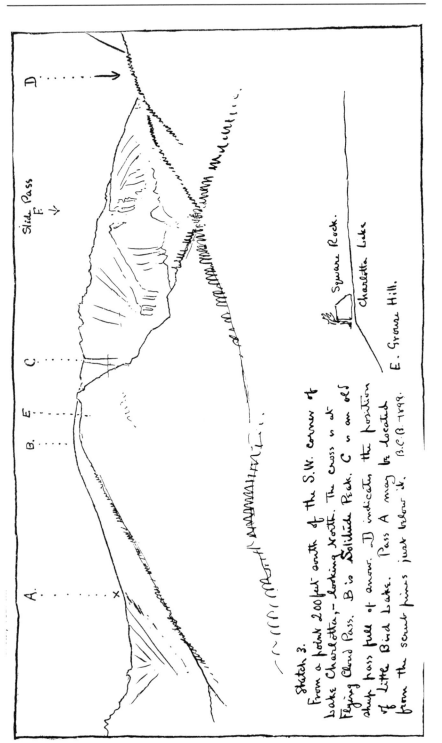

Sketch 3.

From a point 200 feet south of the S.W. corner of Lake Charlotta,—looking North. The cross is at Flying Cloud Pass. B is Solitude Peak. C is an old sharp pass full of snow. D indicates the position of Little Bird Lake. Pass A may be located from the scrub pines just below it. B.C.B. 1899.

E. Grand Hill.

Charlotte Lake.

Square Rock.

The Fin.

The Black Castle. Mt. Rixford.

The Pyramid.

Sketch xo 4. Looking South. B.C.B. 1899.

Knapsack Pass our camp-fire two thousand feet below. Lucy heard me
shout from here. Down the long slope I went with leaps and bounds a
kangaroo would have envied, and in twenty minutes reached camp.

Lucy and the baby had made a good fight against the storm, but the
channelings of the water showed that they had almost been washed away.
Packed in dry blankets, the child sat for several hours under the six-foot
tarpaulin roof quite contented, listening to the thunder and watching
with baby-wonder the accumulating hail-piles—"Just like washing rice,"
she said. Her mother had kept a great roaring fire hard by all day, and
withal no one was the worse for the storm.

One morning Lucy left camp (I stayed with the child) and crossed
the divide at False Pass (see her route dotted on map), descended to the
Eastern Lakes, tramped down northward below the Fin, returned over the
divide by Blue Flower Pass, and walked into camp about five o'clock.
Doubtless she was the first woman ever in that basin. Some friends of
ours visited the region a little later and named the largest lake after her. I
named one of its islands after the infant—Eleanor's Island. I hasten to
add that I should not have done it had she not possessed a suitable name.

Earnestly desiring to find an animal pass to this basin, I explored
every foot of the crest of its northern wall from Kearsarge Pass to Flying
Cloud Pass. The discoveries I made are on the map. Flying Cloud Pass
has certainly been used by sheepmen as an animal pass; but its northern
side is rough and should be seen before being attempted. False Pass and
Knapsack Pass are convenient for foot-travel, but impossible for animals.
False Pass has a very steep and very long descent on the north. I
descended once along the channels of the northeast face of Mt. Rixford,
but I cannot recommend it. It is dangerous. Slide Pass appears to have
been used by sheepmen; but here again one should work out his route
before attempting to take animals over it. Not very far to the west of Slide
Pass is a narrow gate through the crest, and this also the sheepman has
undoubtedly used, though whether for pack-animals or sheep only, I cannot say. It was a mere ribbon of steep snow on the north when I visited it.
Blue Flower Pass is my own private discovery, and I was much pleased
with it until, after monumenting its northern side almost down to the
basin's bottom, I came to a passage through bed-rock on edge. I worked
an hour or two building steps here, but still I cannot report it as passable.
But a certain amount of work—not more than a few hours, I should

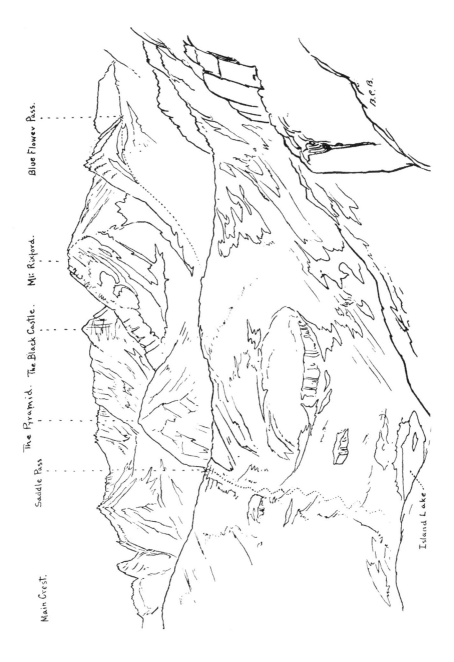

Main Crest. Saddle Pass The Pyramid. The Black Castle. Mt. Rixford. Blue Flower Pass. Island Lake B.C.B.

Sketch no. 6.
The Fin: Wonder Lake at the left. Looking East - from point j on map. BC B

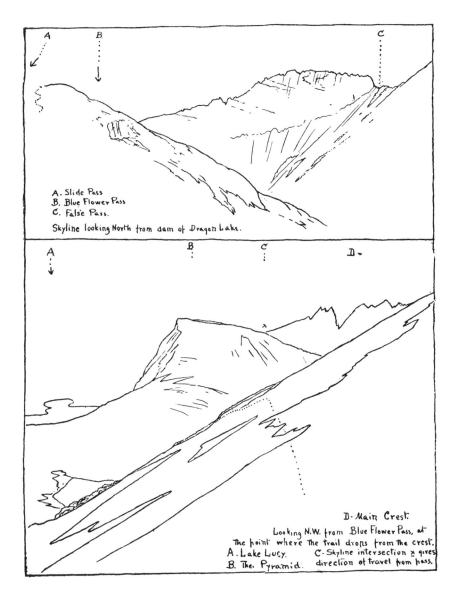

A. Slide Pass
B. Blue Flower Pass
C. False Pass.

Skyline looking North from dam of Dragon Lake.

D- Main Crest.

Looking N.W. from Blue Flower Pass, at
the point where the trail drops from the crest.
A. Lake Lucy.   C- Skyline intersection x gives
B. The Pyramid.   direction of travel from pass.

say,—ought to make it possible. The southern approach to this pass is not very difficult,—that is, for real mountain animals.

As to the map herewith, it will be found quite practicable to travel by, though no doubt in such things as the relative sizes of lakes it is very funny. Moreover, there are a great many more lakes in the basin than are shown on the map. Taken in connection with the topographical sketches, it should enable any one, without loss of time, to go to any part of the basin. It is to be hoped that another season will see found or made a reliable animal trail over this basin's southern wall. Once down to either the eastern or the western group of lakes, there would be no serious difficulty in moving pack-animals almost anywhere. The western lakes are on a sort of shelf, and must he some six hundred feet higher than the eastern chain. At either group plenty of feed is to be found; and the defacement and destruction by sheepmen have been less here than in any place I have visited. My first thought was, "*This* is the kind of High Sierra that John Muir talks about in his book."

Mr. Geo. W. Naylor, of Independence, (forest ranger,) told me that an "old prospector" once told him that twenty years ago he had taken his animals over this divide just north of Bullfrog Lake. On the strength of this I made a special search for his pass, but failed to discover any place where it seemed even remotely possible to put an animal over. Mr. Naylor, after visiting the basin, agreed with me as to its extraordinary beauty, and desiring to have it quite perfect, he next day took his companion, and between them they carried over a pail containing a dozen trout, which fish they liberated in the hitherto fishless waters of Lake Lucy. And, by the way, speaking of trout, three years ago I carried up from Bullfrog Lake nine large trout and put them in the Kearsarge Lakes Having this summer investigated the matter, I can report that they flourished, and that now there are trout in every lake between the Main Crest and Bullfrog Lake. Mr. Naylor made this true this summer by taking fish away up to the last glacial pond just at the northwest foot of University Peak.

Mr. Naylor heard of a pass into this northern basin by way of its western wall—somewhere near Ultima Lake. Being determined to get in there to camp, he took his animals and disappeared, aiming to cross the first divide somewhere a mile or two west of Flying Cloud Pass, and, descending thence on the western side of the basin's western wall, to cross that wall, as I said, near Ultima Lake. As he never came back, I suppose he got in. This basin could no doubt be reached with animals by crossing over from the Copper Creek Basin into Paradise Valley, ascending to the head of that, thence following its eastern fork, and from that turning up to the south, where the basin's drainage stream comes down. I have no doubt this was often done by sheepmen. But it is a dreadfully roundabout, difficult, long way. Moreover, the trail that leads down into Paradise Valley is almost impassable now, and by the time the sheepmen have ceased for a year or two to use it, it will practically cease to exist. Trails of this sort have never been monumented, and a few seasons will see them overgrown, washed out—in fact, lost. This is a matter the Sierra Club should promptly and effectively interest itself in. Next season should be entirely devoted to trail-marking.

All the altitudes herewith reported are simply my estimate. Mt. Rixford, however, must be excepted. I found Dr. Rixford's record on that, and the height was therein given as 13,500 feet.

The Ascent of the North Palisades

Joseph N. LeConte

Originally published in the *Sierra Club Bulletin*, vol. 5, no. 1, January 1904

Of all the vast area of the High Sierra, without doubt the wildest, most magnificent, and most difficult of access is that portion about the extreme sources of the Middle Fork of King's River. This stream above its junction with Goddard Creek (the "head of navigation" for the average camp outfit) drains a basin of about one hundred square miles, nearly all of which is above the timber-line, and which includes about its rim some of the highest points in the State. Through the midst of this rugged area the Middle Fork cuts a profound cañon in granite and black volcanic rock, many points on the west side rising five thousand feet above the stream. This cañon trends almost due north and south. From its edge, extending back four or five miles to the east, is a rough plateau scored by deep transverse gorges which pour the melted snows of the Main Crest into the river. On the north the basin is hemmed in by the Goddard Divide between the King's and San Joaquin rivers, and on the west by a huge spur of the latter terminating in Woodworth Mountain. Except to a man afoot, all these cañons and divides are impassable from the west and north, though it is reported that the Main Crest is crossed by a sheep-trail at a point about six miles north of the Palisades.

To the mountain-climber the main chain of the Palisades is by far the most interesting field of action. For a distance of ten miles this portion of the Main Crest presents toward the west an almost unbroken precipitous front of from two thousand to three thousand feet. At its southern end Split Mountain rises to an elevation of 14,146 [14,058] feet above sea-level, and, though easy of ascent, the difficulties of reaching its base had until a year ago prevented an attempt to climb it. Farther north the Middle Palisade touches 14,070 feet, and is still unscaled. At its extreme northern end the mass culminates in a magnificent group of peaks, consisting of the North Palisade (14,282 ft.) [14,242], Mt. Sill (14,198

ft.) [14,162], Agassiz Needle (13,945 ft.) [Mt. Agassiz, 13,891], and Mt.
Winchell (13,817 ft.) [13,768]. These are the North Palisades, and until
the ascents described in the following article were made none of their
summits had even been attempted.

The Palisades were first mentioned and named by the members of the
California Geological Survey in 1864. Professor Brewer in his report says:
"At the head of the North (Middle) Fork, along the Main Crest of the
Sierra, is a range of peaks, from 13,500 to 14,000 feet high, which we
called 'the Palisades.' These were unlike the rest of the crest in outline
and color, and were doubtless volcanic; they were very grand and fantastic in shape, like the rocks seen on the Silver Mountain trail near Ebbett's
Pass. All doubts as to the nature of these peaks were removed after
observing on the east side of the crest, in the Owen's Valley, that vast
streams of lava had flowed down the slopes of the Sierra, just below the
Palisades."[1]

About 1875, the members of the surveying parties under Captain
Geo. M. Wheeler, recognized the great height of this part of the range,
and determined the altitude and position of two of its high points by triangulation from the "Virginia Base," calling them the N. W. and S. E.
Palisades.[2] These correspond to what are commonly known as the North
Palisade and Split Mountain, and their heights as given by him are
14,275 and 14,200 feet [14,058].

In 1877 [1878] Mr. Frank Dusy, mountaineer, and pioneer of the
Middle Fork Sierra, worked his way to the base of the Palisades, and
explored the head of the river. In 1879 Mr. Lil A. Winchell, of Pine
Ridge, visited the Palisade region, and named the highest point Dusy
Peak, the next point north Mt. Winchell, after Professor Alexander
Winchell, the geologist, and the most northerly of the group Agassiz
Needle.

In 1895 Professor Bolton Coit Brown obtained his first glimpse of the
Palisades from the summit of Woodworth Mountain, eight miles to the
southwest, and called the highest pinnacle of the northern mass Mt.

1. Geological Survey of California. J. D. Whitney, State Geologist. Vol. 1,
   Geology, p. 393.
2. Geographical Surveys West of the 100th Meridian. Capt. George M.
   Wheeler, in charge. Table of Geographical Positions, etc., p. 19.

Jordan. In 1896 I took the liberty of naming the second highest point Mt. Sill.

The party of the California Geological Survey made no attempt to visit this region. In 1875, Mr. Gustave Eisen and party, of San Francisco, made a knapsack trip up the Middle Fork and Palisade Creek, and climbed one of the points near the Middle Palisade. This and the ascent of Split Mountain already referred to were until last summer the only records of actual ascents amongst the Palisades. To capture the summit of the North Palisade, therefore, had long been a great desire of mine, and a number of trips through the mountains to the west and south of the peak, only furnished a still further incentive to make the attempt.

In the spring of 1903 plans were laid for a trip to the North Palisades. Messrs. James Moffitt and James Hutchinson were to be of the party, men of much experience in High Sierra climbing, and, what is equally important, experienced in the method of traveling necessary in this sort of region. So, after bidding good-by to our Sierra Club friends of the Whitney and Williamson climbs, Mrs. Le Conte and I crossed the Harrison Pass and joined our companions in the King's River Cañon on July 12th. Here also we met Messrs. Robert and John Pike, who decided to join the party.

The start was made at noon of the 17th, and the following evening saw us once more in our beautiful Simpson Meadow, where we remained two days to rest, fish, and prepare our packs for the trip ahead. We reduced our outfit to the simplest possible dimensions, took our three small burros only for packing, and left our little tent and all bulky and heavy articles behind, On the morning of the 21st we started out early, and followed the trail to Fiske's mine, five miles above, where Cartridge Creek enters the river. Of the rough trip up this cañon I need not speak, as this has already been described in a previous article. We found, however, that all the rock-rolling and brush-cutting of the year before did very little toward improving the route. Triple Fall was made by noon, and we camped for [the] night about a mile or two above without mishap to our pack-animals. Next morning by 10 A. M. we reached the lower end of the Cartridge Creek Lake Basin, and camped again at beautiful Lake Marion, just where the clear stream leaps from the lake over the moraine and into the wild cañon below. [See Color Plate No. 12.]

In order to study out a passable route to the North Palisades, and also to make altitude determinations of the many surrounding peaks, the

THE PALISADES AND VICINITY.

Scale

0   1   2   3   4   5 Miles.

J.N. LeConte
Jan. 1904

afternoon was devoted to climbing a high slate peak just south of the lake. This peak, which has an elevation of 12,712 feet, is on the divide between the South and Middle Fork of King's River, and is the same which Mr. Lindley and myself ascended last summer when seeking a route to Split Mountain.[3] It commands a splendid view of the head-waters of both streams. By 3 in the afternoon we reached its summit, and immediately turned our attention to the North Palisades, which arose in a forbidding array of jagged spires ten miles to the north. The day was

---

3. Marion Peak, 12,719.

cold, and so perfectly clear that with the aid of the telescope of our tran-
sit every rock, chimney, and ledge of the huge wall could be studied with
ease. It now appeared that, although the actual summit of the highest
peak was on the Main Crest, the whole of the great knife-edge did not
constitute a portion of it. Just to the south of the summit a great spur shot
off to the east, joined Mt. Sill, and, turning southward, continued the
Main Crest in that direction. The great wall of the North Palisade, however, continued directly south from the summit for a mile, and then
broke down into some of the tributary canons of Palisade Creek. Between
this wall and Mt. Sill to the east there was included a vast amphitheater
draining into Palisade Creek, and it seemed certain that we could make
our way into this and climb the great snow-fields within, whose glistening
edges could be seen on the very tops of the ridges. To navigate the final
knife-edge to the summit appeared by no means so sure. One deep cleft
in particular worried us, but of course it was impossible at so great a distance to tell whether or not it was passable. The western face of the
mountain appeared to be totally inaccessible, though a few narrow chimneys seamed its savage face. These might, we thought, be taken advantage of as a last resort. The prospect could not be called encouraging, but
Mt. Sill might, at any rate, be taken, and from its summit a great area
could be mapped. For over an hour we stayed on the summit of our peak
studying the chances *pro* and *con,* and had to confess at last that the odds
were against us.

After taking a round of angles to all the prominent peaks in sight,
and feasting our eyes upon the stupendous panorama, doubly impressive
amidst the shadows of the declining sun, we hurried down the mountain,
over long stretches of snow, across fields of jagged slate, and around the
end of the lake to our camp, where Mrs. Le Conte and Mr. Moffitt had
supper ready.

That evening we laid out our supplies for the final trip. These were
cut down to the last extremity. An eider-down quilt apiece, a compact
4 x 5 camera with eighteen plates, a very light plane-table, weighing not
more than a couple of pounds, two Sierra Club register-boxes, a small pot
and frying-pan for a kitchen outfit, four spoons and four tin cups for a
dining-room set, and a rather small three days' allowance of food. After
all things were divided up no pack seemed to weigh more than twenty-
five pounds. The party consisted of Messrs. Moffitt, Hutchinson, Robert

Pike, and myself. Mrs. Le Conte and John were to keep camp till our
return.

At break of day the indefatigable Moffitt was astir and getting breakfast before the rest of us could even get our shoes on. By 5:30 everything
was packed and we were off. Mrs. Le Conte and John accompanied us to
a sheep pass over the north wall of the lake basin, and one of our jacks,
"Spotty," carried our packs for that distance without difficulty. Here the
knapsacks were adjusted to our own backs for the rest of the trip, arid we
struck out north, while the others returned with "Spotty" to camp. The
descent from the sheep pass was into the basin of a tributary of Cartridge
Creek which enters the main stream from the north just below Triple
Falls. First it was over hard-frozen snowfields, and then over huge granite
fragments to the margin of a lonely lake. This, from its shape. we called
Dumb-bell Lake, and made our way around its eastern end,[4] over talus
slopes, and then across the complicated topography of the basin toward
another pass which could be seen on the divide to the north.[5] In the
course of a couple of hours the crest of this was reached by a gradual
ascent from the south, but on the north it broke away in steep chutes
filled with snow. Far below lay another desolate lake walled in by gigantic
cliffs to the east, and the outlet, which entered a deep gorge, was evidently a tributary of Palisade Creek. The immense cañon of this latter
could now be seen cutting thousands of feet deep directly across our
pathway, and on the farther side rose the Palisades, more savage and forbidding than ever. **[See Color Plate No. 13.]** The snow which choked
our pass formed a cornice projecting far over the chute, so it was necessary to first descend by the aid of the rocks on one side, and then take to
the snow-field below. Now a swift glissade was a pleasant rest from climbing over talus, and this let us down a couple of hundred feet in a few minutes. At the shore of our Amphitheater Lake we stopped a moment to
rest and enjoy the wild outlook, **[See Color Plate No. 14.]** and then
entered the cañon through which the outlet stream made its way. The
view down this was now unobstructed. Its confluence with Palisade Creek
was directly opposite that of the stream which drained the huge

---

4. The editor of this volume can attest that at the east end of the lower
   Dumbbell Lake are boulders the size of small automobiles.
5. This pass is just east of Observation Peak.

amphitheater between the North Palisade and Mt. Sill. Our route could
not have been picked better, for all that was now necessary was to
descend to Palisade Creek, cross it, and climb out on the other side as far
as the timber-line before dark.

This all seems very easy on paper, and looks nice and smooth on the
map, but the reality was quite the reverse. The cañon which we now
entered was exceptionally rough. Near its head, falls blockaded the way,
necessitating detours along side ledges. In other places brush choked the
narrow space by the stream, or piles of giant debris encumbered the way.
Luckily, gravitation was in our favor, and we made fair time, finally
reaching the beautiful valley of Palisade Creek by noon.

The cañon of this large stream is typically glacial—a great U-shaped
trough, lined along its bottom with meadows and thin timber. The view
down its course was very fine. Far across the Middle Fork Cañon rose the
black crags of the Woodworth Divide. Great talus-fans and moraines
clung to the mountain-sides above, but the lower slopes were clothed
with verdure and forests of red fir and tamarack. The meadows were
ablaze with flowers; myriads of columbines, castilleias, tiger-lilies, straw-
berries, and tiny compositæ were everywhere. The place was absolutely
untouched. Not since the creation of the forest reserve had human foot
trod this glorious wilderness, and even before that time the sheepmen
who visited the valley must have been few indeed, for not a blaze,
monument, nor corral did we see, and there were but few signs of old
sheep-camps.

Here we stopped for noon. A fire was lighted and tea made in our tin
bucket. Bread and prunes were produced, and we enjoyed a well-earned
rest of two hours. But anxiety as to the outcome of the day's tramp and
the sort of camping-place we might run into before nightfall started us
out all too soon. The way now lay across the valley and up the side of the
great cañon along the course of a tiny stream which we knew drained the
distant amphitheater between the Palisades, five thousand feet above.
Our path at first lay quite a distance to the left of the stream, which we
called Glacier Brook, and the climbing for the most part was through
alpine pastures spangled with flowers. But soon we began to leave this
region of life, and again to enter that of desolation—of rock and snow.
A thousand feet above the valley we passed over the old moraine, and
now the grade of the creek decreased, and we entered a wide glacial
trough—a "hanging valley," tributary to the main Palisade Cañon.

By 4 o'clock we had reached the level of the highest trees, consisting of a half-dozen storm-beaten tamaracks, and there threw down our packs for the night. We were completely shut in by high cliffs, and no glimpse of the Palisades could as yet he obtained.

To cook dinner with nothing but a frying-pan, a diminutive pot, and a tomato-can is an art requiring considerable experience and is not an easy one to acquire. First the stones for the fireplace must be put so close together that it is difficult to make the fire burn at all, and, again, to balance the little pots on rough stones requires knowledge of the laws of equilibrium which can never be gleaned from books on mechanics. The operation, though laborious, was finally brought to a successful conclusion, when we ate canned beef (so-called, but in all probability canned horse) off heated fragments of glaciated granite, and canned tomatoes and coffee in turn from cups. The dish-washing consisted in throwing away the plates and rinsing the cups.

As the chill of the approaching night began to settle over our desolate camp we built a huge fire near a big boulder, cut our stogies in two to prolong their period of usefulness, smoked, and were at peace. The outlook was across the great valley of Palisade Creek and directly up the rugged gorge by which we had descended from Amphitheater Lake. Down its middle tumbled the foaming stream, a long line of silver, lost here and there amongst the talus-piles. Cataract Creek, we called it, and marveled at its wonderful setting. About its head was a mighty array of snow-clad peaks, now flashing in the rays of the setting sun. It was far more pleasant to enjoy this view than to think of the difficult day ahead and of those left behind in camp so far away.

We were up again by dawn the morning of the 24th. After considerable trouble with our primitive stove, we finally got breakfast, and, shouldering camera, plane-table, and lunch, took our way up Glacier Brook, determined to work into the great amphitheater, try the North Palisade from the southeast, and if unsuccessful to ascend Mt. Sill. After an hour's climb over talus-piles, meadows, glaciated slopes, and snow, we obtained a glimpse of the ragged western front of our mountain through a gap in the northern wall of the cañon. Soon this was lost sight of; the cañon turned in behind the Palisade ridge, and we were at the entrance to the amphitheater. The slope of Sill plunged down into it rather precipitously from the east, and was bare of snow, with the exception of three long stripes just below the summit. The side toward the Palisade ridge was, to our surprise, not so precipitous, nor was it rough toward the head on the cross-divide between the peaks. The floor, western side, and head was [sic] covered with a continuous field of snow, changing into ice at the lower end. We climbed over pile after pile of great talus fragments, and gladly took to the snow at the earliest opportunity. At first it was hard and comparatively smooth, but higher up it became indescribably rough. The unequal melting of the snow cut the whole mass up into a labyrinth of great knife-blades, which were sometimes four feet high and two or three feet apart. We were forced to step from blade to blade, balancing on the sharp edges, and often falling into the spaces between. I have frequently seen this ice-blade structure on Sierran snowfields, particularly on Mt. Lyell, but never so highly developed as here. We made straight for the point where the cross-divide joins the Palisade ridge, and our spirits rose as we climbed. The way was clear as far as we could see. Soon the magnificent summit appeared peeping over the ridge ahead. The final approach seemed also passable. We were sure of success,—so sure in fact that I, who was at that moment ahead, called out, "Boys, we shall make it." A dozen steps more brought us to the top of the cross-divide, and in an instant was swept away every chance, every hope of success.

Such a stupendous view I never expect to see again in the Sierra. We were on the edge of a precipice which sank for a thousand feet absolutely sheer to the head of a splendid glacier, the largest in the Sierra Nevada, but never before described. Just to the left our ridge joined the Palisade ridge not more than a hundred yards from the summit, and that last portion was a serrated knife-edge. The only possible route was along this edge, and this might have been feasible had it not been gashed in one place by a notch a hundred feet deep. We spent over an hour here examining every crack in the rock and discussing every possible way out of the dilemma. Hutchinson crossed with danger one small notch of the knife-edge, went to the very edge of the great chasm, and with his field-glasses scanned carefully the opposite side, but came to the conclusion that even had one been able to descend to the bottom, not a single finger hold could be found on the other wall. Furthermore, one could not go around the notch, for it continued on down each side of the mountain as a vertical walled gorge, running out into nothing on the face of the cliff above the glacier.

It was hard to give up when within almost a stone's throw of the top, but it was clearly "no go." We took a long rest, enlivening it somewhat by rolling huge boulders down the precipice on to the glacier. It was really a thrilling sight to watch them go thundering down the cliff, leaping across the bergschrund, and then end over end through the snow till only distinguishable by the snow-foam when they struck. We then turned our attention to Mt. Sill, and after a rough scramble of an hour along the ridge to the east arrived without serious difficulty on that hitherto untrodden crest.

The view in every direction was unparalleled in grandeur and extent, particularly along the Main Crest to the north and south. Close by rose the apparently inaccessible spire of the North Palisade across the profound cirque containing the Palisade Glacier. This latter was of the greatest interest. Its area seemed fully a square mile, perhaps more,—for distances are hard to estimate in such a locality. All along the base of the cliff below was a bergschrund, probably a mile in length. Against the mountain-side the slope of the snow was very steep, but lower down it eased off, and the glacier was crossed by fifteen or twenty crevasses far more perfect and much larger than any I have ever seen on Mt. Lyell. The lower end swept to the right around a buttress of Mt. Sill, and was lost to sight, but farther down were two beautiful lakes of milky white water which contrasted in a most striking manner with the clear emerald lakelets scattered all about. To the south stretched away the long line of Palisades, all guarded by sheer cliffs on the east. Along their bases lay three or four small residual glaciers, which, with the large one, form the head-waters of Big Pine Creek. The prospect to the west was cut off by the jagged crest of the North Palisade, but far to the north rose that airy pinnacle, Mt. Humphreys, and I could not but recall a state of affairs similar to our present one when attempting its ascent in 1898.

The height of Mt. Sill as given by triangulation from surrounding summits is 14,198 feet[14,162], and checks fairly with the reading of the aneroid, 14,100 feet. It is the fourth highest in the range, being overtopped by Whitney, Williamson, and the North Palisade only. We built a monument and deposited therein our Sierra Club register-box No. 43.

About 3 in the afternoon we started down the western face of the mountain. Some difficulty was encountered in getting around immense granite blocks, but finally the floor of the amphitheater was reached without the necessity of traversing any of the rough snow, made doubly difficult on account of the softening effect of the afternoon sun. After turning down into the cañon of Glacier Brook, Hutchinson climbed out of the notch on the west side and examined with the glasses the front cliff of the North Palisade. We then returned to camp.

After supper that evening we discussed the advisability of making an attempt at the western side of the mountain. It appeared a useless venture as well as a rather dangerous one. But finally it was decided to give one more day to the work—to at least creep around the foot of the giant and get an idea of the country at the head of the river.

Next morning, with rather doubting hearts and very sore legs and arms, Moffitt, Hutchinson, and I struck back up the cañon again just after sunrise. When opposite the break in the western side, we climbed from ledge to ledge, and finally reached the notch which Hutchinson had investigated the day before. We could now see the whole profile of the great mountain, consisting of crags and precipices piled up for two thousand feet above a vast talus-field along its base. Evidently the first move was to cross this field and reach a point opposite the summit, whence any chimneys that might exist could be examined. This was a great consumer of time, for the blocks fallen from the mountain were of immense size and often the spaces between were filled with soft snow. By 8:30 the field was crossed, and we now saw the entrance of a great chute, or chimney, twenty or thirty feet wide in places, which cleft the western precipice from crest to base. This was evidently the same which terminated in the impassable notch at the top, and which had been the cause of all our trouble the day before. It was useless to follow it all the way up, even if accessible, for we knew that it would be impossible to climb out of the notch in any case. The rest of the front seemed blank, so there was no choice but to start up and look for a point above where the chute could be abandoned on the left-hand side.

At first the climbing was over loose material, tedious but not difficult. Then we struck the rocky bottom of the gorge, and the trouble began. In some places snow-banks were encountered—not so steep but that toe-holds could be kicked out. The containing walls for some distance were inaccessible, till finally we came to a point where a crack ran up the left side, and immediately above this the chimney entered between perpendicular cliffs of great height. This, then, appeared to be the last chance, so Moffitt and Hutchinson both made determined efforts to get up, but without success. On looking down the gorge, however, there appeared to be a ledge along the wall which had been invisible from below. While the others were trying the crevice, I went down to examine this. It appeared to be the only way out of the difficulty; so the others came down and we started across. The ledge was three or four feet wide, but sloped at a high angle away from the wall, so that crawling along it was a somewhat unpleasant operation. Further along it narrowed to but little over a foot, but fortunately became level. Hutchinson and Moffitt came over soon after.

We were now on the rocky front of the mountain, and a glance above showed a narrow chimney parallel to the big one below. Up this we climbed with the greatest care. Sometimes it was only wide enough to admit a man's body, and we had to work up with knees and elbows. In some places it was filled with clear ice, and great icicles hung directly in the way from some lodged boulder above. These had to be avoided by stepping in the narrow space between the rock and ice, or by finding foot-holds on the walls. After about five hundred feet of this we suddenly came to a widened portion, and there, towering almost in the zenith, a thousand feet above us, was the summit we had so long worked for. Up to that moment we had not hoped for success. Every instant we had expected to be stopped by some impassable barrier, but now on careful examination there did not appear to be any difficulties ahead worse than those that had already been overcome. Oh, the excitement of the minutes that followed! One who has not been in a similar position can never realize our feelings as foot by foot the upward path was won, and nearer and nearer came the tiny rounded cap above. Again we entered a chimney, and again came through in safety. Now we were in a sort of sloping bowl directly below the top. To go straight up was not to be thought of, as the caplike summit almost overhung on that side. We worked up toward the knife-edge just to the south, and instantly the stupendous panorama of precipice, glacier, and desert burst upon us. We were on the main ridge between the impassable notch of yesterday and the top. Even there—even twenty feet below the top we almost failed. The knife-edge was composed of thin blocks standing up on edge, from six to eight feet apart, and equally high. These had to be climbed over one by one, by letting down at arm's-length between two and pulling up over the thin edge of the next. At 11:30 we crawled out upon the crown, victorious at last, after nearly two thousand feet of difficult rock-climbing.

The panorama is nearly the same as that from Mt. Sill, with the exception of the basin of the main Middle Fork, which lay, a lake-dotted plateau scored with cañons, at our very feet. On the other side the course of the Palisade Glacier could be followed farther down than from Sill, and the crest to the north was better shown. The knife-edge to the north of the summit was frightfully gashed, making an ascent from that side wholly out of the question. An approach from the east might be possible, though very doubtful. We had already satisfied ourselves that the southern knife-edge was beyond our powers, so the route up the western front seems to be the only feasible one.

There was no sign of any sort to show that the mountain had ever before been ascended. We built a monument, and left therein our register-box No. 42. My own triangulation places the summit at 14,282 feet, and the aneroid read 14,200, a very fair agreement [12,242]. This puts the peak third in our Sierra.

We spent an hour on the top, somewhat disturbed, be it confessed, by the prospects of the descent. We had taken careful note, however, of the bad places, and were pleasantly disappointed in finding the return but little harder than the climb. In an hour and a half the ledge was reached and safely passed, and soon after three triumphant tramps were toiling over the boulders of the talus-field headed for "home." When at 4 o'clock we pulled into our little camp at the timber-line, we found Pike fast asleep. There was still time to push on to a more pleasant camping-spot; so, packing up the all too meager outfit, we struck out down the creek, and reached Palisade Valley by 6 P.M.

Here in the midst of this little park was an ideal spot for camping. We made our stop on the peninsula between Palisade Creek and Glacier Brook, surrounded by flower-gardens and sheltered by tall tamaracks. That evening we celebrated by eating up practically everything we possessed that was eatable, and wound up by smoking whole and complete stogies, without the painful necessity of cutting them in two.

If we were eager to start out on this eventful trip, how much more anxious were we at its successful completion to return to those who were left behind! So long before break of day Moffitt was stirring around making coffee, for that was about all we had, except a half-cup of mush apiece. But before sunrise we faced the rugged gorge of Cataract Creek and climbed with all the energy that was left. The first few hours were all right, but I confess that for my part I was pretty tired when the pass above Amphitheater Lake was reached. Getting over that villainous talus around Dumb-bell Lake was still worse, and the final pull over the snow to the sheep-pass where we had parted with our camp companions was the worst of all. But the sight of Lake Marion inspired us with fresh energy, and at 11:30 we pulled into camp only to find Mrs. Le Conte and John away. In a few minutes, however, they returned from one of a series of unsuccessful bear hunts.

I have no doubt that others will follow our track to the summit of the Palisades. Doubtless, also, scores from the Club's Outings will climb or be pulled and boosted up its rugged face; but never again will any one feel the inspiration, the excitement, and the glory of success that we three experienced when the first ascent was made.

Colby Pass and the Black Kaweah

James E. Hutchinson
Originally published in the *Sierra Club Bulletin*, vol. 11, no. 2, January 1921

Of many factors which determined for us the region for our summer's outing, there were three outstanding ones: *First:* Mr. McDuffie had assembled for the trip a most congenial and delightful party, and had told us of the beauties and charms of Roaring River Basin and the Kaweah Peaks country. *Second:* It is eight miles, as the crow flies, from the Whaleback in Cloudy Cañon across the Great Western Divide to Junction Meadow on the Kern; it is sixty-five miles by the shortest trail between these same points (via Turtle and Black Rock passes); it is seventy miles by the next shortest trail (via Kings Cañon, Bubbs Creek, and Shepard Pass). Mr. Colby had said that, from the lay of the land, a pack-train ought to go straight across and save two days between the Kings and Mount Whitney. *Third:* On many occasions, from the vicinity of Brewer, I had viewed the Kaweahs—ragged and savage peaks, dominated from every viewpoint by the unclimbed Black Kaweah. There were plenty of other inducements, but what more were required?

Our party[1] gathered at Giant Forest on July 16, and there was met by our pack-train, in charge of Ernest E. McKee, with Onis Imus Brown assistant packer and cook. Later during the trip we were to be joined by three other members.[2] Before leaving the forest we climbed Moro Rock and there obtained that most wonderful view of the Kaweah region and the Great Western Divide, and, through the notch at the head of Deer Creek (10,700 feet), the lowest saddle north of Coyote Pass, got our first

---

1. Mr. and Mrs. Duncan McDuffie, Mrs. William Knowles, Mr. F. C. Torrey, Mr. Charles A. Noble, Mr. Charles A. Noble, Jr., Col. W. H. Williams, Mr. J. S. Hutchinson.
2. Mr. and Mrs. Arthur Elston, Mr. Vernon Kellogg.

view of the Black Kaweah—in the sunset light looking fierce, threatening, and defiant. On the morning of July 18 we left for Roaring River, taking the "J. O." Pass trail and stopping over at Clover Creek for a trip to Twin Lakes. Some of the party ascended Silliman, the most prominent peak of the Silliman Crest and one commanding a broad and extended view of the Great Western Divide. Again, from here, the Black Kaweah was the most dominant peak in the whole horizon. Upon arriving at Roaring River we found Mr. and Mrs. Ralph Merritt in a beautiful camp just above the bridge. We established our camp a mile above them, in Cloudy Cañon, a short distance above the junction of Deadman (elevation, 7600 feet). From this point it is possible to make many delightful side-trips—Moraine Meadow, Avalanche Pass, Sphinx Lakes, Josephine Lake, Sentinel Dome, Mount Brewer, etc. Another trip which I would suggest, but I am not sure that it can be made, is along Glacier Ridge—a wonderfully glaciated ridge dividing Cloudy and Deadman cañons. One very fine trip which should not be missed is up Deadman Cañon. We wished to explore this cañon with some degree of care, and so decided to take our pack-train and spend one night at its upper end. In this cañon are (sic) a number of beautiful meadows filled with wonderful wild flowers. After traveling for an hour you come to the grave of a French sheep-herder, murdered there in 1887. It is this grave which gives the cañon its name. Our camp was made in an ideal spot, on a glacial bench, with a wonderful outlook in all directions and near a point where the stream comes tumbling down from Bird (or Dollar) [Big Bird] Lake. That night, long after dark, we were delighted by a most unexpected visit from Mr. Le Conte, who dropped in on us from Horse Corral Meadow.

The next morning some of the party returned with the packs to our Cloudy Cañon camp, while the rest ascended to the head of Deadman and crossed Glacier Ridge into the headwaters of Cloudy Cañon. From near the head of Deadman, looking back, one obtains a view of the finest U-shaped glacial cañon in the Sierra. The view as you cross the ridge into Cloudy Cañon is most impressive, for you have the Great Western Divide from Brewer to Sawtooth laid out distinctly before you. We were particularly absorbed with the stretch from Milestone to Triple Divide, because we knew that somewhere there—just where we could not tell—lay the saddle which Mr. Colby believed to be passable. The saddle between Triple Divide and the next peak north—a very red mountain— looked best, but we knew it was not the place we were after. Mr. Merritt had told us that Dr. Rixford with a party of five had disappeared up Cloudy Cañon about ten days before, incidentally looking for Colby Pass. As the party had not returned, he surmised that they had gotten out of the cañon, possibly over that pass. While we were at our point of vantage on Glacier Ridge we chanced to notice across a snow-field just below us, on the Cloudy Cañon side, rather fresh hoof-prints. Following these we found they led, by a very steep and rough trail, to Miner's Pass and then along the ridge westward to the Elizabeth Pass of Stewart Edward White. Of course, we did not know whose tracks these were, but immediately thought of the Doctor's party. At this point we had reached our nearest approach thus far to the Black Kaweah, four miles distant, and it certainly appeared a rough and treacherous peak—sheer walls across the whole northern face, and its knife—edge scarred and broken by great clefts.

From Miner's Pass it was a long descent of 4700 feet and a long distance back to our Cloudy Cañon camp, going, as we did, the whole length of Cloudy Cañon; but the trip was full of inspiring views and points of interest. To see the Whaleback alone is worth a long trip into the region. [See Color Plate No. 15.] It was just dusk when we reached camp, quite fatigued; but a very excellent dinner, culminating with one of Mrs. Knowles' celebrated tapioca puddings, was the end of a perfect day.

From our observations taken when crossing Glacier Ridge, we knew that Colby Pass could be reached only by first getting into a large basin east of the Whaleback. Accordingly, on July 31, we moved to Upper Cloudy Camp (elevation, 9100 feet), at a meadow just west of the north end of the Whaleback. Merritt had told us that sheep had recently been over a new trail leading eastward out of Cloudy Cañon half a mile or so north of Whaleback Creek. McDuffie followed this and found that it led up toward Table Creek, and not into the Whaleback Basin. He thereupon cut across an intervening ridge, southward, and followed up Whaleback Creek until he looked into the basin. Returning, he reported signs of very old sheep-trails here and there on the northern end of the Whaleback, but nothing continuous.

During the afternoon Brown and I explored all across the northwestern shoulder of the Whaleback. The whole slope was dotted with misleading monuments leading in all directions. After a very long search, a way through was found, but there was one terribly bad place where a trail must be constructed. We then went up into the Whaleback Basin. The route first followed up a rather narrow cañon near the stream, then crossed to the north side, went over some projecting buttresses, and afterward, descending, crossed through some willows to the south side. Here the walls recede and the country opens into a large-sized basin with a fair meadow. There are no trees except on the north and northeast sides of the basin. We explored for a possible camping-place, and located one, tentatively, on a glacial shelf about 200 feet above the meadow, on the north end of the basin, beside a stream which comes down from the north. We then returned hurriedly to the bad place in the trail. It certainly was bad. After working at it for a couple of hours, I asked Brown if he would get the animals through, to which he made one of his favorite and characteristic replies: "There ain't nothin' holdin' me back, is there?" Just below this place a large dead tree blocked the only possible route, and this would have to be cut out on the following morning. Upon reaching camp and reporting progress, there was much rejoicing, for all knew that if a camp was established in the Whaleback Basin we could readily explore every saddle, crack, and notch in the ridge for a way across.

The bad place referred to was like a zigzag stairway, very steep indeed, and up a rocky chute, or chimney. At first there was a straight stretch upward about thirty feet, close beside a rocky wall; then an abrupt turn back for fifteen feet up to a little ledge; then another abrupt turn of twenty feet, with a final jump-up of three feet over a slippery rock. The turns were so short that the animals could barely make them, and extreme care had to be exercised to prevent their stepping off into space. The packs were not heavy, for at least half of our outfit had been left at our permanent camp. McKee and Brown were supervising the ascent and asked me to make a try-out with one of our best mules, a spirited animal. Taking the lead-chain, I started up the stairs. The pack was not wide, but halfway up the first stretch it struck the rock-wall; the mule lost his balance and started over backward. I braced myself for the shock, but was jerked completely off my feet. The poor mule landed on top of his pack in the rocks at the foot of the stairs. We removed the pack and tried again with only the saddle on, McKee taking his turn at leading, but the animal had lost his nerve and in a moment was again on his back at the bottom. No damage, however, was done, except a broken saddle. By this time the mule was trembling like an aspen-leaf, and we turned him loose, with the idea of taking him up the following day. Next we tried one of the best horses, and in an instant he was lying on his back in the rocks, the pack under him and his legs pointing upward. Only one animal made the ascent with his pack. A second one got halfway up and then was unpacked. In every instance, at the last stretch, the animals were steadied with ropes about their necks, for fear they would turn over, an act which would have been absolutely fatal. The mule which made the first attempt, in ten minutes after the incident, had forgotten all about his troubles, was searching for the choice morsels of grass growing in the rocks, and when all the others had gone up went through without difficulty.

Above this stairway is a small flat area, where we repacked, and by two o'clock we were in camp on the glacial shelf at the north side of the Whaleback Basin (elevation, 10,000 feet), a wonderfully beautiful spot in a grove of trees beside a fine stream (a small branch of the main stream), the water plunging down in. beautiful little cascades and waterfalls, interspersed with fine little pools, and surrounded by an innumerable variety of wonderful wild flowers. From this shelf we could look south up the full length of the Whaleback Basin and southwest across the meadow to the knife-edge crest of the Whaleback—from beginning to end a succession of weird-looking gargoyles, pinnacles, and spires, particularly noticeable as the rays of the declining sun shone through and across them. The afternoon was spent in exploring up a ridge which bounds the Whaleback Basin on the northeast. From this ridge we got a good view of Milestone and of the great cirque described by Mr. Colby, also of a long stretch of the crest line; but even now, with powerful glasses, we deliberated long and earnestly as to which was the real pass. We looked down on an unmapped lake, a beautiful sheet of water, two-thirds of a mile in length by one-third in width.[3] **[See Color Plate No. 16.]** Colby had questioned the possibility of getting around its shores; so from our point of vantage we examined carefully with the glasses the north shore of the lake. It appeared to be impassable-a smooth granite buttress, about midway along, extending from the cliffs above out into deep water. Possibly one could get around by climbing up 500 feet over the buttress. On our return trip to camp we followed the southern shore of the lake, starting at its eastern end. By very careful maneuvering one could take animals around the southern shore, with the exception of just one place near the eastern

---

3. Colby Lake.

end, where a huge rock-slide has come down, blocking the route for one hundred yards or more.

That night it was decided that on the following day we would explore afoot up to the alleged pass to see how far the animals could be taken. Brown and McKee would take their horses as far as possible. These two men had entered into the quest for a pass with great zeal and enthusiasm. McKee's brother Earl had been up the Kern-Kaweah on foot to a point not far from the pass, and Ernest wished to connect up with his brother's trail. Brown was always in for trying anything once—the more difficult, the better. He had never been in the Kern and wanted to get there. The idea of opening a new route appealed to their imagination.

Having explored the south side of the lake the day before and found it impassable, we took the north side. Those on foot had reached the middle of the north shore when the horsemen arrived, having ridden all the way from camp. So far, so good. Then came the slick buttress running down into deep emerald waters. A steep cleft choked with boulders ran a little way up the slope to a horizontal shelf five feet wide, which in turn ran fifty yards clear across the buttress. Brown and McKee immediately set to work to remove the boulders from the choked cleft, and in a short time had their horses on the shelf. From here the traveling across the buttress was comparatively easy. This shelf is the only possible route around the shore of the lake.

A short distance beyond the shelf is an extensive willow thicket, watered by many little branches of a stream which tumbles down from a good-sized lake above. McKee plunged through this on his horse, following the remnants of an old circuitous sheep-trail. Brown rode his horse along the shore-end of the thicket, on a shelf in the lake, the water reaching up to the stirrups.

The course from here is up a small rather rocky gorge, with here and there signs of an old sheep-trail. Farther along the way leads into an extensive rock-pile, and it took Brown and McKee some little time to work their way through. Above the rock-pile the country flattens considerably and opens into a narrow alpine valley, with tiny streams running through mossy banks. Here and there were a few scattered albicaulis. The alpine valley leads directly to the base of the last steep rocky ascent. This ascent rose probably 1000 feet in elevation to the supposed pass, and for the whole distance lay at an angle of forty degrees. The way was up a broad chute 300 feet in width, bounded north and south by rocky walls, gradually converging as they neared the saddle. The forty-degree slope was composed of rocks and boulders of all sizes, scattered about promiscuously and all imbedded in loose granite, gravel, and sand. In a few places patches of snow lay in the chute. Those afoot ascended rapidly, using here and there the remnants of an old sheep-trail which had withstood the ravages of slides and weathering, looking back now and then to see how the horsemen had progressed. Each time we could see that they were coming steadily on. An hour's climb brought us to the summit (12,000 feet), and for the first time we knew it was the pass. It lies about one and a half miles from Milestone and is the first real saddle southwest of that mountain. It is about three miles in a straight line southeast of the northern end of the Whaleback. By our trail it is about five. The east side was an easy, gentle slope down toward Milestone Bowl, and then on down to the cañon of the Kern-Kaweah. The pass once gained, the rest would be easy. We all waited at the pass for an hour, enjoying the view and watching the men as they built stretches of the frail and then moved their horses gradually upward. They moved, slid, and rolled tons and tons of rocks. None was too large for them to tackle. Sometimes a small avalanche would go sweeping down, perhaps carrying away portions of the trail already built by them. They were as strong as giants, and the high altitude seemed to make little difference in their energy. Someone jokingly remarked that the topographical maps would have to be altered to meet the changed conditions wrought by these assiduous trail-builders.

After watching the trail-workers for an hour or more, until the men were perhaps one-third of the way up the slope, the members of the party decided to return to camp. I remained to lend encouragement to the trail-builders, assisting as best I could, and frequently taking photographs as the work progressed. Little by little the horses were gotten nearer and nearer the pass—now twenty-five feet, now fifty or even one hundred feet at a stretch. At exactly 1:25 we reached the pass and heard from far in the distance a mighty shout. Our party at the lake far below had been watching with glasses as the advance was made up the rocky slope.

From the pass to Junction Meadow (via the Kern-Kaweah) the way was open. Professor Dudley had brought animals up the stream. Abernathy had been up to the pass with burros. Earl McKee had been up from the Kern afoot, and had reported the going fairly good, except at the lower end of the river, where packs must be carried a short distance. The only question remaining was: Could the pack-animals be brought up the last thousand feet to the pass? Our saddle-horses had been led up, but could the pack-animals navigate the same trail? There were two particularly bad places in this slope—one, where a large boulder projected into the trail so that the stirrups struck in passing; the other, where two large boulders came together too close for the packs to pass.

The return to our camp at the Whaleback Basin took about two hours. Reaching there we found that McDuffie had returned down Cloudy Cañon to our main camp to greet our newcomers and to escort them up to the basin camp the following day. He left word that we should decide whether the pass should be attempted with the packs. That night around our rousing camp-fire we discussed the advisability of the attempt. The unanimous vote was "Yes."

What is more glorious than these evenings in camp?—the twilight fading into dark, and then the utter darkness beyond the camp-fire's glow; the absolute stillness, save for the crackling fire with its myriads of firefly sparks; the murmuring brook near by; now and then the crash of a rock from the Whaleback cliffs across the meadow; then there are good friends gathered in the camp-fire's genial warmth, listening as Mrs. McDuffie reads thrilling tales of James Capen Adams, mountaineer and grizzly-bear hunter, Clarence King, and other wild tales of adventure;— the fire dies to glowing coals, and as the moon rises over the great wall of the Western Divide, flooding the basin with soft, mellow light, each one seeks his tamarack bedchamber for a peaceful sleep, to dream of untrodden trails, unpassed passes, and unknown Kern-Kaweahs beyond. At such times, truly "All's well with the world."

The next morning at daybreak McKee and Brown were off with the pack-animals, headed for our lower camp, and the men of the party were to meet the pack-train near Cloudy Cañon upon its return and help over the difficult place at the stairway. Colonel Williams and I returned to the rough place and did some further work on the staircase. We also spent more than an hour exploring all over the face of the slope for a possible way around. Many times we thought we had found it, but inevitably were led to some smooth granite slope where only blasting would make a trail. We then carefully monumented a good route all the way down to Cloudy Cañon, and on the east side of the crossing placed a pile of stones on a large boulder. The crossing is at the northern end of the meadow, just at the edge of the timber.

McDuffie, with the Elstons and Vernon Kellogg, reached our Upper Cloudy Camp at five o'clock, and shortly the pack-train arrived. By 5:45 we were at the staircase. Getting the packs and animals beyond this took until eight o'clock. While repacking, darkness overtook us and it commenced to rain.

We had sent our new arrivals ahead, giving them the general direction and the location of our camp, telling them that they should be in camp by seven o'clock. After repacking, we followed, going fairly rapidly until we reached the lower end of the Whaleback Basin. By this time it was pitch dark. In the daylight it was easy going, winding here and there in serpentine fashion through the rocks and by the meandering stream flowing deep in mossy banks, here and there twisting and turning between boulders thrown down from the cliffs of the Whaleback. For a time the flash-light aided us, but soon the maze became so complicated that we were completely tangled up and had to retrace our steps many times and start anew. It was a most exasperating experience, for we kept falling into the stream and getting into pockets where the horses could not proceed. The lights of several camp-fires were seen on the shelf above, and we could hear the shouts of those in camp; but to get through the inky blackness and over the uneven and uncertain meadow was desperate sort of work.

At 9:30 McDuffie and I led the last of the pack-train into camp, feeling that the day's real labors were ended. As we approached we heard a shout from out the darkness of the meadow below, only to find that our newcomers had not arrived, but were lost in the darkness of the region below. A warm welcome! We got the flashlight and lanterns, and by continual calling and signaling located our friends among the rocky talus on the opposite side of the meadow.

By 10:30 our friends were welcomed to a roaring camp-fire, and, after getting into dry garments, we all partook of a hearty and much-relished dinner. We then sat about the camp-fire and listened to all the latest news, read very welcome letters, and shortly after midnight retired. As the camp-fire died down the whole of the Whaleback Basin was lighted by the glow of the full moon, making a weird and strange sight.

The next morning, after a late breakfast, we laid our plans for the day. The camp should be moved up to the north shore of the uncharted lake, and McKee and Brown would take some of the pack outfit up to the pass and cache it, thus lightening the load for the final ascent to be made the succeeding day.

Triple Divide Peak—a peak well and attractively named—thrust its head up above the tail of the Whale at the southern end of the basin, plainly visible from our bench camp. We knew that the view from that peak would be well worth while, so the two Nobles and I decided upon the climb and planned to join the rest of our party at the new camp at the lake above. In the clear mountain atmosphere the peak looked dose at hand and as though it could be reached in a bee-line up the Whaleback Basin, across the tail of the Whale, and thence across an intervening depression. It was a long climb to the crest of the tail, and then to our consternation we were standing on 400-foot cliffs impossible of descent. As a result, we had to veer to the east away from our bee-line course, climb over the top of the red peak lying northeast of Triple Divide, go down to the saddle between the two peaks, and then by the Triple Divide knife-edge climb to the summit—a long, arduous trip, but worth many times the exertion required to make it.[4] A snowball which I crushed on the topmost point went part into the Kern, part into the Kings, and part into the Kaweah. At our very feet to the west was the source of the Kaweah River, which in a distance of twenty-five miles descends nearly 12,000 feet to Three Rivers, at an elevation of 800 feet, making probably the quickest and most rapid descent of any of the streams on the western slope of the Sierra.

At the saddle, between Triple Divide and the red peak, we found foot-prints and a handkerchief filled with roots. Robinson Crusoe was not more surprised at Friday's prints in the sand. Had Dr. Rixford crossed here?—and, if so, where had he gone?[5]

---

4. This was a first ascent.
5. NOTE.—Since returning home, Dr. Rixford tells us that he crossed here, carrying his packs to the saddles and then descended a thousand feet to a lake on a shelf high above the Kern-Kaweah. Here his way was blocked by some cliffs and he was forced to camp, without feed for his burros and no fuel larger than gooseberry bushes. He thinks a trail can be found, but in his limited time could not work it out. The next day he returned over the same route and left Cloudy Cañon by Miner's Pass. It was his tracks we had seen when on Glacier Ridge.

Returning from Triple Divide, we took a direct course toward the west side of the Whaleback, climbed a talus-slope up the tail of the Whale to a low notch, descended into the Whaleback Basin, and thence to the unmapped lake. It was late when we came over a shoulder just before reaching the lake. The alpenglow cast a glorious pink over the Great Western Divide before us and brought out in great detail the pass for which we were headed on the morrow. Young Noble, a good climber full of energy, had led the trip practically all day and was ahead. Suddenly he shouted: "They're at the pass!" Sure enough, high up on the rocky slope below the pass, we could faintly see Brown and McKee with the tiny pack-animals moving slowly upward. Now and then they would stop for further trail-building. Finally they reached the two projecting rocks of which I have spoken as too close for the packs to pass, and shortly, through the glasses, we saw them unpacking and caching the outfit. Just at dusk they started down, and in half an hour (an incredibly short time for the distance), just as darkness had settled, rode into camp, on the north side of the lake. (Elevation, 10,500 feet [10,595].) Plans were made for an early start. The packers said it would be necessary to build the trail in the two places where boulders obstructed the packs. Accordingly, early the next morning Williams and I started ahead with shovel and mattock to make the places passable. In an hour we were at work and kept it up steadily for two hours, filling in and raising the trail between the two closely converging rocks so that the packs would clear them, and building up and around the other projecting boulder. At 10:15, looking far down, we could see the pack-train just leaving the lake. At 12:45 thirteen people, nine pack-animals, and four saddle horses stood on Colby Pass amid great rejoicing. After a delightful luncheon, with raspberry sherbet as a dessert, a monument was built and in it Mr. Kellogg deposited the following record:

August 5, 1920.

This pass was crossed from the Roaring River side, to-day, by a party of thirteen persons with thirteen animals (four saddle animals and nine pack animals). The pack train was in charge of Ernest E. McKee of Badger and Onis I. Brown of Lemon Cave. There was no trail nor any indications of the previous passage of animals over the pass, except for the traces of a sheep trail. A trail was worked out by the packers and some members of the party in about eight hours, on August 4 and 5. The

passage was made without accident to any animals. The
members of the party were:

Mr. and Mrs. Duncan McDuffie, Berkeley, Cal.
Mr. and Mrs. Arthur Elston, Berkeley, Cal.
Mrs, Wm Knowles, Oakland, Cal.
Mr. James Hutchinson, Berkeley, Cal.
Col. W. II. Williams, Oakland, Cal.
Mr. Chas. Noble, Berkeley, Cal.
Mr. Chas. Noble, Jr., Berkeley, Cal.
Mr. Fred Torrey, Berkeley, Cal.
Mr. Vernon Kellogg, Stanford University.

From the pass to the Kern-Kaweah River a fairly well-monumented trail follows down the north branch of that stream. The pass itself is level for fifty yards; then comes a gradual slope to the lower end of Milestone Bowl. Continuing, it leads through a fine alpine meadow in a hanging valley particularly fine, for all the way you have the wonderful snow-clad northern slope of the Kaweah Range right before you. Then you reach the forested area. As any course is here possible, we plunged down into the cañon and camped in a beautiful spot on the river just above Gallats Lake and below a large meadow with the stream meandering through it. (Elevation, 10,000 feet.) That night we celebrated with a grand repast and called it "The Feast of the Colby Passover"—and McDuffie was our Moses leading the Exodus into the Promised Land.

The next morning four of our party—Elston, Williams, and the two Nobles, who had pressing engagements at home—left us amid expressions of great regret from everyone. We all had planned to move down on the same day, but the most wonderful fishing that ever was induced the rest of us to remain a day longer. The Kern-Kaweah has had a perpetual closed season, being closed at its western end by the precipitous walls of the Great Western Divide and at its eastern end by the boulders in what Professor Dudley called the Kern-Kaweah Pass; but for our party it certainly was an open season, and we never had such fishing before.

The following day we moved down to Junction Meadow. The trail, such as it is, follows down the north side of the stream. It is monumented rather imperfectly, but with care can be followed. In some places there is rough rockwork, in others it is brushy, but altogether is traversable by good animals. About a mile from Junction Meadow we reached some cascades and falls, where the river makes a very precipitous descent. Here the trail is forced away from the river and up a long rocky and steep

chimney to the north. This is the Kern-Kaweah Pass. It zigzags back and
forth again and again, is steep, but perfectly passable until within fifty feet
of the top, where it is blocked by some large boulders. Here we had to
unpack and carry our outfit to the top. The animals were gotten up with
the assistance of ropes, a very necessary precaution to prevent their turning over backward. Finally, they were all at the top without mishap, but it
was very exciting work for a time. By five P.M. we had made camp in
Junction Meadow (elevation, 8100 [8,036] feet), eleven miles by our trail
from our Upper Cloudy Camp.

I will not dwell upon the details of our trip down the Kern to Funston
Camp, to Moraine Lake, and finally to Buena Loma Camp on the
Chagoopa Plateau at the base of the Gray Kaweah. This region has been
ably described and is well known to most Sierra Club members. From
here the party went by trail to the extreme northwestern end of the Big
Arroyo, to camp as near as possible to the Black Kaweah. I wanted to get
an intimate and close-up view of the Kaweah Range, and so Mr. Torrey
and I skirted around the base of the peaks on the Chagoopa Plateau, following here and there an indistinct and poorly monumented cattle-trail
until it ended in a rocky talus-slope in the third recess from the east,
about opposite the middle Kaweah. From here we still went westward,
keeping on a level, the going pretty rough and absolutely impossible for
animals, until we reached the cirque which heads at the southern base of
the Black Kaweah. The country here became more open, with small scattering meadows, and we soon saw signs where cattle had been brought up
directly from the Big Arroyo. The descent from this point into the Big
Arroyo was long and tedious. By two o'clock we had joined the others at
the extreme head of the Big Arroyo, about a mile below the Nine Lakes
Basin and not more than half a mile south of where the head of Deer
Creek breaks through the very low notch in the Great Western Divide to
which I have referred. Here we had an alpine camp, in a delightful little
grove of trees (elevation 10,300 feet), at a point very near the Black
Kaweah.

The sight of the Black Kaweah had thrilled us again and again as we
had circled the peak, and McDuffie, Brown, and I wanted to climb it.

Mr. Farquhar had viewed the peak from various sides and told us he
thought the most feasible line of attack would be by the buttress and
knife-edge running out from the summit toward the west, I had carefully
examined this knife-edge with the glasses from the north, at Miner's Pass

and Triple Divide Peak, and also, the day before, from the south, when Torrey and I were skirting the southern base. It looked pretty fair, but I must confess there were some deep, ugly gashes in it, which did not appeal to me greatly. From our camp we could see that the top of the western buttress could be reached by some stiff climbing up one of several smooth avalanche-polished grooves. Upon reaching this top we would then have a fairly near view of the summit of the mountain and could decide on our future course.

The following morning McDuffie, Brown, and I were off at 5:40, carrying with us for emergency fifty feet of rope. In two hours we were at the top of the buttress. The view of the peak from this point was absolutely appalling—the knife-edge running up to the peak, and the peak itself seamed, cracked, scarred, and broken by weathering as on no other mountain we had ever climbed; the whole ridge appeared to be disintegrating rapidly. McDuffie jestingly said we had better hurry over before it should fall to pieces.

From our viewpoint, the best possible route appeared to be along the knife-edge; but again we saw the ugly clefts in several places. One in particular appeared on our side to be most uninviting, but the thought that possibly the north side at that place might be sufficiently broken to get a foothold led us on. We went up and down, around, across, over, and under boulders and broken slabs of granite, always on the alert to prevent slipping and overbalancing, every muscle tense and ready to respond. Our footsteps followed a most uncertain zigzag course, and had they been plotted would have indicated anything but a temperance movement. The way those ragged rocks were broken, splintered, massed, and piled together, helter-skelter, would have rejoiced the heart of a cubist artist. Again and again I was reminded of the cubist painting in Mr. Torrey's home—"The Nude Descending the Stairs."

Slowly, very slowly, we progressed along the knife-edge, up and down, around clefts and breaks, always in doubt as to what was fifty feet ahead of us. Finally, at a point perhaps a quarter of a mile from the summit and six hundred feet below it, we came upon the deepest notch of all, the one which had been visible from both north and south. It was not more than fifty feet deep, but its sides were almost vertical and perfectly smooth. For a long time we worked at it, carefully going down each side of the mountain until at the bottom of the notch, but with no way to get onto the knife-edge again beyond the cleft. The whole situation looked hopeless and desperate. From our position here we could get a long, sweeping view of the whole north face of the mountain. It was practically vertical for a thousand feet down onto an extensive snow-field, and we turned away for all time from any hopes on that side.

We then surveyed the southern side of the knife-edge. It was steep enough, but nothing compared to the northern side. The only ray of hope lay in the possibility that if we could get down on the southern slope for several hundred feet, we could then work around toward the east, get more nearly under the main peak, and then by chance find a favorable chimney running up toward the summit. In an hour we had descended far down on this southern side. Here the slope was somewhat more gentle and we were able to work around on various shelves, finally coming to the largest of several chimneys running up in the general direction of the summit. This chimney was pretty well broken up, so that one could get finger and toe holds, but in many places it was worn smooth by the avalanches of rock, snow, and ice which for ages had shot through it. It lay at an angle of sixty degrees, but fortunately kept leading in the desired direction. The greatest care had to be exercised each instant to prevent the starting of rock-avalanches. Brown was a hundred feet ahead. I heard a warning shout, "Look out!" and knew something was coming. I ducked my head behind a boulder just in time to prevent its being hit by a rock the size of a football, which came tearing down. The rock struck my knapsack a glancing blow and bounded off.

After two hours' climbing we again reached the knife-edge and looked over into the deep abyss on the north side. Right above us, two hundred feet to the east, towered the summit. Our chimney now swung directly around to the southeast and narrowed up considerably. Soon we were in a tiny notch on a small buttress running out southwest from the main peak and not more than twenty-five feet from the summit. Here, unintentionally, we started a small avalanche. It shot down in a north-westerly direction, increasing in momentum and volume as it progressed, and in a few moments we heard it thundering down the chimney south and back of us—the chimney by which we had ascended—making a complete turn.

After eight hours of continuous climbing, at 1:45 we were at the summit (13,752 ft.) [13,765]),[6] and spontaneously set up a mighty shout of joy. The peak stands in the midst of a tremendous amphitheater formed by the multitudinous peaks of the Great Western Divide and the peaks of the main crest. We looked into the whole region traversed by us during the three preceding weeks and saw the route we should follow returning to Giant Forest. Immediately below us to the south and west lay the deep depression of the Big Arroyo; on the northwest lay the Nine Lakes Basin; to the northeast lay the Kern-Kaweah Cañon; and to the east we looked along the ragged, jagged crest of the Kaweahs.

The only sign of life having been there before was an eagle's feather on the extreme summit. This we carried away as a trophy. After lunching and feasting on the superb view, we built a monument three feet high, thus making our mountain one foot higher than the next Kaweah Peak to the east. Then a flag-pole was constructed from the legs of our camera tripod, a white handkerchief was attached, and a flag was left floating from the summit. In the monument we deposited a tobacco-can containing the following memorandum:

> *August 11, 1920.—Left camp one mile below Nine Lake*
> *Basin at 5:40 a.m. Attempted to climb along N.W. ridge*
> *but impassable notches prevented. Then dropped down*
> *about 400 feet into the southern cirque and ascended the*
> *chimney which reaches the northwest ridge 100 feet*
> *N.W. of the summit. Arrived at summit at 1:45 p.m.*
>
> > *Duncan McDuffie, Berkeley, Calif.*
> > *Onis Imus Brown, Lemon Cove, Cal.*
> > *J. S. Hutchinson, Berkeley, Calif.*

At three o'clock we started down, following the same chimney by which we had ascended. This work was most trying and tiresome, requiring greater care than the ascent. When we reached the point where we had first entered the chimney, the question arose should we again climb five or six hundred feet over the buttress to the west and descend to camp by our morning's route, or should we continue down into the cirque immediately below and south of us, past a snowbound lake, around the southern end of the buttress, and down into the Big Arroyo. We were

---

6. Another first ascent.

tired of climbing, and so chose the latter course. Then came some rockwork as dangerous as any we had thus far encountered. Our chimney ended in high and abrupt benches and shelves, together making a drop of two or three hundred feet. It took us many long, anxious moments to work our way down to the cirque. At one place near the bottom the rope was used, but I am not at all certain it was essential; possibly there was a way around. The cirque was reached at the top of a snow-field lying there in the form of a huge wish-bone, pointing directly up toward our chimney. I mention this wish-bone, as it may in the future identify our line of ascent. Of course, a snow-field is apt to be a fleeting landmark. The Lake of the Lone Indian near the divide between Fish and Mono creeks was so named because of a perfect Indian head silhouette of snow in the bluffs above the lake; but a few years later, when I was there again, not the slightest trace of the Indian was left. However, with the wish-bone it may be different, for a photograph of the Kaweahs from Sawtooth, taken by Mr. Farquhar in 1912, shows exactly the same wish-bone to which we descended, and we all know that the snow-cross on Mount Tallac persists from year to year.

By the time we reached the cirque the sun had long since left it. It was very cold and the snow was frozen and rough. Then came jagged rocks and talus-slopes about the lake. Continuing in a southerly course, we finally struck some meadow-land and a fine grove of trees on the edge of the Big Arroyo. Here would be a good place to camp as a starting-point for the mountain, provided one could get up the steep benches and shelves above the wish-bone. In some places we had slid down where one could not possibly ascend, but probably these places could be avoided. From the grove of trees referred to we turned directly west around the end of the buttress, and after a long, tiresome descent, part of the way over sharp rocks, we reached camp just at dark, having been out fourteen hours.

Between our camp and Giant Forest lay three days of travel through as fine, beautiful, interesting, and exciting country as can be found in the Sierra, but I must hurry through. One day took us to a group of little lakes below Black Rock Pass. From here, with our glasses looking far across the Big Arroyo, we could see the white flag fluttering in the sunlight on the summit of our mountain. The next day took us across Black Rock Pass (elevation, 11,500 ft.). This is a strange and unusual pass, and should always be ascended from the east, for by so doing you will save one thousand feet in elevation. If you doubt this, look at the contour map. From this pass we went down, down, down Cliff Creek, more than six thousand feet in eight miles, through Redwood Meadow to the Kaweah River for the night, and then, the next day, across the deep gorge of Buck Cañon and up and up an old, unused, overgrown trail to Alta Meadow, where, at sunset, from that wondrously beautiful meadow, we gazed long and intently at the Black Kaweah towering six thousand feet apparently out of the deep abyss of Buck Cañon at our very feet. A few hours the next morning brought us to Giant Forest and the end of the trail.

And now five months have passed, and we still lift our eyes unto the mountains from whence cometh our help, and what do we see?—the wondrous afterglow lighting the high points of the trip—Silliman, Brewer, Triple Divide; the inspiring camps of Roaring River, Kern-Kaweah, and Big Arroyo; the unmapped lake; Colby Pass; and last, but not least, the once defiant Black Kaweah floating the white flag.